Drugs and Minority Oppression

Also by John Helmer

Urbanman: The Psychology of Urban Survival (Editor)
Bringing the War Home: The American Soldier in Vietnam and After
The Deadly Simple Mechanics of Society
Mere Chattels: Social Policy Toward Women and Children

Drugs and Minority Oppression

JOHN HELMER

A Continuum Book THE SEABURY PRESS ● NEW YORK

The Seabury Press
815 Second Avenue
New York, N.Y. 10017

Copyright ©1975 by John Helmer
Designed by Carol Basen

Printed in the United States of America

Library of Congress Cataloging in Publication Data

Helmer, John.
  Drugs and minority oppression.

  (A Continuum book)
  Includes bibliographical references and index.
  1. Drug abuse—United States. 2. Minorities—United States. 3. United States—So-
cial conditions. I. Title.
HV5825.H43   362.8'4   75-2114
ISBN 0-8164-9216-6

FOR OPAL AND LOUIS
AND IN MEMORY OF JAMES AGEE

Contents

List of Tables

List of Figures

Preface

This book is the third in a series on the social and economic dynamics of class conflict in America. The fourth is planned to be a more technical sociology of heroin use and the heroin trade and will analyze data collected in New York from 1973 to 1975.

Practical limitations have made it impossible to bring these books together in one. Both focus on labor markets and labor-market stratification as the underlying dynamics of class organization and class conflict. But whereas the present book emphasizes the relationships between broad changes in market conditions and changes in public *policy* on drugs, the subsequent one will develop a theory of labor-market stratification to explain changes in the pattern of drug use itself. This extends the topic to cover working-class crime in general, which has been undergoing major structural changes in the past four or five years,* and to deal also with mental disorder and suicide in the same social context.

Work on this book was materially supported by the Drug Abuse Council in Washington, D.C., which commissioned me to undertake a broad study of sociological and psychological theories of drug use. It is a pleasure to acknowledge the generosity and expert advice provided by the council, through Thomas E. Bryant, president, and James V. DeLong, director, though this should not be taken to mean that the interpretations and conclusions in this book in any way represent the council or its approval. They are my own.

For great personal support I am indebted first of all to Norman Zinberg, and then to my colleagues at the Research Center for Economic Planning, particularly Thomas Vietorisz.

Joann Platt and Marjorie Harrison worked to produce the manuscript.

Finally, there are friends, all lost, some taken away, who helped teach me the spirit—Jerry Berndt; Nicolas Boulte; Ron Freda; Jimmie Longwood, of the *S.S. Cleveland* on the Yokohama–Hong Kong run.

---

*For example, Francis A. J. Ianni, *Black Mafia, Ethnic Succession in Organized Crime,* New York: Simon & Schuster, 1974.

Drugs and Minority Oppression

Chapter I.

The Vice's Cycle

In 1971, in a speech on crime and domestic affairs, then-President Nixon declared narcotics to be Public Enemy Number One.

The drugs, which in the hands of the likes of Lucky Luciano, Meyer Lansky and Santo Trafficante had elevated them high up in that galaxy of American evil, the public enemies list, now collectively surpassed even their preeminence. Fact was that Luciano was dead and his successors less than a match for his entrepreneurial talents; Lansky was ailing and barely a step ahead of the indictment and extradition warrants with which Federal Court had been hunting him all over the world; and Trafficante's grip on the Caribbean and Latin American trade was no longer the same effective corner on the world market it had been in the fifties.

The business of supplying and delivering the stuff had become— what to say?—more democratic than ever before in the century of the American trade, with Southeast Asian farmers and Hong Kong middlemen selling drugs to anyone with the cash to buy, and independent dealers operating on the streets untaxed by the established mafia syndicates and needing nothing from the French connection.

But there was anonymity and a lack of drama in this legion of fresh faces. The anarchy of free enterprise was not as gripping in the public imagination as the monopoly conspiracies and masterminds of the past had been. Drug dealers didn't stare down from the posters on the post office wall nor hold their own on the FBI's ten most wanted list. The crack police were hunting a handful of leftist incendiaries or half-crazed aircraft hijackers, and narcotic agents preferred as a matter of policy to make a hundred marijuana arrests than to trap a single high-level heroin dealer. There were more headlines for marijuana arrests, and better press meant more promotions which meant better pay.

It stood to reason, then, that for the federal government alone to spend 164 million dollars that year tracking down a narcotics trade worth 650 million, and subsidiary crime reputedly valued at another 650 million for more than a quarter million addicts, plus another 366 million on drug treatment, counseling, and rehabilitation services*—no anonymous, native-born, unsyndicated $3,500-a-week trader with a modest amount of air travel in and out of Hong Kong or Paraguay could fit the bill as the most heinous public enemy America had at the time. In the mythology of these things, nothing but the drug itself would suffice. And so it happened that the most effective analgesic known to man and the best cough mixture ever compounded almost exactly a hundred years after its unprescribed use was first legislated a crime in California, became the number one outlaw in the land.

This is a book about the mythology of narcotics that has grown up in the past century, how and why it has grown, the particular purposes it has served, and not least of all, its relationship to the truth—the truth about the drugs themselves and the truth about the people who have used them.

Most of these myths are not now nor ever were simply the figments of an individual's imagination, either unintentionally false out of misconception or ignorance, or else deliberate lies. Had that been the case, the falsehood would have been easy enough to expose long before this, and it would be unlikely that much the same notions that characterized expert and popular opinion about drugs a hundred years ago would still be conventional wisdom today. Nevertheless, it is characteristic of this mythology of narcotics to believe that scientific knowledge has replaced lay ignorance and prejudice about narcotic drugs and their functions, when this is not what has happened at all.

It is simple enough to say at the outset that this is a story of several

---

*Expenditures are for fiscal year 1972. The estimated outlays for 1975 are to be nearly 50 percent higher. See Sibyl Cline, *The Federal Drug Abuse Budget for Fiscal Year 1975* (Washington, D.C.: Drug Abuse Council, Public Policy Series 5, July 1974), p. 2

The estimated values of the narcotics trade and crime related to it have been extrapolated from several sources, in particular, George F. Brown and Lester Silverman, *The Retail Price of Heroin*, Arlington, Va.: Public Research Institute, 1973; and a number of papers by Max Singer of the Hudson Institute, Croton-on-Hudson, New York. They are highly speculative, and are noted here only to indicate how much narcotics officials thought they were chasing with what they were spending.

generations of American people who smoked, sniffed, swallowed, or otherwise ingested compounds and derivatives of opium, including some recent synthetic forms such as methadone, cocaine, and marijuana, all of which have been described, at least until now, as narcotics. The story is part history, inasmuch as most of the events described took place in the past, and part sociology, because the principal focus of the story is on the classes of people who used the drugs rather than on individual drug use as such, and because the story attempts to explain public attitudes and social and legal policy in terms of an enduring and violent conflict between these classes.

There has always been sufficient evidence to make the mythology of narcotics believable, if not verifiable, but in virtually no instance has the evidence been of both the necessary and sufficient kind. Apart from its veracity, the mythology has played a dynamic role in identifying the sides and measures to be taken in the broader social conflict in which the drug issue has invariably been embedded, conflict has typically been between competing elements of a local or regional labor market, when what has been at stake is the preservation of wages in times of acute economic crisis. Labor markets, wage differentials, business cycles, unemployment—these look, at first glance, to be matters far removed from the consumption of narcotics. Notwithstanding appearances, it is the objective of this book to illustrate just how the power and persistence of the drug mythology has derived from its role right in the middle of these things, as motivation and rationalization for the methods used to settle economic conflict and put down the popular unrest that has caused the conflict.

Once the myths can be examined in this context it will be seen that they are made up of three types of information in roughly equal parts. They contain *misinformation,* which is the partial truth that leads to false conclusions; *disinformation,* which is the falsehood that will be readily believed; and *information,* the truth which, when set beside the others, will be overlooked, discounted, or ignored. These myths are not the invention of individuals acting singly or in organized groups, for even when claims about drugs can be traced to particular individuals, their widespread dissemination and credibility depend on factors that have been beyond the ability of even the most calculating of conspiracies to influence or vary. There are liars and there are conspiracies of a sort in this story, but identifying them is not as important as understanding the context in which these myths play a part, as well as understanding the social forces which ultimately determine how they function and what the end result will be.

No deception on so great a scale, enduring for so long a time, can be satisfactorily reduced to a conscious conspiracy, even of such otherwise likely candidates as the American Medical Association and the old Federal Bureau of Narcotics, any more than the widespread consumption of the drugs can be laid to the ingenious plans of a singular public enemy or his mafiosi. The reader is best advised to believe those who appear in this story as being capable of wishing such conspiracies of deception and of attempting them, while at the same time not to credit them as individuals with the full achievement of the mythology in fixing public opinion and, through that, the policy decisions of the courts and legislatures.

The principal myths are:

1. *The consumption of narcotics was widely diffused throughout American society, at least until 1920.* It is widely believed that not until the Harrison Act of 1914 and consequent Supreme Court rulings prohibited the unregulated use of the drugs did narcotics become concentrated in the working class. Before that legislation the typical narcotic addict is thought to have been middle-class, female, and living in the rural areas of the country. The addiction was involuntary, based on ignorance of the true contents or addictive effect of opiate-based patent medicines and tonics. According to this myth, the pattern of working-class or lower-class narcotics use—which has been the acknowledged one since 1920, along with the related delinquency and crime required to finance drug purchases on the black market—have been the *effect* of the legislation, and an unintended effect at that.

The terminology of class employed here, which will be used throughout this book, is intentionally simplified. Still, the occupational, educational, and income differences which today conventionally distinguish the working class from the middle class apply throughout the period, although, naturally, detailed specification of the criteria would show the result of a steady rise in the relative size of the white-collar work force, general upgrading of educational credentials, and improvement of incomes.

In order to distinguish trends in the distribution of narcotics use, I will regard the middle class as being composed of persons who work as proprietors, professionals, or in technical and managerial functions or who hold what are generally thought of as white-collar occupations. Education and income are higher than the average. The lower, or working, class (the terms are used synonymously here) covers the varieties of blue-collar work, where education and income are at or below average. The dynamics of class and class conflict, which will be spelled out at greater length later on, focus on the differences in labor market power, which are contingent on work skills and union combination and are typically associated with differences of race or ethnic background. These factors will require that we discriminate between different elements of the working class, but for the moment, a simplified class picture will suffice.

Social class is vital to the interpretation of this history, for the truth is, narcotics use in America has always, both before and after the Harrison Act, been predominantly a *working-class* phenomenon. This has been a specific *cause*, not a general consequence, of narcotics prohibition when it has been enacted.

2. *Present public policy toward narcotics is an inheritance of the irrationality, ignorance, or confusion of the past and can now be superseded and reformed by rational and scientific solutions.* The truth is that, from the beginning there has always been reasoned scientific support for both prohibitionist and nonprohibitionist positions, as well as for policies with punitive and medical solutions. Expert evidence on narcotics may have changed—though this too is exaggerated, and the extent of the progress achieved over the years is almost as mythical— but the role of science and the expert is little different now from what it was, say, at the time of the British Royal Commission on Opium of 1890 or the American Philippine Commission inquiry of 1906. Not ignorance but selectivity has determined narcotics policy and will continue to determine it. Scientists are no more reformist than conservative and no less partisan than the rest. Two aspects of this partisanship must be understood. The first is the economic expansion of the medical profession to command the sale and supply of all medical services, including drugs. The second is the expansion of police powers, under political authority, to control and coerce all aspects of working-class behavior, including drug consumption. The first required the economic elimination of the old patent medicine industry, which was accomplished by 1910; the second depended on the reinterpretation and subversion of the Bill of Rights, a process that continues today.

3. *Addiction is the inevitable outcome of prolonged narcotics use, and that addiction itself, a physiological condition chemically induced, deprives the addict of his capacity to control consumption, let alone stop it, which impels him to irrational extremes of behavior, including violent crime.* The truth is, from the very beginning, the consumer's control over the size of dosage and frequency of use has varied over a very wide range. Today, and virtually since 1920—at any point in the range, at any dose with whatever frequency—use of the drug is called

addiction. But intermittent, or occasional, use, regulated by social norms and self-willed without internal compulsion, physiological symptoms, or irrational behavior during withdrawal from the drug has been observed regularly throughout the twentieth century, among Indians as reported to the Royal Commission on Opium, among native Chinese by the Philippine Commission; among Chinese in America, as we see in Table 2.1, it was thought that occasional users outnumbered the regular or addicted ones by more than two to one. The Vietnam War has confirmed officially what has long been known, that heroin addiction, whatever it is, is reversible in a matter of days or weeks without coercive deterrents or medical treatment, with conscious volition instead and without noticeable aftereffects. With the return of the Vietnam addict, researchers have only just begun to find evidence of the occasional controlled use of heroin among conventional users—where it has been all along.[1]

These, then, are the foundations of the mythology of narcotics. No account of the drug problem in America today nor policy formula for dealing with it, whether in favor of prohibition or against, in favor of harsher criminal sanctions to deter narcotics use or gentler clinical therapy to overcome it, does not draw on these myths. They are the instruments of public deception, and deception is the mainspring of public policy. To interpret these myths at their source and analyze them in their social context is vital and urgent if the deception is to stop turning its predictable and destructive cycle.

Public concern about narcotics use and drug addiction is a repeating thing.[2] The record of press agitation, of legislative debates and enactments points to a recurrence of this concern every 20 or 30 years during the past century.

We are in such a period now. Typically it begins when the problem is discovered anew. The first stage is the mass dissemination of that fact, speeded through society by the terrible fright that it produces. But since discovery also involves criticism of the existing public institutions whose job it is to manage the problem—such as doctors, police, and prisons—this discovery is met with sharp denials from those in authority. Stage one generally concludes with their credibility shot to pieces.

Stage two involves the formulation of a theory of the problem and its causes, plus measures to deal with it. These often threaten the power of the existing drug authorities, if "new policy" means new people or new institutions to implement the measures. Since policy depends both on theory, to make it palatable, and power to make it work, there is a tight nexus between theory and power. It can happen, therefore, that the ambition for power is a strong stimulus for the development of theory in this area, and the acquisition of new power is usually accompanied by new theory to rationalize a new system. Theoretical innovation in such situations is dubious perhaps, as the continual reappearance of the mythology of narcotics shows, but the systems for administering and controlling drugs are highly competitive and have changed radically from period to period. Thus the present period has seen bitter fights for sovereignty over the drug problem, at first between federal agencies and local governments, until control finally went to a new bureaucratic instrument, the White House Special Action Office for Drug Abuse Prevention (SAODAP).[3]

The third stage involves the routinization of theory and policy. The institutional challenge is over with, and the winners get the chance to test their claims that the political and bureaucratic struggles of the earlier stages are paying off, that the cause for concern is being liquidated. At this stage a certain optimism begins to appear. Former Attorney General Kleindienst told police officials in 1972 that "there never has been a time when Federal efforts have been so effective against the drug traffic," and that the President "has some solid results to show for this tough policy."[4]

The fact that these periods of concern do recur and that they are alike in many respects, as I will show, suggests that the problem itself is a recurrent one. If this is true, of course, the stage of optimism with which each period concludes is as cyclical and illusory as the other forms in which public concern manifests itself. Just how the dynamics of public concern actually affect the dynamics of narcotics use is not clear, although, since neither the agents of public opinion nor the authorities have a sense of the history of the narcotics issue, and because this history has not until recently begun to be written, it is a lot easier to imagine that the concern, when it arises, is effective in reducing the problem to a size that is manageable.

In the longer, historical perspective this seems less true. The problem, and the concern about it, as it is reflected in public policy, appear to pursue more or less independent courses. True, they are functionally related, of course, but not in the way common sense would indicate.

I said that new institutions for dealing with narcotics addiction will bring with them new theories of the problem and how to deal with it. The novelty here is more apparent than real. Consider three images of the addict, drawn from several distinct periods of concern.

Many females are so much excited sexually by the smoking of opium during the first few weeks that old smokers with the sole object of ruining them have taught them to smoke. Many innocent and over-curious girls have thus been seduced.[5]

If instead of these girls, adolescents of either sex—or indeed individuals of any age—are substituted in the observation, the analysis is reduced to the opinion that the use of the drug is immoral, a vice, and that at the initiation of drug use, what happens is that the innocent are seduced.

In 1905, in a report to Congress which was influential in establishing the legislative course on narcotics for the next 10 to 15 years, a committee of the Philippine Commission reported the testimony of one witness:

. . . judging from experience, one must say that moral sensitiveness is deadened, or the activity of the brain concerned in the aesthetic sense suffers with the brain generally. Moral torpor and indifference gradually supervene, and this is most noticeable in those who previously to the habit had in every way an exceptionally immoral character. But the moral state varies, for the unfortunate victim under the influence of the drug is not the same person as when he is suffering from the pangs of deprivation. . . . The fact is that the majority of persons seek the aid of opium to refine their sensuality.[6]

There is confusion here as to whether the drug acts on the brain and in a physiological sense produces "moral torpor," or whether using the drug itself is evidence of moral failing, or whether the consequences of drug use in the addict's behavior (elsewhere Dr. Lin mentions unwillingness to work, inability to control oneself) are what produce the immorality and vice. But the same theory appears again during World War I, this time in an article by an army doctor who had interviewed enlisted men whose drug use (cocaine, opium, heroin) had been uncovered by the military authorities:

. . . in the majority of all cases there is *some inherent or acquired moral weakness,* otherwise the man would not fall in the first instance. His particular peculiarities of make-up are not removed by any form of medical treatment and if he uses drugs to any appreciable degree it is entirely probable that the power of moral restraint is permanently damaged.[7]

King was a little surer than the earlier witness that "moral weakness" leads to drug use and is not simply a consequence of it, although the consequence is to reinforce the weakness and make it irreversible. It is important to note that once the problem is defined morally, it is effectively removed from *all possibility* of treatment. As we shall see, such a perspective leads to a policy of quarantine and imprisonment for all drug users.

In an important recent article on heroin addiction—important because one of the authors is the newly appointed chairman of the President's National Advisory Commission for Drug Abuse Prevention and because it illustrates what the Republican Administration promises to implement in this area—the image of the addict is still cast in the moral mold; only the words are different:

> The addict is intensely present-oriented. Though "dabblers" or other periodic users may save heroin for a weekend fix, the addict can rarely save any at all . . . almost none have the *self-control* to go to sleep at night leaving unused heroin behind. . . . How many addicts living this way can manage a reasonably normal family life and work life is not known, but clearly many cannot. Some become heroin dealers in order to earn money, but a regular heavy user seldom has the *self-control* to be successful at this enterprise for long. . . . It is this craving for the drug, and the psychological states induced by its use, that are the chief consequences of addiction; they are also the most important consequences about which, ultimately, one must have a moral or political view. . . .[8]

Today it is philosophically harder for us to accept the idea that as a society we should make people show self-control or be moral, unless their vice causes harm to others. James Wilson repeats the recurring theme that drug addicts are hedonists, though the old connection between that and the demand for sexual gratification has dropped out of sight, since researchers have shown that, in fact, the use of opiates *reduces* erotic interest and drive.[9]

Pleasure remains seductive, though:

> The simple fact is that heroin use is intensely pleasurable, for many people more pleasurable than anything else they might do. . . . All of us enjoy pleasure; an addict is a person who has found the supreme pleasure and the means to make that pleasure occur.[10]

To some, this is immoral enough—it is pure hedonism—to justify depriving addicts of their liberty,[11] but in the present stage of social evolution, the enforcement of morals seems too coercive and autocratic, at least when the moral is stated in absolute terms. A utilitarian defense is necessary, instead. The typical utilitarian approach to the narcotics problem is the same one today it has always been: *narcotics cause crime.*

Dr. Boone, a long-time resident of Shanghai, told the Philippine Commission inquiry in 1905:

> I see no difference in the effect of the drug upon Europeans and Chinese. Its moral effect on the Chinese is often to make him a criminal. Opium smokers are prone to lying and to acts of malicious mischief, such as incendiarism, etc. The police courts of Shanghai show that the use of opium and crime in Shanghai are intimately associated.[12]

The same argument was extended to the use of cocaine by Hamilton Wright in 1910. Wright was probably the person most responsible for the passage of the Harrison Act four years later and the initiation of the federal drive against drugs. "This new vice, the cocaine vice, the most serious to be dealt with, has proved to be a creator of criminals and unusual forms of violence, and it has been a potent incentive in driving the humbler negroes all over the country to abnormal crimes."[13]

Note that what is alleged here is not merely an association or correlation between drugs and crime—which might, of course, be the effect of another factor again—but rather that drug use actually inspires the criminal to act and is the root cause of such acts.

Captain King sticks to the straight associational claim:

> The fact that men do begin the use of drugs through associations formed in the "red light" districts is established. . . . As further evidence in confirmation of the dangers above attributed to association with this class of women, I cite the following: At certain posts large numbers of soldiers appeared to be becoming seriously delinquent, as evidenced by the numbers coming here [U.S. Disciplinary Barracks] from organizations stationed there.[14]

Wilson is more careful to distinguish criminal behavior before drug use and after, but as he makes clear, to make the utilitarian case for suppression of narcotics use, it is not necessary to establish the exact direction of the relationship so long as its existence, and the consequent harm to others, can be verified:

Despite the fact that many addicts were criminals before addiction and would remain criminals even if they ended their addiction, and despite the fact that the theft losses to addicts are considerably exaggerated, there is little doubt that addiction produces a significant increase in criminality of two kinds—stealing from innocent victims, and selling heroin illegally to willing consumers.[15]

Once the fact of harm to general social welfare is established, the warrant for a policy is out. What the policy will be has always been determined by the theory of how drug use is acquired individually and spreads socially, and this—the theory of contagion—has scarcely changed since the 1880s. If drug addiction spreads like an infectious disease, the theory goes, the way to stop it is to identify the infected and lock them up so they can neither go on "infecting" others nor cause the social damage that justifies a quarantine as strict as prison.

Kane, in 1882:

It was soon found that smokers coming East were constantly making converts, so that in a few months' time small and large towns like Truckee, Carson, Reno and many others, each had their smoking dens and their regular customers. Each new convert seemed to take a morbid delight in converting others, and thus the standing army was daily swelled by recruits.[16]

An American Federation of Labor pamphlet of 1902:

The police have largely broken up these [Chinese] laundry opium joints, but there are hundreds, aye thousands, of our American boys and girls who have acquired the deathly habit and are doomed, hopelessly doomed. . . . Is it right or just to knowingly expose our children or the children of our neighbours to such dangerous contamination, even though it be not direct . . . an evil so entirely destructive to our domestic ideals?[17]

King again:

Experience here confirms me in the belief that many persons, at least early in their use of drugs are very pleased with their effect and enthusiastically spread the doctrine. . . . This, in my opinion, forms the most important chapter in the whole matter; . . . nothing can be more potentially harmful in [an army] company than one or two drug users, who may readily corrupt twenty or more men in a relatively short time. Hence, a more constant and earnest effort to weed out every user at the earliest possible moment is positively indicated. . . . Practically the only hope that exists for a permanent cure in the case of either morphine or cocaine users is the placing of them in an environment where it is difficult or impossible for them to get the drug. It is also important that the environment be such that they will have the moral support of more strongly endowed persons who have their interests at heart.[18]

In 1951, to the Federal Commissioner of Narcotics, H. J. Anslinger, this meant bluntly that "the immediate need in New York is not education but a quarantine ordinance which would confine these users in a controlled ward of a city hospital until they are pronounced cured by medical authorities."[19]

Finally, in Wilson's paper, the same theory points to the same result:

In the great majority of cases, not only was the new user turned on by a friend, but the friend himself was a novice user still exhilarated by the thrill of the high. . . . Suppose that law enforcement was directed at the user rather than the dealer. Taking users off the streets in large numbers would tend to reduce the demand for, and thus the price of, heroin. . . . Suppose, finally, that coupled with law enforcement aimed at known users there were a selective strategy of identifying and restraining the agents of contagion. . . .[20]

These excerpts articulate a remarkably unchanging ideology of drug use, a system of beliefs which identifies the addict in a combination of moral and psychological terms, illustrating the process by which addiction spreads in quasi-medical language and underwriting a range of enforcement policies with the utilitarian argument that addiction causes social harm.

This last element is the key to the punitiveness that has characterized narcotics policy from the beginning. If the harm done by drug addiction were suffered only by the addict himself, then notwithstanding the antihedonism of our culture, prison would not be the place to deal with him. This is perfectly evident in the treatment given morphine addicts early in the century, who happened to be physicians or who chanced to occupy relatively high social status. Alexander Lambert, then president of the American Medical Association and a highly influential public advocate of drug prohibition, went so far as to turn class differences among addicts into two distinct treatment policies. "It is usually a just differentiation," he told the AMA narcotics committee in 1921,

> that the heroin addict is of an inferior personality compared with morphinist . . . morphine is the drug of the stronger personality. . . . The social and public health problems of the narcotic drug question are practically confined to the addicts of heroin and cocaine, and their hospitalization and after-care. The problems of the morphine addicts belong more to general medicine and are more easily solved and show no tendency to become a social menace.[21]

The plain fact, and one I will return to again, is that the lower- or working-class addicts used heroin or cocaine, often both, and the middle- or upper-class addicts, principally medical men among the few there actually were, used morphine. The latter group were designated by Lambert and the AMA committee as being "otherwise normal," viewed with sympathy rather than moral condemnation and proposed for private medical treatment that might involve, at least initially, maintenance of the habit. According to the committee's report, the working-class addict was either a "correctional case," a "mental defective," or "social misfit." Prison was the mode of treatment recommended.

The importance of social class in both the theory of addiction and the determination of policy is not easy to pinpoint because it is so often expressed in quasi-medical or quasi-psychological terms. Lambert's "inferior personality-stronger personality" is typical; King, speaking of soldiers, spoke of drug users as being "defective individuals,"

> inherently so; a few of them definitely insane, most of them, however, belonging to the great borderland between mental stability and definite mental disease or positive defect. . . . A medical writer has referred to these people as "second-class human beings." They seek to slide through life with the least difficulty possible, with few or no cares and no responsibility and the minimum effort, mental and physical.[22]

As late as 1951, Harold O'Keefe, the chief of social service at the Lexington (Kentucky) hospital for addicts, repeated the stereotype of the working-class addict as if it were a well-established psychological datum:

> His dependency upon drugs seems to encrust the element of general dependence in his character, providing a kind of moral lethar-

gy. Frequently the result is a well-nigh spineless being in whom the sinews of personality are flaccid at best.[23]

Lethargy, flaccidity, laziness, passivity, inordinate sensuality—these are recurring images of the addict. The point here is that this stereotype was applied *only* to the working-class addict—and not only the addict, for it was and is still applied to the working-class individual in general.

"The addict is intensely present-oriented" is the way Wilson and his colleagues summed him up. But this trait is also commonly invoked to describe or account for working-class involvement in promiscuous sex,[24] violent gangs,[25] in juvenile delinquency in general.[26] Combined with other character traits, it has been adopted in a theory of working-class political attitudes and behavior, among which are support for strongmen in government, patriotic wars, militarism, and the strict enforcement of morals—in sum, what has come to be called working-class authoritarianism.[27]

This is not the place to dispute all of these claims at once. I want to point out, however, that they are all related to a central organizing myth, that the function of this myth is to legitimize and bolster the defenses in law, custom, and morality that middle-class America has built to protect the inequities of wealth and value on which it feeds. An attack on one part of this myth can accelerate the demise of the whole, thereby exposing the social injustice it hides.

Once the class bias of narcotics law and policy can be seen, however, the utilitarian case for it can no longer be regarded as philosophically neutral or objective. As the quoted excerpts above illustrate, so long as the policy issue is confined to the crime that results from addiction, the general social good is clearly enhanced by a reduction of both the incidence of crime and its cause. If, however, the criminal activity into which narcotic users step or fall is the consequence of an altogether different pattern of choice for working-class addicts—if, to be exact, inequality of income and social well-being between the classes makes the criminal choice more *likely or necessary* for the working-class addict than for the middle-class addict—then the policy of crime reduction will in no way alter the balance of social evil that the initial inequality represents. Indeed, to the extent that inequalities of this kind go together with narcotics use, the narrow application of utilitarian principles in this case simply adds to the sacrifices one class of society must make to improve the net balance of satisfaction for the other.

This, in a general way, is what in this book I intend to establish concretely. It will not be enough to show that the picture of narcotics use that has prevailed to date has frequently been founded on error or misconception. The recurrent nature of elements of this picture—of the mythology of narcotics, in short—suggests that what is at stake here is more than the correction of well-intentioned errors. Fundamentally, what is involved are the conflicting conceptions of social justice and the bitter struggle to implement them that is going on.

Chapter 2.
The Chinese Opium Crusade

There are many ways to take opium, and smoking it has been the Chinese way since the end of the seventeenth century. The practice was a small and geographically limited one in the beginning, confined to the coastal province of Fukien and the offshore island of Formosa. But early in the nineteenth century new pressures of trade caused a vast increase in the supply shipped to Chinese coastal merchants who, in turn, stimulated popular consumption and the diffusion of the habit up and down the coast, as well as inland.

Trade pressures were primarily from the British, who were the suppliers, and secondarily from the Americans, who were among the shippers and go-betweens. Cultivation of opium was how the British had financed the colonial administration in Bengal, and for the merchant companies involved, trade in the drug with China earned double profits—once when the drug was exchanged in Canton and Shanghai for silver, tea, and silk and again when these were landed and sold on the London markets.

The rising Chinese merchant class also stood to multiply its profits as the popular demand for opium grew. Inland, they bought tea and silk at low local prices and bartered them with the foreigners on the coast for the drug, whose real cash value depended on the merchants' ability to resell it to consumers at double (or more) the price. The profitability of the opium trade to the Chinese was an essential element in the expansion of the British trade. Without the coastal merchant to act as the comprador, or agent, for the drug supply, trade between the Europeans and China would have been too one-sided to endure, since, apart from opium there was initially little the Chinese could or would have wished or needed to buy from abroad as fair exchange for their tea and silks:[1]

China was force-fed opium, to be sure, as all the textbooks of nineteenth-century imperialism aver. As we will see many times over, supply preceded demand. In one sense of the old-fashioned economic law, the supply created its own demand.² It took a class of native Chinese and a unique role for opium as a medium of exchange, a form of money, along with the expectation of high profits among the Chinese compradors, to establish such a vast market for opium in China.

As it developed, the Chinese opium market was divided along clear lines of occupation, wealth or class. Most Chinese consumers, and the largest number of the most regular users, were poor peasants on one hand and wage laborers on the other, living in cities like Canton and Shanghai. According to one witness at the Philippine Commission inquiry, urbanization significantly increased the extent of opium use. Testimony by both Chinese and Europeans in China confirmed the class distribution: "the wealthy class in China, as a rule, does not smoke opium; the habit is largely confined to the poor. Among the smokers the proportion of the significantly well-off may be 20 percent; of the poor, 80 percent."³ This was equally true outside the homeland, among the Chinese in America, who started coming to California during the gold rush period in the early 1850s.

Between 1852, when the migration across the Pacific began to grow heavy,⁴ and 1863, when the gold mining for which they came was virtually played out, the Chinese immigrants were typically the younger sons of landowners without primogeniture rights of inheritance or many others living above rural poverty but with a stake too small to enlarge their wealth. They were usually not from laboring origins. Their stake, while small, insured that their interest in mining in California was independently capitalized. They paid for their own passages and brought capital with them to invest. In 1852 the total amount invested by Chinese in Californian commerce alone was estimated at $2 million.⁵ The number of wage laborers among the Chinese in the early period was low. As can be expected, if opium use was confined to this class, there is no record of its use among the first generation of immigrants in California. Not even recurrent incidents of anti-Chinese rioting and propaganda during the 1850s produced a single instance of the kind of claims about opium use that became commonplace 20 years later. Indeed, there is no mention of opium-smoking until the mid-1860s. None of the sources already cited have placed the beginning of the habit any earlier.⁶ There are no reports of the widespread opium use until the mid-1870s, when anti-Chinese demonstrations and the campaign to cut off immigration began in earnest. This period, roughly 1875 to 1880, is the first of the great antinarcotic crusades in our history. It is marked by the first attempts to legislate against drug use, which, as I will show, were closely related to the economic goals and motivation of the exclusion drive.

Getting rid of the Chinese had been spasmodically popular as an issue since the earliest arrivals. The conflict in the mining fields in the mid- to late-fifties reflected the slow but inevitable deterioration of the economic position of the independent white miners, prospectors like the Chinese themselves who had immigrated to the West with a small amount of capital, the traditional poke and burro, a partner or two perhaps, and much optimism that small-scale entrepreneurship could be vastly profitable. Of course, the surface gold did not last long. The deeper the miners had to go into the ground, the costlier their mining became. Water was expensive, as was blasting and sluicing equipment, and the new technology for such mining gave the large companies an important advantage. So the illusion of riches passed, and in the new economics of mining, the prospector had little choice. Without the capital to sustain himself, he could either lay down his pick altogether or swing it for the companies which could afford to stay in business. Wage labor came hard to men who aspired to independence, and naturally they vented their spleen on the companies which were taking over their claims. They were also ready to attack the Chinese in the mining fields, not because the Chinese were responsible for reducing the economic condition of the whites but because the Chinese were prepared to accept the terms of wage labor dictated by the companies to an extent that the white forty-niners were not. This, in turn, meant that the companies could afford to drop the wages of the white laborers, as long as there was a ready supply of Chinese who, if not happy, were at least willing to accept it. To stabilize the labor market in the mining fields and hold the line on the level of wages, the whites turned their attack from the source of economic power to the source of labor competition, and attacked the Chinese to drive them off the fields.

Calculated hostility of this kind, plus continually diminishing returns to mining, led to a drying up of the earlier petite bourgeoisie Chinese immigration around 1863–64. Between 1862 and 1863 California's gold production fell by more than half, and for the next four years more Chinese left the country than entered it.

After 1867 the newcomers were prepared to work. They had no assets; they had borrowed to finance their passage and would take any job that would help them pay off the debt. They were the perfect solution to the California employers' problems, the chief of which was the high cost of white labor. In a number of cases Chinese were introduced during the mid-1860s to break strikes against the Central Pacific Railroad, and other railroad companies followed suit. Anti-Chinese agitation was fairly rare, though, during the 1870s, at least for as long as the scarcity of labor and high wages held out for white workers, conditions that depended on a high rate of railroad construction.

As major lines were completed during the seventies and construction slowed down, labor scarcity turned to surplus and wages began to drop. An increasingly diversified economy in California was able to absorb this labor and cushion against wage declines, but around 1876 the economy began to suffer from competition from industries in the East whose access to California markets had been increased, by the completion of the railroads and the resulting drop in freight rates.

Especially hard hit was San Francisco, the center of California's manufacturing industries. To a large degree these industries had been built on Chinese labor, whose availability, passivity, and low price made them essential. This was also true in labor-intensive agriculture, especially fruit-growing and truck gardening in and around the city. By 1880, the Chinese in California were distributed among a variety of occupations, but in terms of concentration they dominated boot and shoe, cigar, and brick manufacture and were quite visible and economically important as relatively high-skilled labor in agriculture and fishing.

This high visibility, achieved by concentration rather than by large numbers overall, again precipitated anti-Chinese agitation. As the economic depression in the city deepened, both small manufacturers and the white labor force focused their attention on Chinese "competition" as being responsible for the conditions of low wages and high unemployment. As Chiu has shown,[7] the pattern of concentration of Chinese labor was the consequence, not the cause, of the low-wage (as well as the low-price-per-good) condition. White laborers, especially those with an independent-miner background, were unwilling to work at low wage levels of agricultural and industrial work and certainly not while railroad construction was paying a premium.

The economic basis of ethnic antagonism is clear:

Technological changes led as well to a hierarchy of profits. Large capital was concentrated in trades enjoying a high rate of investment returns, as in railroads and factory manufacturing. Small capital was crowded into fields where profit was low and diminishing. Caught in this process, apprehensive over the loss of their status as independent producers, lacking any understanding of the workings of "economic forces," small manufacturers of cigars, shoes, and clothing rose to vent their anger upon a scapegoat, as had the independent miners in the 1850's.[8]

Urban industrial workers had little in common with the small manufacturers, but, like them, they felt that unemployment and low wages had been caused by the Chinese. This feeling was reinforced by strong class antagonism as it became clear that the large capitalists of the area, the railroads and the mining companies, were *not* in favor of excluding the Chinese. Indeed, they argued that Chinese labor was the basis of California's rapid economic growth.[9] At first, farm elements were not hostile to Chinese labor, although interests diverged between large and small, often family, farm producers who were locked in conflict with the railroads over freight and land prices. The farmers chose to side with the white urban workers against "big business," and exclusion of the Chinese was the touchstone of the alliance.

It is worth reconstructing the political-economic picture in some detail in order to illustrate the kinds of pressures that were being brought to bear against the Chinese at the beginning of the first antiopium crusade. It is also important to understand the nature of the economic and political crisis into which the Chinese immigrants, especially the urban workers among them, were thrown by the depression of the late 1870s.

Among the first generation of Chinese immigrants who had weathered the decline of surface mining, a number had succeeded in building up their investment in commerce or small industry. Sizable profits were made by Chinese merchants in supplying the large construction gangs of the sixties and seventies. The second-generation, or laboring, immigrant may have had some hope of paying off his debts and going into truck gardening, the cigar business, or a laundry himself, but the worsening economic conditions after 1875 killed his chances.

The depression split the Chinese community down the middle. Generally, the merchants and petite-bourgeoisie group from the first wave of immigration had the assets with which to weather the economic pressure and falling profits, but the economic conditions depressed the Chinese laborer's wages and employment chances even further, thus deepening his debt and leaving him with fewer means for meeting the conditions of his immigration contract. The result was that Chinese laborers turned to the merchants as the employer of last resort and as the only available source of food and credit during prolonged unemployment.

The Chinese merchant class had other sources of income. During this time the incentive to shift to them was greater than at any time in the history of Chinese immigration. These were essentially the provision of illicit services. The first was sex, the second gambling, and the third opium.

At the time, the vast majority of Chinese immigrants to America were men.[10] Later, by the Act of Exclusion of 1882, the wives of all but the wealthiest Chinese were officially barred from entering the country. In 1870 there were nearly 13 men to each woman. During the next decade and the spurt of immigration in the first few years of the 1870s, the sex ratio grew wider until, according to the census of 1880, it exceeded 21 to 1. Trade in sex was inevitable, and the established sources of capital in the community were in a unique position to finance and conduct it.

Since white women were also scarce in California at the time, the demand for prostitutes drove the price of sex beyond what a Chinese laborer could afford, even supposing that cultural differences and latent racism on both sides were not sufficient to make the trade unacceptable. What was needed were Chinese prostitutes. To this end, capital was needed to pay for the recruitment and passage of girls from China to the United States, as well as to take care of the police payoffs and other overhead involved. Individual merchants or associations therefore undertook the contracting, often attracting girls in Canton and Hong Kong with offers of marriage, and set up houses for the trade.[11]

Gambling was provided in these and other establishments. In the conditions of tighter money, faro, fan-tan, and other games of the long shot offered the isolated, indebted, unemployed Chinese laborer his only chance to maintain his solvency. Under the circumstances in which the owners of the gambling houses were also the employers of legitimate labor, credit in the form of wage advances was made available, since it increased their control over the laborers. This was used, in turn, to depress real wages further and simultaneously raise the profitability of licit and illicit enterprises.

Now consider the opium trade. From 1871 to 1879 the average annual imports of smoking opium to the United States were 52,716 pounds. In the single year 1879, 60,648 pounds entered the country officially. The next year this shot up 27 percent, to 77,196 pounds, the largest single rise for the decade. Between 1880 and 1884 annual imports averaged 139,504 pounds, that is, more than two and a half times the earlier level.

What was happening?

The conventional explanation, and the one Hamilton Wright adopted retrospectively in his Report on the International Opium Commission in 1910, blames increased demand. As he saw the situation, the rise in imports of smoking opium reflected the increased demand for it from the larger numbers of Chinese arriving in the United States. We know that these numbers were increasing between 1868 and 1876, but the following year the number of arrivals dropped sharply, while that of those leaving increased. For the next four years the outflow rose steadily, and in 1880 there was a *net* outflow of over a thousand.

That the demand for opium existed among the Chinese in the mid-1870s and increased thereafter cannot be doubted, but it appears that the increase on the demand side *was preceded by* an increase on the *supply* side and that this was virtually unrelated to what was happening to the Chinese in California. What was involved, instead, was a complex network of speculation in the international opium trade which, coming on top of deteriorating economic conditions in California, encouraged opium importers in the United States, that is, *Chinese* importers, to introduce larger quantities of the drug for sale than ever before.

During the 1870s Persian-grown opium, which for years had trickled into China along the overland route through Bokhara, increased in volume to the point where the British administrators in Bengal, although they had no way of determining the exact size of the Persian imports, began to fear for the health of their monopoly. Chinese cultivation of the poppy was also becoming extensive, and significantly, from the consumer's point of view, its quality was beginning to approach that of the best Indian product.

Although the volume of Persian and Chinese opium in the late seventies was only a fraction of the Indian, the fact that it existed and was expanding had serious repercussions in the highly speculative conditions of the Indian industry.[12] Since the British colonial exchequer depended so heavily on a profitable opium trade, protection of the monopoly was considered essential. So the viceroy and his administration decided on a vast expansion of output, to allow the unit price to fall if need be, all in order to drive the competing opium off the market.

This tactic reached its zenith in the trade of the year 1879–80, when, altogether, 95,000 chests, or 15.2 million pounds, of opium were exported to China. Following this, both competition in the China market and fluctuations in opium acreage in Bengal, as well as drought and other factors, led to a steady decline in the volume and value of the trade.

As a market for opium, the United States was insignificant compared with China (annual imports of crude and smoking opium in 1880–84 were less than 3 percent of the Indian exports to China).[13] Nevertheless, the climate of changing expectations regarding the trade interacted with other speculative interests to produce the sharp rise already noted.[14] To traders burdened with a growing Indian surplus, the American market was a minor, but convenient, outlet. To shippers and clipper captains operating between the Chinese ports and San Francisco, new cargo was needed once the flow of Chinese began to reverse itself. For the voyage from Hong Kong or Canton to San Francisco, the numbers of immigrant passengers fell by over 50 percent in 1877 alone. But the key element in this situation was the behavior of the Chinese merchants operating, for the most part, in San Francisco. The economic depression that had struck the city precipitated a special crisis for them, and the expansion of the opium trade offered a way out.

From the beginning of the immigration, the Chinese had established many associations among themselves. These were the *tongs*, and were originally based on a clan, or kin, connection, occupation, or the region from which members had come. They served several functions—as fraternal and mutual-help groups, as quasi-unions to represent their members in collective bargaining or in negotiations for jobs, as community policing agents, traditional courts of arbitration, and trade associations. While the name, or clan, *tongs* functioned as loose mutual-aid societies, the trade *tongs* operated as tight cartels regulating every aspect of a particular industry, allocating raw materials, fixing prices, providing insurance, and generating commercial and investment credit. There were also *tongs* that represented most of the political and ideological tendencies then current in China.[15]

Tong leaders kept a tight rein on their organization, while the organizations themselves regulated and maintained a fairly rigid hierarchy of power, wealth, status, and prestige throughout the Chinese community. For instance, the economic controls imposed by the trade associations were particularly useful to members in dealing with the non-Chinese world. They were also so tight that their effect was to eliminate what little chance for social mobility there was among the Chinese at large. There was little likelihood, for example, of a laborer rising to become a merchant. The one gap in their power, however, was the illicit trade in sex, gambling, and drugs.

How legal and illegal enterprises were joined together and managed by the *tongs* at the time cannot easily be known.[16] It is likely that some legitimate traders were forced by their *tong* associates, either directly or through protection payments, to help finance the brothels, casinos, and opium dens. The gangs supplying protection often supplied a bona fide service, for the threat of violence from whites in the Chinese quarter of San Francisco was a real and constant one. To the extent that the first generation of immigrants retained control of the major *tongs*, however, those lower-class Chinese whose aspirations for wealth and power were checked by the existing system sought to branch out and specialize on their own. Selling protection was the first step. What was evolving in the mid-1870s, then, were a number of specialized "criminal" *tongs* composed of members who were excluded from any other trade by the ruling groups.

These *tongs* fought violently with each other to establish exclusive territories and areas of operation. With the onset of the depression they appear to have competed with elements of the ruling *tongs* to introduce and then control the trade in opium. The outcome of this struggle was victory for the criminal *tongs*, a clear split by 1890 between the criminal and the legitimate trading *tongs*, and the elimination of overlapping or competitive operations. Several years later, at the turn of the century and for 20 years more, the two groups battled for economic control of Chinatown. This resulted in victory for the legitimate side when Chinatown changed from serving sex to serving chop suey.[17]

At the same time, there were many legitimate *tong* interests which needed no pressure to direct their investment into criminal operations. The majority of these organizations were not the evil conspiracies they were accused of being by the anti-Chinese press and agitation of those years. Some may, however, have specialized in the illicit trade and some may not, but the connivance of many of the legitimate traders in financing the importing, processing, distributing, and sale of opium cannot be doubted.[18]

There were good reasons for this, quite apart from the profits to be made from the business. Remember that the period 1875–1880 was one of deteriorating economic conditions for most Chinese laborers. There were few alternatives. They could leave the United States; they could move out of California to other parts of the country, looking for work; or they could stick it out in California, relying on credit and other help from the *tongs*.

To the merchants, exodus was more of a threat than was depression, because it removed for good the very basis of Chinese enterprise: cheap labor. Opium may have been offered as an inducement to stay (close to the source of supply), and there is fragmentary evidence that opium rations were specified for this purpose in the terms of some labor contracts.[19] But we know that the big increase in opium imports took place during a decline in the Chinese population, so it seems likely that the importers intended to initiate a demand for the drug that did not already exist.

Wright, whose report was based in part on "inquiry amongst the leading Chinese in this country," stated that the opium habit was acquired by the immigrants *after* they arrived in this country and not, as others have claimed, before they left China.[20] In his study of the *tongs,* Reynolds also came to the conclusion that the Chinese did not bring opiate use with them, but that instead, it had begun in the United States because "the basis for their temperance was largely removed in America."[21] By this he meant a combination of factors—a psychological predisposition to use the drug and the absence of traditional kin structure and normative bonds which might have inhibited drug use.

There is no telling what exactly *motivated* the individual Chinese then to smoke opium in the United States. Even when drug users are more readily available to respond to this question about motivation, rarely is there a decided answer, and even when one exists, it doesn't *sufficiently* explain the phenomenon. At any rate, we do know that at the end of the last century, perhaps 35 percent of the immigrant population smoked with some degree of regularity. This is Wright's estimate, based on interviews and hearsay evidence which he further broke down into three categories of use.[22]

TABLE 2–1

Characteristics of Opium Use Among Chinese
in the United States, circa 1900

Category of Use	Consumption by Weight	Number	Percent
Heavy	6 pounds per year	12,000	10
Light	1½ pounds per year	18,000	15
Social	1 ounce per year	12,000	10
		42,000	35

This should be treated as a hypothetical maximum, although, whatever the real numbers were, there can be little doubt that for the next half-century the Chinese were represented in the population of narcotics users out of all proportion to their total in the general population.[23] The timing at the very beginning is important. Using the same rough estimates again, it is possible to show how the aggregate number of Chinese users and the prevalence rate changed between 1870 and 1890. The tabulation is based on four assumptions: (1) minimal smuggling of the drug; (2) all smoking opium imported in that form and not prepared in the United States from gum opium base; (3) all opium smokers Chinese; and (4) all heavy Chinese smokers. Variation in any of these, or in combination, would radically alter the aggregate and rate estimates, and there is no telling whether such variation was equal and constant in each period. Both the 1880 and 1890 estimates do come close, however, to the 10 percent "heavy smoking" rate figured from different sources by other authorities.

TABLE 2–2

Prevalence of Opium Use Among Chinese
in the United States, 1870–90

	1870	1880	1890
Total Chinese population in U.S.	63,199	105,465	106,488
Annual average imports of smoking opium, for the previous five-year period (lbs.)	21,666	58,653	64,465
Number of opium smokers at an estimated 6 lb. each per year	3,611	9,776	10,744
Prevalence rate (percent)	5.7	9.3	10.1

Notwithstanding the likelihood of error, the strong suggestion here is that there was a substantial jump in opium smoking among the Chinese between 1870 and 1880. Most of this increase was concentrated in the depression years, 1875–80, when the major rise in imports occurred. But significantly, as will be seen, this took place *after* the first antiopium legislation had been enacted in the country (the city ordinance banning its use in San Francisco).[24]

At this time it required only a tiny fraction of the Indian opium output to make a substantial difference in the situation in the United States. In this context (that of calculations independently arrived at by growers, shippers, buyers, distributors, and consumers) the drug served several functions. The combined effect of the bottom falling out of the sweatshop industries and the intense anti-Chinese campaign threatened to destroy Chinese capitalism by driving its labor force away and bringing manufacturing and trade to a halt. At this time, then, the prospects for a trade in opium coincided with the deterioration of the conventional Chinese economy; simultaneously the deterioration of the general economy put large numbers of Chinese workers out of work, making them dependent on the *tongs* for employment or welfare.

Opium was looked on, first, as having the potential to compensate for the general decline of profits, employment, and income. Given an initial level of demand, no matter how moderate, the legitimate traders in Chinatown were in a position to use opium in lieu of money wages to pay their employees, in effect, to deflate wage levels while at the same time inducing the workers to stay in San Francisco close to the source of supply, rather than leave for the East Coast or for the homeland. Opium also offered an alternative source of income to gambling and prostitution, which were declining as the economy worsened. With many unemployed Chinese seeking jobs, the "criminal" *tongs* were able to recruit new members to sell the drug at the same time they were paid, at least in part, with a supply of the drug for their own use.

There is no good way to tell how far recruitment to drug use was determined by the expectation of profit out of the trade or by the need for an analgesic and soporific as potent as opium. The order and timing of events are important, however, in order to establish just how speculative importation was in 1879 and the following years, for they reveal that use of the drug was propelled by powerful economic forces. Consumer demand no more explains the development of the market, with all the economic and social ramifications it then had, than individual desire for any good ever explains aggregate level of supply.

Chinese laborers had to enjoy smoking opium in order to continue doing so, of course, but insofar as opium was so valuable that, like gold or money, it could be exchanged for almost any other good, consuming it could also have reflected the simple desire for consuming wealth.

Having identified these functions of the drug, it would be misleading not to repeat that the spread of opium would not have developed outside the peculiar economic conditions in which the Chinese, both petite bourgeoisie and working class, were forced to live. To take another example, in the Mississippi delta a strong effort was first made during the 1870s by white planters to attract Chinese laborers to working on the cotton plantations. The purpose was to displace black sharecroppers (who had, under early Reconstruction, gained the power of the franchise and were threatening to use it against the political supremacy of the planters): "The apolitical noncitizen coolie, it was thought, would be a step back toward the more docile labor conditions of slavery times and would also destroy all arguments about the indispensability of Negro labor to the Southern way of life."[25]

The experiment failed, for several reasons. The number of Chinese attracted was small. Once the real terms of plantation labor became clear, they abandoned the work; having done this, they were able to build up successful grocery businesses of their own. Essentially it is a story of the Chinese, initially laborers, breaking out of the constraints of what has been called a split-labor market.[26] It stands to reason, then that we would find no evidence either of opium use among the Chinese in the delta or even of *accusations* that it existed and was a public menace.

In California, however, only a small minority of the Chinese achieved any kind of economic independence. Most were the hapless victims of the split-labor market in which, during the 1870s, the higher-paid (white) labor combined with small farmers and manufacturers to force out the Chinese altogether.

The earliest agitation for exclusion had been directed against Chinese miners when the pickings grew slim for independent prospectors. There is no mention in the record of anti-Chinese rhetoric of the time that the immigrants used opium or passed the habit on to whites. Not until the mid-1870s did talk of this kind become noticeable, and from what we already know of the movement of immigrants and opium during the depression years, it is evident that increased public consciousness of the habit came before its increased diffusion. In other words, opium-smoking was simply part of the stereotype generated by antagonism between the races.

The earliest connotation of opium use was not an intrinsic one. There was no claim, for example, that it was harmful directly. Its use indicated, rather, how different, foreign, and unassimilable the Chinese were as a group. A California Senate report of 1877 stated flatly: "the whites cannot stand their dirt and the fumes of opium, and are compelled to leave their vicinity."[27]

In 1875 San Francisco passed a city ordinance against opium-smoking and the operating of dens for that purpose. The following year a similar ordinance passed in Virginia City, Nevada. Concerning this ordinance Kane offers the testimony of a local physician on the reasons for the legislation:

> Opium smoking had been entirely confined to the Chinese up to and before the autumn of 1876, when the practice was introduced by a sporting character who had lived in China. . . . He spread the practice amongst his class, and his mistress, "a woman of the town," introduced it among her *demimonde* acquaintances, and it was not long before it had widely spread amongst the people mentioned, and then amongst the younger class of boys and girls, many of the latter of the more respected class of families. The

habit grew rapidly, until it reached young women of more mature age, when the necessity for stringent measures became apparent, and was met by the passing of a city ordinance.[28]

This, of course, is the classic theory of contagion, but there is no way of knowing how much of it was rumor, how much was true, and how much was mere rationalization for the broader aims of the anti-Chinese agitation.

The Chinese opium crusade is such a clear illustration of the role of class in these developments, however, for it occurred when there was no precedent for a legal ban on narcotics and when no one believed that the drug or its use per se was harmful or dangerous. Just how unformed the ideology of opium was is evident in the testimony, given sometime after the ordinance went into effect, of a number of authorities who were more familiar than most with the drug and the Chinese predilection for it. Seward, who was strongly opposed to the exclusion campaign, examined the criminal statistics for Chinese in California. While acknowledging prostitution, gambling, and a certain amount of extortion, corruption of police, and internecine feuding, he did not mention opium use.[29] This was in 1881. A few years later, Richmond Mayo-Smith, a political economist, noted the evidence of opium-smoking but qualified it: "which latter vice, however, seems to be less of a public nuisance than drunkenness, for it simply stupefies the victim instead of exciting him."[30] Even later, before the Philippine Commission, the examining physician of the New York Life Insurance Company in Shanghai told the commissioners that he readily permitted opium users the life insurance they applied for, on the ground that "Chinese can use opium moderately for years, indeed for a lifetime, with no ill results."[31]

The point to be emphasized is that the ideology of opium during the period in which the first antinarcotic legislation in the country was introduced specified virtually nothing about the drug or its effects. That antiopium laws were put into operation and that notions about the drug being harmful and dangerous were expressed and eventually believed is indicative of a class ideology in the making, although the character of the class conflict that stimulated the ideology is not simple.

The principal factor involved was the existence of a labor market split less by skill or the characteristics of industrial organization than by race, for the latter, much more than the former, set the pattern for determining wages. The Chinese, whatever their skill level, were paid less than whites. This labor market was the creation of the railroads and the mining companies, which hired labor agents in Hong Kong and Canton to recruit immigrants. Indeed, it was the creation of California capital as a class, whether individual elements actively initiated immigration or not. By no stretch of the imagination can the non-Chinese working class be held responsible for that. Its members were basically correct in identifying tendencies toward the dual wage market as a form of class threat from the start, with the potential for undermining existing working-class wage levels and subverting the power of class unity in collective bargaining.

The primary event that precipitated the campaign against the Chinese and against opium was the sudden onset of economic depression, the high unemployment levels, and the disintegration of working-class standards of living. Again, if blame must be leveled for that, it rests on the small, urban manufacturers whose rate of profit depended not on technological innovations, expanded capital investment, improvements in productivity, and because of these, lowered unit costs—all of which might have protected them against economic reversal—but rather on cheap labor alone, first female and child labor and then, because they were found to be more productive and easily disciplined, the Chinese. Once the railroad wiped out the geographical protection of this industry from the more sophisticated mass production of the eastern United States, the price of manufactures had to fall, and with that went economic stability. In other words, the depression was a crisis of small capital, combined with the decline of employment in railroad construction.

Hostility toward the Chinese was the immediate result, although the race issue did not, in fact or in time, serve the interests of the white working class or the small entrepreneurs. Neither group realized this, and among the working class the defense of the Chinese by the railroad and farming interests automatically reinforced the determination to expel them. The opium issue, which was one of the many variations on this theme, was part of the general ideological response to labor market failure, reflecting the extent to which the secondary labor market, with its Chinese concentration, offered no "work relief" to the unemployed, insecure, white working class. The ideological role of the anti-opium campaign was to get rid of the Chinese. It had a practical consequence—providing a legal basis for unrestrained and arbitrary police raids and searches of Chinese premises in San Francisco. Ostensibly to identify opium dens, these raids served the same purpose as that of the vigilantes in the mine fields, against Chinese encampments in the mid-1850s.

I have defined the function of the antiopium campaign at one level of class conflict. Had the economic conditions not deteriorated, inciting agitation against the Chinese, the particular inducements to develop the trade in the drug among Chinese capitalists would not have arisen. They, no less than native American capitalists, depended on the continued exploitation of the immigrants at low wage rates, and this, in turn, created a second level of class conflict tied to the first. At the second level the drug was also a class weapon, in that it depressed the real level of working-class wages and living standards, although in the broader, multilevel context, recruitment of workers for the opium trade was, for them, an effective and rational response to the economic bind. They would become pawns in the competition between the *tongs* for economic hegemony in Chinatown—cannon fodder, in fact, when the competitors took to their guns—but that was in the future and probably would not have affected the calculations of the Chinese anyway.

Though the California antiopium legislation had little effect at the time (there turned out to be much more effective ways of opposing the Chinese), analysis of what took place shows a pattern which has repeated itself in nearly every period of active agitation on the drug issue ever since.

Chapter 3.
Blacks and Cocaine

The second national campaign against narcotics ran, with ups and downs in what newspapers like to call public hysteria, for roughly 15 years, that is, from 1905 to 1920.

In that time Congress passed three major pieces of antinarcotics legislation—the Pure Food and Drug Act of 1906, the 1909 act "to Prohibit Importation and Use of Opium," and the Harrison Act of 1914—and then, along with a number of court decisions broadening the scope of the legislation and police powers to enforce it, fixed the national policy of prohibition on narcotics down to the present day.

The background for this was a concoction of myths which, in this instance, is the sociological term for lies and deceptions which took many sincere people in, a background that performed much the same covering role as did antiopium propaganda for the Chinese exclusion movement a quarter of a century before, except that this time the target was enlarged to take in blacks and working-class whites of immigrant origins. The underlying pattern of economic crisis and class conflict was repeated; only the political dynamics were different. An irreversible force (the medical profession) met a corruptible object (the legal profession).[1]

What the Pure Food and Drug Act did was not ban narcotic drugs but only require that when medicines contained them, that fact and the quantity would be clearly labeled on the package. Actually the popular agitation that culminated in the 1906 act was concerned only incidentally with the consumption of drugs. In the event, the measures dealing with the opiate and cocaine contents of patent medicines were inserted into the bill at the last moment. Its Congressional sponsors and the man who drafted it, Dr. Harvey Wiley of the Bureau of Chemistry in the Federal Department of Agriculture, favored the measures but did not consider them as important or as likely to pass as the food adulteration provisions, which were the heart of the legislation.[2]

The bill drew support from a variety of forces. One of them, which was to have a roundabout, but telling, effect on the narcotics story by the time of the Harrison Act, was the medical profession. For most of the nineteenth century doctors had been practicing their medicine without much popularity or prestige and in competition with pharmacists, druggists—in fact, anyone with the imagination or capital to risk in offering his services or products for the cure of ailments and disease. By 1900 two developments had begun to transform the once laissez-faire free enterprise in cures. One was medical theory after Louis Pasteur had refocused attention in diagnosis and pathology on the *parts* of the body rather than the body as a single entity. This, in turn, spurred specialization and division of labor within the medical profession, while at the same time the number of medical graduates began to multiply fast.[3]

Meanwhile, the patent medicine industry had grown to such size in output, dollar sales, and the capital needed to sustain operations that it was no longer easy for the lone entrepreneur to make good. The newspaper and advertising industries had generated much of their revenues over the years from the marketing of patent medicines, but by late in the century competition had become so intense that the cost of mass advertising campaigns had reached the point where the large capital investments necessary to launch a new product began to limit the entry of newcomers to the field. In short, only the large companies could survive, and economic concentration was already well advanced before the 1906 act which accelerated it.

The increasingly self-assertive medical profession contested the provisions of the legislation with the drug manufacturers, whose economic power had become more and more centralized. What was at stake was control of the market in medical services. So long as *anyone* could offer medical treatment by marketing a patented formula of his own invention, the doctors' accreditation and the legitimacy this was intended to carry were subject to indiscriminate competition in the marketplace. Pharmacists and druggists, who also claimed a special position on similar grounds, could earn nothing for the scarcity. The price of their skill was thus squeezed, in addition to their being between the doctors as prescribing agents and a welter of drug and medicine suppliers, whose repute depended on marketing and advertising campaigns and not on the efficacy of their products.

The economics of this system made everyone a charlatan. The 1906 legislation did not change much, not even the quality of medical goods and services; it simply reduced the ability of some groups to supply the goods and services and divided the market up between those who were left—organized doctors and a diminishing number of drug companies, with a system of licensed retailers in the middle. Nor did the 1906 act, as is often claimed, stop the abuses of the patent medicine industry; it merely helped rationalize its economic structure and legitimize the output, the effect of which was higher prices and greater profits in the pharmaceutical business.

Opium, heroin, morphine, and cocaine were at the time the principal analgesic drugs in use. The fight to control them, which the American Medical Association had begun in 1905, reflected the profession's determination to take over greater control of drug production and supply than was granted it in the provisions of the 1906 act.

Hamilton Wright, a medical scientist specializing in tropical diseases, was the principal representative of the prohibitionists in the profession; practically speaking, both the 1909 and 1914 acts were his doing.

Since 1908 Wright had been deputized by the State Department to represent the United States in negotiations with the Chinese for controlling their own opium problem and at a number of conferences the United States sought to convene to regulate the international traffic in opium. The Report on the International Opium Commission, was written by him following meetings of the Shanghai Opium Commission in 1909. Before the commission had even adjourned its proceedings, Congress passed an act to tighten controls over imported opium, which prohibited the entry of the drug in a form intended for nonmedicinal use and limited the entry of approved shipments to 12 designated ports.[4]

Initially the State Department's concern with opium stemmed from a desire to block the importation of Chinese supplies of the drug into the Philippines which, at the time, were under American colonial administration. The report by a committee of the Philippine Commission, issued in 1906, stimulated the government to act on the problem of foreign traffic, and Wright was responsible for linking this aspect of policy with draft legislation he proposed for dealing with domestic consumption in the United States. He told the House Ways and Means Committee in 1910:

> The opium problem in the United States as it now stands needs to be confined by a triangle. One side of that triangle has been laid

down by the act of last February. The importation of opium prepared for smoking and of other forms of opium except for medicinal purposes is prohibited by that act. If the proposed act about to be submitted, or some other act of Congress to control the manufacture and interstate traffic in the drug passes and is approved, the second side of the triangle will have been laid down. The third side may be made from an internal-revenue act that will prohibitively tax the manufacture of smoking opium within the United States.[5]

It took four more years for Wright's triangular policy to be implemented, but when it finally was, in the form subsequently known by the name of the bill's sponsor in committee as the Harrison Narcotic Act, Wright had extended the provisions to include all of what he called habit-forming drugs, including the opium derivatives morphine and heroin and the pharmacologically unrelated cocaine. Trade, prescription, or consumption of these drugs were not prohibited under the new law, not at first, for it was designed as a revenue measure and provided only for registration of the channels through which the drugs passed at each stage of trade, from importation of the raw material to final consumption, and the levying of registration charges and tax on each of the groups involved, from manufacturers to medical practitioners and retail druggists. Regulations later issued by the Treasury transformed the act into the blanket prohibition that Wright had originally intended, including the prohibition against doctors prescribing the drugs to maintain existing habits.

Wright himself believed that two things were basic to the case for narcotics prohibition. The first was that the use of opium in one form or another, either by smoking prepared gum opium or by injecting morphine or heroin, was widespread in American society. He made a special point of social class. Smoking opium, he wrote in 1910, "had steadily spread to a large part of our outlaw [sic] population *and even into the higher ranks of society*" (my emphasis). Even worse was the so-called cocaine habit, "the most threatening of the drug habits that has ever appeared in this country," which "apart from the outlaw population, threatens to creep into the higher social ranks of the country."[6]

To some extent Wright put the blame for this on irresponsible dispensing practices by medical practitioners, along with a "certain amount of ignorance as to the danger in the use of opiates."[7] That being the case, he reasoned, the medical profession would be responsible—in effect, wholly responsible—for rescuing the country from the danger by curing those with drug habits involuntarily or otherwise acquired. This was the second fundamental tenet of his belief—that addiction to opiates or cocaine was a disease of a recognizably pathological character and that it could be cured by medical treatment.

Such a belief depended on evidence of the way in which the drugs affected the body, and a great deal of then fresh clinical research appeared to provide it, along with recipes for a variety of treatments.[8] One of them had been developed for use in a private New York sanitarium by Charles Towns who had also applied it, with reputedly great success, in the Philippines and China. Wright was so impressed that he attached it to his report to the State Department at the conclusion of the Shanghai meeting. It was also taken up by Alexander Lambert, a Cornell professor and associate of Wright's, and, crucially, the medical advisor and friend of President Theodore Roosevelt. Because of their powerful network of government contacts, official assignments within the government, their spokesmen role for the American Medical Association on the drug issue, and close association together, Wright and Lambert deserve to be regarded as the founding fathers of American drug policy.

The immediate effect of the Harrison Act was, in one sense, the realization of the medical profession's long-standing aim: to gain control of drug production and supply. Musto describes the result as "almost a monopoly for physicians in the supply of opiates to addicts."[9] What happened was that the act licensed the doctors to prescribe the drugs, but it did not limit the purposes for which the prescribing could be done. The result was that doctors took to the trade as the old patent medicine salesmen had done before 1906, offering drug supplies at a premium price in the name of progressive withdrawal or just plain habit maintenance.

Wright and Lambert had conceived of medical control of the drug trade—but not in these terms. They supported *total* prohibition, even of maintenance doses, because they thought they knew what led people to consume the drugs, what caused their addiction, and what would without fail cure them of it. Total narcotics prohibition, as it came into force in 1919, produced sharp dissent and opposition among practitioners dealing with drug users, but it reflected Wright's and Lambert's position exactly. Lambert was elected president of the AMA in 1919, and his position on drugs was the official AMA one.

This has frequently been characterized as a retreat by the profession from what is loosely called the "medical approach," as distinct from the "police approach" to drug users. In fact, the two were never alter-natives in the original Wright proposals but from the very beginning complemented each other. For Wright from the beginning and later Lambert consistently distinguished among drug users between the "outlaw population" and the "higher social ranks." The first part of their case for narcotics prohibition was that addiction was spreading from one to the other, increasing the size of the former with recruits from the latter. The second part of their case said quite simply that those who would be cured could be cured—if drugs were completely prohibited. For example, Lambert, who tested the Towns cure at Bellevue Hospital in New York, never believed that curability extend-ed to the criminal element. The punitiveness that is generally associat-ed with the "police approach" was the policy he espoused for that ele-ment or type of addict. What this amounted to was a distinction of so-cial class, expressed in terms of the drug involved, or the "personality differences" between groups of drug users.

It is usually a just differentiation, Lambert told the AMA narcotics committee in 1921, "that the heroin addict is of an inferior personality compared with the morphinist . . . morphine is the drug of the stronger personality . . . . The social and public health problems of the narcotic drug question are practically confined to the addicts of heroin and cocaine, and their hospitalization and after-care. The prob-lems of the morphine addicts belong more to general medicine and are more easily solved and show no tendency to become a social menace."[10] The working-class addict, as I indicated earlier, was either a "correctional case," "mental defective," or "social misfit." Prison was the recommended mode of treatment.

It seems so natural now—to some, reasonable—that the nonmedical use of these drugs should be prohibited totally and that the prohibition should be backed by the threat of prison. At first, though, Wright, Lambert, and their associates in the federal government and the AMA found it difficult to convince those responsible for enforcing the ban and applying the sanctions that, as a general rule, an individual didn't have the freedom to consume whatever drugs he chose or that in the particular case presented to the court, the individuals charged were guilty of any crime other than the exercise of this freedom of choice.

An Oregon district court, for example, ruling on the conviction of a Chinese for selling opium, acknowledged at the height of the first opi-um crusade that the target of the prohibition was not the drug per se but the particular and characteristic user: "Smoking opium is not our vice, and therefore it may be that this legislation proceeds more from a desire to vex and annoy the 'Heathen Chinese' in this respect, than to protect the people from the evil habit." The conviction was sustained on the grounds that "the motives of legislators cannot be the subject of judicial investigation for the purpose of affecting the validity of their acts."[11]

To uncover what these motives were for each major episode of narcotics prohibition and to identify the real targets among drug users marked for prison—this is how I will approach the history of the policies and laws, but lawyers took no such approach in the early resistance to prohibition. Essentially it was fought out in the courts on the constitutional issue. How far could the police powers of the state be extended over individual behavior such as opium use or tobacco and alcohol use which involved similar and parallel legal struggles and in which supposed basic personal rights were involved?

The fight to stave off state and police control of the alcohol trade was already virtually lost by the time of the first antiopium legislation, but mere possession of alcohol, for consumption rather than sale, was successfully defended by lawyers and sustained by judges until at least 1915.[12] During the same period, possession of narcotics—in virtually every case, possession of opium by a Chinese—failed to make or win such a defense. Instead, courts in Oregon, Washington, and California decided that it was up to the state legislatures to decide what public harm there was in use of a drug. When it was argued that this was much worse than alcohol consumption, the courts accepted the distinction. In the case of Yun Quong, who was convicted in California in 1911 for possession of opium, the lower court said bluntly:

> Liquor is used daily in this and other countries as a beverage, moderately and without harm, by countless thousands . . . whereas it appears there is no such thing as moderation in the use of opium. Once the habit is formed the desire for it is insatiable, and its use is invariably disastrous.

In letting the decision stand, the state supreme court held that the evils of opium might well be worse, but that it was *sufficient* that legislators were not acting unreasonably *merely to think so.*

> The validity of legislation which would be necessary or proper under a given state of facts does not depend upon the actual existence of the supposed facts. It is enough if the law-making body may rationally believe such facts to be established. If the belief that the use of opium, once begun, almost inevitably leads to ex-

cess may be entertained by reasonable men—and we do not doubt that it may—such belief affords a sufficient justification for applying to opium restrictions which might be unduly burdensome in the case of other substances, as, for example, intoxicating liquors, the use of which may fairly be regarded as less dangerous to their users or to the public.[13]

After World War I had begun in Europe and as the United States edged toward intervention, the hyperpatriotism, the widespread paranoia about German-speaking Americans and the rumored fifth column of spies, and the determination of the Wilson Administration to dragoon a substantially unwilling population into war and either subvert or destroy the opposition—all were circumstances making the time poor for the Bill of Rights and for constitutional guarantees of personal liberties. Legal resistance to the prohibition of alcohol collapsed, and the Volstead Act instituted the decade and a half known as Prohibition by outlawing the possession of liquor. This was upheld by the United States Supreme Court in 1919. At the same time a succession of Treasury Department regulations enlarged the prohibition on narcotics, and again the Supreme Court held that this was permissible under the Harrison Act and supported the original Wright-Lambert policy that simple maintenance of a drug habit interfered with the cure and therefore must be banned.[14]

What was subject to police power, as now construed by the courts, was whatever legislators or the vast, if manipulable, public thought to be harmful to public welfare, whatever that might be. Gone was the earlier limitation that the harm be demonstrably and directly injurious to society; gone, too, was any requirement that the damage to welfare be proved. In their places was the force of public opinion, right or wrong, which, as a practical rule, amounted to the force of medical opinion, again right or wrong. But, as indicated, research findings could be used to support either side of the prohibition issue, so that there was no way clear to decide between sides—not, at least, on scientific grounds. What became public opinion then, or what this was generally understood to be, and what became public policy cannot be explained on their scientific merits, simply because the merits were evenly divided. If there was a connection between opinion and policy, it had to be a *political* one, of people and opinion mobilized for particular policy objectives. The story of each episode is the account of how this was done and what the objectives were.

A commentary on the evolution of police power indicated just how far, by 1914, legal policy on the issue had departed from the guarantees in the Bill of Rights:

> As each litigation arose, the judges could follow no rule but the rule of common sense, and the Police Power, translated into plain English, presently came to signify whatever, at the moment, the judges happened to think reasonable. Consequently, they began guessing at the drift of public opinion, as it percolated to them through the medium of their education and prejudices.[15]

In this way it happened, then, that the machinery was set up, principally by leaders of the medical profession but with lawyers in the supporting role, to mobilize whatever community resources were available to attack or punish the social groups or forms of behavior that these politically commanding elites considered dangerous or threatening. The next step in the story is to illustrate which groups were newly singled out during this period and to show that the conventional rationales for narcotics policy at the time, in particular those provided by Hamilton Wright, were almost certainly untrue and known to be untrue by a number of people who advocated them.

The point I am making is that several latent forces and interests (in the political-economic sense of the term) were acting on the policy-making process throughout the period. The fact that one of the results was the foundation of a narcotics policy in the United States does not necessarily mean that the individuals and groups which laid them down did so in response to a manifest need for narcotics control per se. If we ask what was the evidence of a drug problem during the period 1905–20, we will find, as we did in analyzing the first episode, a visible gap between what the problem really was, what its dimensions were supposed to be in public opinion and whose interests were served, and what was accomplished by the adoption of the policy when it came.

There are three distinct drug "problems" in the historical record. One was a sharp and noticeable increase in the number of adolescent drug users between 1910 and 1915. The evidence for this is found in court, hospital, and prison records. A judge of the Court of Special Sessions, in New York, reported that in 1916, 18.9 percent of drug cases presented to him were under 21 years old and that between 1916 and 1921 this was the peak year for that age group.[16] W. A. Bloedorn, who analyzed drug addiction admissions to New York's Bellevue Hospital from 1905 to 1916, found that most of the cases were concentrated between the ages of 21 and 23:

> When we take into consideration the fact that most addicts have

been constant users of the drug for at least a year and in many cases for several years before admission to the hospital, we see that a large percentage began the use of drugs while they were still minors.[17]

There is no way to be sure how general, or how unusual, this phenomenon was. Bloedorn's evidence indicates that among users of morphine, opium, and cocaine at Bellevue, the average and modal ages were significantly more than those among the heroin users, that the annual admissions rates for the former drug groups peaked in 1913 at the latest, and that there was a sharp and continuous rise in the admissions rate for heroin users from 1913 to 1916, the last year studied. This suggests that something unusual may have been happening and that the rise in heroin use and the fall in the age of the users were parallel, related phenomena.

Kane was one of the publicists during the first episode (see Chapter 2) who claimed that the young, especially young women, were particularly susceptible to the opium habit,[18] but Bloedorn's evidence belies this.[19] For opium addiction he found two age peaks at the 24–26 and 36–40 age groups (a total of 74 cases), for morphine a flat and even distribution between the ages of 24 and 40 (1,393 cases), and for cocaine, a single peak at 27–30 years (53 cases).[20]

Rosenblutt, who was the superintendent of a New York State reformatory in 1914, has stated that he had more "youthful dope users" at that time than in any period since, including the period of the second adolescent "epidemic" between 1949 and 1951.[21] Without being specific about the age of the users, Perry M. Lichtenstein examined a thousand cases of addiction among New York City prison inmates and reported a substantial rise in the proportion of addicted inmates from 1909, together with the fact that "the greatest increase has been within the last year (1913–14)."[22] "The number of young people addicted is enormous. I have come in contact with individuals sixteen and eighteen years of age, whose history was that they had taken a habit-forming drug for at least two years. This includes girls as well as boys."[23] Dr. Ernest Bishop, who was in charge of drug addicts at the city workhouse on Blackwell's Island, testified before the New York State Joint Legislative Committee in 1916: "I remember when victims sent to us were men, some of them aged, but now they are chiefly young men and boys."[24]

The second drug problem that can be identified between 1905 and 1920 is the prevalence of drug use, primarily heroin and cocaine, in the armed services during World War I. This is probably a consequence of the first problem, insofar as the same young men who were exposed to drugs between 1910 and 1913 were likely to enlist or be drafted for service during the war.[25]

Leaky and an anonymous reviewer of his study of heroin users reported the existence of the habit among naval enlisted men in 1915–16. Concerning the social background of such men, the reviewer noted that they had a "history of having been in reformatories for petty crimes; others are members of gangs. Others live with prostitutes. . . . They give a history of a bad record at school and afterward were unsuccessful [i.e., unemployed]."[26]

Kolb and DuMez cited Army statistics for the entire period of wartime mobilization, those men rejected for service because of mental diseases—a total of 72,323. Of these, only 3,284 were identified as drug addicts. In addition, they quote the testimony of Colonel Pearce Bailey, the chief of neurology and psychiatry in the medical corps, who told them that "there was very little traffic in drugs in the camps in this country and in France, as practically no cases of any addiction were reported among the soldiers."[27] After allowing for some underestimation on the part of Army examiners ("the error . . . must have been small"),[28] Kolb and DuMez concluded that "the Army findings are the most important in indicating that the youth of the country are not addicted in great number."[29]

In fact—and this pattern was repeated in official military briefings on the matter during World War II, in Korea, and in Vietnam—the Army was deliberately misleading in its use of statistics, and the conclusions Kolb and DuMez drew were unfounded. The place to look for reliable statistics, such as they were, on drug use among enlisted men during the war was in court-martial and discipline records. Although they represent only the number of drug users who were caught, the total proportion of soldiers likely to have used drugs was significant.

King, whose findings were based on a study of over 2,500 prisoners in the Army Disciplinary Barracks between 1914 and 1915, estimated that at least 4 percent of the military prison population were drug users, and no less than 1 percent of the total enlisted population were the same:

It is my opinion that the use of drugs (chiefly cocaine and heroin) during the period under consideration has been greater than has been believed. . . . It seems that the majority of users coming under our observation began its use after enlistment. A smaller proportion before enlistment. Regarding this point, often no very definite evidence is obtainable.[30]

Extrapolating these percentages to the total number of enlisted men who served during the war suggests approximately 35,000 drug users, a number large enough to have made a drug problem visible to the military authorities.[31] Since King, whose study was the most detailed on the subject, also argued that drug use was contagious, the potential threat to military discipline was magnified several times over. In circumstances where drug use was particularly concentrated, the threat extended to the efficiency and reliability of entire units.[32]

The important point here is that these two problems were almost exclusively working-class in character. King presented background material on eight cases, none of which appears to have had more than eight years' schooling and most of them a history of paternal alcoholism typical of working-class families. Bloedorn identified drug use as particularly a problem of "the large centers of population":

> There can be no doubt that overcrowding, congestion, insanitary surroundings, and a lack of facilities for healthful recreation are predisposing factors in drug addiction . . . with this sort of environment the drug habit is considered to be highly contagious, particularly among minors.[33]

According to Lichtenstein (whose sample was of prison inmates), "the greater number are of the gangster type and consequently are mental and moral degenerates."[34] It is reasonable to guess that both this "type" and the delinquents referred to by Leaky were of working-class origin.

I have not considered either race or ethnicity of the drug users identified so far. There is not much doubt about identifying the military users as white, but the adolescent population is more difficult to identify. It was almost certainly not Chinese. In New York, according to Lichtenstein, the three most common groups, by ethnic origin (heroin users only), were American, Italian and "Hebrew-American" (Jews born in the United States to immigrant parents).[35] Among the 159 arrestees whose names were reported by the *New York Times* in the first 24 months after enactment of the city's antinarcotic legislation, the Towns-Boylan Act, Jews were especially prominent. They appear to have dominated the street trade in drugs in Brooklyn where Samuel Greenberg, known as the "King of Cokies," was arrested for possession of cocaine in July 1914.[36] Italians or combinations of Italians and Jews ran sales networks in lower Manhattan (the Bowery and the Lower East Side) and in the Tenderloin (6th and 7th Avenues, 30th to 39th Streets), which, according to the *Times*, was "supposed to be the center of the drug traffic."[37]

What is missing here is any sign of drug users from the "higher social ranks," to use Wright's phrase; yet scarcely a contemporary survey of American drug use has not accepted his characterization that the drugs were *evenly* distributed throughout the society, at least until the Harrison Act.[38] After Wright and until 1928, the most authoritative source was *The Opium Problem* by Terry and Pellens, in which they collected survey and questionnaire results from a series of reports going back to the mid-nineteenth century. These consistently suggested that narcotic addiction has generally been the result of overmedication by anxious patients and irresponsible doctors or accidental in cases where the addict was unaware of the identity of drugs he or she consumed. Terry and Pellens also claim that the typical addict was more likely to be female than male, white than black, and middle rather than working class.

Many of the surveys quoted *excluded* working-class residential areas from investigation altogether. The surveys of Michigan (1878) and Iowa (1885), for example, omitted the major cities in those states from consideration. "With the usual vicious elements of city life eliminated," according to Hull,[39] and with "underworld influences such as prostitution, gambling, etc., largely . . . eliminated," Marshall reported,[40] it should not be surprising that a distorted profile of drug abuse emerged. Questionnaire returns were particularly low—48 percent for Marshall and 9 percent for Hull. Conclusions about the social class of addicts were derived from highly selective sources of information. "We are confident," wrote the reporter for the American Pharmaceutical Association's survey of 1903, "that the use of narcotics is increasing. . . . While the increase is most evident with the lower classes, the statistics of institutes devoted to the cure of habitués show that their patients are principally drawn from those in the higher walks of life."[41]

What the early reporters failed to distinguish was the unusual from the routine pattern of drug use. It shocked them to discover pockets of heavy opiate consumption among the village ladies of the Midwest or in medical suites of the big cities. It was equally shocking, equally visible, because it was well publicized, but it was equally unrepresentative in the aggregate, when heroin use today is discovered among middle-class students in well-to-do communities. There is little doubt that it can happen now (see Chapter 5) or that it was happening, as Terry and Pellens regarded it, at the beginning of this century. But it is nevertheless likely that, when counted into the overall prevalence of opiate and cocaine consumption, this pattern was just as exceptional before the Harrison Act as after it. When viewed closely, the rationale for the act and the total prohibition that resulted from it—at least so far as Wright can be believed in stating what that was—had next to nothing to do with the purported morphinism of doctors or the opiate addiction induced among middle-class consumers of patent medicines. Claims to this effect were part of the campaign to manipulate public opinion concerning the dangers of the drugs, while the true target of the prohibition was much the same as it was in the first opium crusade.

Drug use among blacks in the period was a special and distinctive problem. Because of the heated opinions it generated, let us consider it in detail.

Wright expressed the popular view in 1910:

> It has been stated on very high authority that the use of co- caine by the negroes of the South is one of the most elusive and troublesome questions which confront the enforcement of the law in most of the Southern states . . . the drug is commonly sold in whiskey dives, and it seems certain that a large quantity of the liquor sold in these illicit places is laced with cocaine. The combination of low-grade spirits and cocaine makes a maddening compound.[42]

Lichtenstein also reported that cocaine was the preferred drug among black prison inmates in New York in 1914.[43] Two years later the physician attached to the Harlem Prison claimed that there were 15,000 "boy addicts" in Harlem alone.[44]

The most common belief was that "cocaine is often the direct incentive to the crime of rape by the negroes of the South and other sections of the country."[45] It would also make "criminals more efficient as criminals. Beyond this point it brings on the state of fear or paranoia, during which the (cocaine) addict might murder a supposed pursuer."[46] The chief of police in Washington, D.C. wrote in 1908 that "the cocaine habit is by far the greatest menace to society because the victims are generally vicious. The use of this drug superinduces jealousy and predisposes to commit criminal acts."[47] Finally, the drug "transforms otherwise safe and tractable citizens into dangerous characters, and in most instances wrecks the individual and all dependent on him, as well as jeopardizes the lives of many."[48]

The connection between cocaine and rape is crucial in this context, for allegations of black sexual assaults on white women were frequent throughout the South and in the northern cities in the later war years. On August 1, 1914 the *New York Times* reported that "a young man, who has not been identified, went insane from cocaine poisoning in Battery Park last evening and ran about like a madman. He seized several women who were taking the air on the benches and soon the park resounded with their screams."[49] During the "Red Summer of 1919" such charges precipitated lynchings of blacks all over the South, as well as major race riots in Millen, Georgia, Longview, Texas, and Washington, D.C.[50]

Apart from press allegations and the ex cathedra pronouncements quoted above, what evidence was there of the link between blacks and cocaine? Actually, very little.

E.M. Green, who examined admissions to the Georgia State Sanitarium from 1909 to 1914 (a total of 2,119 blacks, "by far the larger part coming from the rural districts and from small communities"), found only three cases of narcotic addiction among black patients, in contrast to 142 "drug psychoses" among whites. Of the three, cocaine was used by itself once and once in combination with morphine and alcohol. The third case involved the opiate, laudanum.[51] Green emphasized that his findings ran contrary to public opinion:

> In view of the frequent statements made by the daily press and the generally accepted opinion regarding the use of liquor and drugs by the negro race, it may be of interest to review the table showing the forms of psychoses found in 2,119 negroes admitted. By this table it will be seen that alcoholic psychoses are found three times as often in the white as in the negro. . . . As is the case with alcohol the cost of cocaine precludes its habitual use, for cocaine unfits an individual for work, and when work ceases money with which to purchase the drug fails, so that the habit does not become established. It may be that in communities in which the negro is more prosperous, drug psychoses are oftener found. . . . [52]

Although blacks in the northern cities were hardly prosperous, they enjoyed higher wage rates than southern blacks. Two studies of Washington's institutionalized population—one of 175 workhouse inmates and another of patients treated in the Washington hospitals from 1900 to 1908—indicated that the number of cocaine users at the time was very small compared with the size of the alcoholic or even the opium addict population, and no particular concentration of blacks was observed.[53]

Of course, there may be a large error of estimation in relying on institutional figures, if it is supposed that blacks would be less likely than whites to seek or receive treatment for cocaine addiction at sanitaria or hospitals. But it does appear that the picture shown in institutional counts such as these matches that given by such observers as the police.

Bloedorn, for example, provides evidence from admissions statistics of Bellevue Hospital that cocaine use in New York peaked in 1907 and dropped quite sharply between 1908 and 1909, remaining at a low level through 1916 (no breakdown by race provided). An almost identical pattern was reported by the chief of Washington's police, who described the cocaine problem as reaching "alarming proportions" around 1906–1907, but that following the passage of the Food and Drug Act, it diminished substantially: "my information is that the sale of cocaine is about one-tenth of what it was before the present law went into effect."[54] Again, no notice was taken of racial characteristics, but the implication to be drawn from the Homes Commission reports is that few officials regarded the use of cocaine as either an especially black problem or, after 1909, as serious as the problem of heroin use (which began to intensify in the subsequent 12 months).

Why, then, did Wright, who had read these reports, insist that "the misuse of cocaine is . . . the most threatening of the drug habits that has ever appeared in this country" and that the principal carriers of the threat were black?[55] What could have caused blacks to use cocaine in large enough proportions to create the impression that they, in particular, were addicted to the drug?

Cocaine was first marketed widely in America in patent medicines. *Tucker's Asthma Cure, Agnew's Powder,* and *Anglo-American Catarrh Powder* were cocaine-based preparations, and the names indicate what they were for. It might be argued that one of the reasons for thinking the use of narcotics was greater among working-class people was that the incidence of tuberculosis and bronchial diseases such as asthma, pneumonia, and influenza conditions like catarrh were higher for them than for the middle class. There is no information that makes it possible to compare the illness and mortality rates of blacks and whites within the working class in this period. It is possible, however, to show that a general comparison of the races makes it clear that blacks were much more likely to suffer from these diseases than were whites.

In Washington, for instance, a large discrepancy between the mortality rates of whites and blacks occurred for pneumonia (ratio of white deaths to black, 1:3.3). Other diseases for which this or higher ratios obtained included tuberculosis of the lungs (1:3), "abdominal tuberculosis" (1:4.1), "pulmonary hemorrhage" (1:6.1), infant diarrhea and gastroenteritis (1:3), malaria (1:4), and typhoid (1:1.8). The only medical conditions for which the white rate exceeded that of the black in Washington had to do with drinking, alcoholism, delirium tremens, and cirrhosis of the liver.[56] This means that in conditions of relative poverty, when doctors and hospital treatment were either physically or financially inaccessible, blacks can be expected to have sought relief in the only thing readily available to them—the patent medicine. How they spent their money should show this, although there are some problems with the evidence. W.E.B. DuBois collected a variety of family budgets from black families in Philadelphia in 1896, Atlanta (1900 and 1909), and two small towns in Ohio and Virginia (1903 and 1897). In some cases the outlay for medicine was indicated, but in most it was lumped together with the doctor's bill or labeled "sickness." Most of the itemized budgets reflect the occupation and living conditions of laborers or farmhands. For them the proportion of income spent on medical needs ranged from 3.8 to 5.6 percent.[57] It is impossible to say, however, how representative the individuals picked by DuBois were of both the urban and the rural blacks of the time.

These percentages may be compared with the figure for 143 families, Polish and Lithuanian, who lived and worked in the Chicago stockyards district in 1909–10; 1.6 percent of their total expenditures went for medicine and doctor's services.[58] This is low by comparison, and especially so in light of the fact that the working-class disease, tuberculosis, was worse then in the stockyards ward than in all but two others in Chicago, causing a third of all deaths, and that infant mortality was also so high that one child in three did not live beyond two years.[59] In this instance the susceptibility to illness was about as high for whites as for blacks, but blacks appear to have spent more money for relief.

The President's Homes Commission sponsored a similar survey of family budgets in Washington during 1908, which resulted in a breakdown of expenses according to the income group to which the families belonged. Since it is clear from other evidence in the report that black families were disproportionately concentrated in the class with income of $500 or less, the results demonstrated what has been anticipated so far; that blacks, being more likely than whites to suffer sickness, spent a larger portion of their income than whites on patent medicines.[60] What is surprising about the report is that families with the least income spent more of it than those with the most on such medicines. This, then, was the first likely source of cocaine for blacks.

Another source which may have made its use evident and distinctive enough to encourage formation of a racial stereotype was in soft drinks with a cocaine base. The Coca in the original Coca-Cola, produced in Atlanta at the turn of the century, stood for the coca leaf, the plant from which cocaine is extracted. In a report on soft drinks issued by the federal government in 1908, over 40 brands of soft drinks were identified as containing the drug.[61]

Drinks of this kind were first introduced in the South during the 1880s. Their appeal spread throughout the country, although the greatest demand remained in the South. They were widely advertised as remedies for headache and as general tonics. Since they were considerably cheaper than either liquor or cocaine, they may have been especially popular among blacks who could not afford the others. This being so, and assuming that the drinks were potent enough to stimulate a habit for them, it is conceivable that the link between blacks and cocaine may have been established here.

Nowadays it is hard to imagine Coca-Cola leading anyone to commit rape. Nevertheless, government officials used to talk about "the prevalence of the so-called 'coca cola fiend' . . . becoming a matter of great importance and concern."[62] In the thinking of the South at the time, if the fiends were black, it seemed quite conceivable that they would attempt to force their sex on white women. But documentation is hard to find; it may not even exist. Government analysts of the soft drinks never identified their contents beyond the generic label, extract of coca leaf; its potency was never measured chemically nor tested in experiments on the human side effects. In other words, there is only the word of a single pharmacologist that notable side effects might have existed, and for all his professional zeal in the anticocaine crusade, there is nothing but words to show for the alleged drug problem.

It is possible that another factor may have been at work stimulating cocaine use in the South—the prohibition of liquor. Between 1880 and 1910 prohibition had spread from state to state, most rapidly and extensively in the South, and there were press reports that one of its effects was to increase the use of drugs as a substitute for liquor.[63] On the other hand, it is known that consumption of alcohol by blacks was far less than that of whites, so that prohibition was less meaningful to them. Even at the price Wright quotes for cocaine in 1910 (25¢ per grain),[64] few blacks working as sharecroppers or as unskilled laborers could have afforded it regularly and still have eaten and paid the rent.

The fact is that Wright, the chief authority for the claim of a black cocaine problem, was reporting unsubstantiated gossip, and knowingly misrepresented the evidence before him. The best evidence available indicates that, whether it was among blacks or whites, cocaine use peaked in 1907 and went sharply down thereafter. The import figures Wright quotes bear this out: in 1907, 1.5 million pounds of coca leaves entered the country, but the next year the amount was less than half that.[65]

During World War I, circumstances combined to increase the supply of cocaine, notwithstanding the restrictions introduced on imports in 1909 and on the sale and possession of the drug by the Harrison Act. Hostilities increased the demand in Europe for cocaine as a surgical anesthetic while at the same time cutting the Europeans off from their source of supply, which was in Central and South America. Until 1914 most raw materials for processing the drug were shipped in and out of London or Amsterdam, but once Atlantic shipping became the target of submarines the primary entrepôt became New York.

In 1915 C.E. Vanderkleed, a representative of a Philadelphia drug concern, told a *New York Times* reporter in Berlin that the war was good for the American drug business if it would take advantage of the scarcity in Europe and the disruption of established trade and production patterns. It "affords the U.S. the chance to become the drug and chemical center of the world."[66] What happened was close to the prediction, as coca leaves were diverted to New York, which, in turn, created the opportunity to divert cocaine from legitimate to illegitimate trade.

This would explain the allegation by Dr. Royal Copeland, New York's Health Commissioner, that in January 1919 more cocaine was sold in the city than in all of 1918 and that in February the demand was even greater.[67] However, this is the only evidence from the press or elsewhere that the use of the drug had risen since 1907. Moreover, Copeland did not say or imply that the users were predominantly black.

Throughout 1919 the papers became curiously silent on the race of cocaine users, curious because stories of black sexual assaults were legion, and racial tension was frequently whipped up by the press to the point where it actually precipitated racial violence in a number of places.[68] Although lynch mobs murdered 78 blacks in 1919, many of them accused of rape,[69] and although three of the major city riots also involved claims of sexual assault by a black man on a white woman, cocaine was rarely mentioned as a contributing cause. Instead, the blame was laid on socialist and radical agitators, members of International Workers of the World, the Bolsheviks—even, in one well known case, on Harvard graduates.[70]

We learn something important about the mythology of drugs from this. Just as it was pure invention that Bolshevik agitators had led blacks to riot in 1919, so it was an invention that cocaine was "a potent incentive in driving humbler negroes all over the country to abnormal crimes."[71] Both functioned as myths to explain how it could happen that otherwise docile, passive (*humble* is Wright's word for *inferior*) black people would react against the impoverished condition in which they were confined.

In these years this condition, along with that of the entire working class, fluctuated, each paralleled by evidence or claims of a new drug problem. Unemployment rose sharply between 1907 and 1908 (the peak of the first cocaine problem), between 1913 and 1914 (the beginning of the heroin problem), and again between 1919 and 1921 (when cocaine and the opiates were reputedly involved once more).[72]

The war itself stimulated the reconstruction of the northern labor force by inducing the large-scale emigration of blacks out of the rural South to man the labor-scarce urban economy. As this economy changed with postwar demobilization from a condition of labor scarcity to labor surplus, the tension between working-class whites and blacks rose as the necessity to compete for jobs and declining wages was forced on them.[73] Rape, crime, and drug addiction were elements of the hostile stereotype that emerged in this conflict; their relation to true conditions was immaterial. Actually, this, the first generation of blacks to become urbanized and leave the farms for the work in Chicago, Washington, and New York, did not respond to the new conditions by widespread drug use or involvement in illegal enterprise. That came in later generations. It had already been established in public opinion by the ideology of narcotics that they had—some 35 years earlier. The assault on white women, like the Bolsheviks' attack on patriotism or the crazed antics of the cocaine fiend, were all elements of a common ideology designed to justify and legitimize the repression with which black claims for equality were met. As I have said, the conflict over social justice is what the story of narcotics in America is about.

Chapter 4.
Mexicans and Marijuana

Marijuana was effectively outlawed as a matter of national policy in 1937 when Congress passed the Marihuana Tax Act.[1] Although it had been written into draft versions of the Harrison Act 23 years earlier, it was omitted in the final version and then dropped more or less out of sight—and out of federal mind—until the early 1930s. For instance, during the twenties medical and police officials in New Orleans, anxious for information about the drug, were told by federal agencies that they had none to provide.[2]

A number of Western states did pass antimarijuana statutes in the mid-1920s, and where none existed, various laws on the books were adapted for the purpose.[3] Users could be arrested in some places and charged with disorderly conduct, and in Illinois sellers of the drug were prosecuted under a statute dealing with the sale of tobacco substitutes.[4]

By and large, though, the authorities were not concerned with marijuana at the time, especially since in the first flush of Prohibition, after the Volstead Act of 1919, there was so much else to be concerned about. In 1932 the Federal Bureau of Narcotics reported that marijuana was being used by Mexicans in the Southwest and West, but it minimized the extent to which this should have caused alarm. The bureau's commissioner, H. J. Anslinger, recalling his policy in the early thirties, told an interviewer that marijuana was a minor problem compared to heroin and that its use was confined to the Southwest—"we didn't see it here in the East at all at that time."[5] Still, in 1935 Anslinger decided to back new federal legislation against the drug, and by 1936 he was ˙˙˙ᵗⁱf ving to its menace nationwide.

˙˙witch has been variously interpreted as a power play by ˙˙mprove his own image while at the same time, improving the public standing of his agency vis-à-vis J. Edgar Hoover and the FBI.[6] In addition it was a response to growing political pressure from the Southwest to put a federal ban of marijuana on the books and federal agents in the field. Anslinger has indicated that this pressure originally came from the local police, then the state governors, from them to the Secretary of the Treasury, and from his office to Anslinger's bureau.[7]

According to accounts of the legislation by Musto and by Bonnie and Whitebread, it was the Mexicans who were the root cause of local concern. Both quote an illustration of this from among Anslinger's testimony at the hearings on the Marihuana Tax Act, a letter from the editor of the *Daily Courier* in Alamosa, Colorado, written in 1936:

Is there any assistance your Bureau can give us in handling this drug? Can you suggest campaigns? Can you enlarge your Department to deal with marihuana? Can you do anything to help us?

I wish I could show you what a small marihuana cigarette can do to one of our degenerate Spanish-speaking residents. That's why our problem is so great; the greatest percentage of our population is composed of Spanish-speaking persons. . . .

While marihuana has figured in the greatest number of crimes in the past few years, officials fear it, not for what it has done, but for what it is capable of doing. They want to check it before an outbreak does occur.

Through representatives of civic leaders and law officers of the San Luis Valley, I have been asked to write to you for help.[8]

In April 1930 the population of Alamosa County was 8,602; according to the census it had risen to 10,484 by 1940.[9] In 1930 the Spanish-speaking part of this (almost entirely Mexicans) was 507—that is, less than 6 percent of the total.

This is hardly the majority implied by the letter-writer, unless he was talking about large numbers of transient workers who moved in at the peak of the harvesting season. But even then, they would not have increased the total more than once over, and at a thousand the Mexicans would still have been outnumbered by more than seven to one.[10] Of course, to a predominantly American-born rural community of north European origins, the annual migration of Mexican labor might have seemed like a deluge.[11] Like dozens of communities in Colorado and the neighboring states, though, Alamosa for over 10 years had depended on the Mexicans for most of their field labor and maintenance and construction work. But at the low wages they were paying the farmers were prepared to stomach the unpleasantness of having Mexicans around and to tolerate whatever "trouble" they might cause.

Why the change of mind, then? Why was marijuana viewed so seriously in 1930 but not before? What benefit to Alamosa did federal legislation against the drug offer? As it turned out, in the first three years of enforcement of the act, federal agents made 2,528 arrests.[12] That is not many for a problem described as national in extent, and not all of them could possibly have involved Mexicans.[13] There is no record of how many arrests were made in Alamosa, yet by 1940 the number of Mexicans in the county had dwindled to eight.[14]

No one can say whether the drug law and stepped-up enforcement started the exodus, merely helped it along, or did not affect it at all. We will see that in counties where the record is clearer, the marijuana law was only one of many instruments used by state authorities to deal with the "Mexican problem," and it was not the most effective one. But only on the surface was the problem one of drug-inspired crime. At bottom it was an economic problem, for what changed the attitude toward marijuana from benign neglect to anxiety for law and order was the unemployment crisis of the Depression. This is what made the people of Alamosa think that 507 were *too many* Mexicans for the county's health and that customs which the laborers had brought with them and which had been overlooked in the past, such as smoking marijuana, were now a serious threat to the community.

Public concern about marijuana grew because Americans wanted to drive the Mexicans back over the border, for reasons which had nothing to do with the nature of the drug or its psychological effects. All the same, a theory about the evils of the drug—linking its use and supply to being Mexican—was invented with the results that hostility toward the Mexicans began to seem a little more reasonable and public policy to remove them that much more acceptable.

There were those whose beliefs about the dangers of marijuana were formed independently of any contact with Mexicans or prejudice toward them.[15] In the history of Anglo-Mexican relations during this period, drugs have only a small place, but in the history we are considering—the history of drug use and policy in America—the problem of Mexican labor and the unemployed surplus after 1928 is the key factor in determining what became public policy and ultimately the law on marijuana we still live with.

To show this, it is not important whether exactly the same people who believed the worst about marijuana were also caught up with the

Mexicans in the economic crisis, just as it is fruitless to try to prove that Alamosa got rid of its Mexican population by booking them on drug charges. Had it not been for the Depression, marijuana would have remained part of the hostile stereotype of Mexican behavior without there being too much public concern about it. What then happened differed from place to place, depending not so much on how prevalent marijuana use was, but on how the economic crisis affected the local population. This is the sense in which it can be said that the ideology of narcotics grew out of the condition of the working class at the time and that it served to bolster the interests of certain social groups against others in an episode marked by the sharpest class conflict in our history.[16]

World War I, which had recruited blacks for industrial labor in the urban North, also drew a large number of Mexicans into the United States for the first time.

During the Mexican revolutionary period beginning around 1909, there was a substantial increase in the recorded inflow across the border, but as refugees who felt threatened by the revolution, they were more middle- or upper-class in background than were the immigrants of the later period, who were mostly rural peasants unable to gain a living from the land.[17]

The war cut off the flow of European immigrants, and farmers and planters in the West were unable to compete with the North for black labor. The white work force available for agricultural work was depleted by enlistments, the draft, and the high-wage condition of the war industries, and, as we saw, the yellow work force had been effectively limited 30 years earlier. The alternative, short of allowing wage rates to rise, was to import Mexican labor.[18] This began in earnest in 1918, with the sugar beet companies taking the initiative. As a result of their pressure the federal contract-labor laws which had prohibited direct recruitment of labor in Mexico were suspended, at first for farm work and then shortly after for railroad maintenance and mining.[19]

There was a great influx of immigrants from Europe immediately after the war. Largely because of the social conflict and economic dislocation in the aftermath of the war, Congress decided to introduce an immigration quota in 1921. Permanent legislation to this effect was passed in 1924, but because of pressure from the Mexican government and employers in the Southwest, Mexico was not among the nations limited.

That year, 1924, was the peak for Mexican immigration; 105,000 were recorded coming in and only 3,572 going out. The following year was also much heavier than immigration experts had predicted when the quotas were being drawn up, and the first of a series of attempts to restrict the immigration was introduced in the United States Senate. This had the support of American Federation of Labor locals in Cali-fornia and throughout the Southwest, although not until 1928 did the AFL national convention support restriction. Other groups in favor of the Mexican quota included the American Legion, schoolteachers, small independent farmers, and a variety of nativist patriotic organizations.[20]

Opposed to the quota were steadily expanding California farm interests in Washington, including the publisher of the *Los Angeles Times,* railroad and mine employer groups, and at the national level, the U.S. Chamber of Commerce, the American Farm Bureau Federation and the National Grange.[21] Nothing illustrates so succinctly the class conflict latent in this issue as does the lineup here. Employers were successful until the end of the 1920s in blocking Congressional action, but the situation after 1930 led to a more local pattern of action in which employers and labor were aligned differently.

In the decade 1920–30 nearly 90 percent of all the Mexicans in the United States were in four states–Texas, California, Arizona, and New Mexico. Texas, which had just over half in 1920, just under half in 1930, had a 78 percent increase over the decade. California received fewer Mexicans, but the percentage increase was much greater—200 percent. The totals in 1930 were Texas, 683,681 (11.7 percent of the state) and California, 368,013 (6.5 percent).[22]

A survey of crime and delinquency among Mexicans in Texas, written in 1930, concluded that they "show delinquent tendencies less than their proportion of the population would entitle them to show."[23] Most of the figures obtained on arrests, court appearances, and prison populations were for 1929, a year of labor scarcity in the state; they covered rural and urban counties, including San Antonio, the largest Mexican center in the country after Los Angeles.

The author of that survey referred to the belief, common at that time, that Mexicans committed the bulk of the state's crimes:

> In no instance have I found this impression borne out by a study of the facts. This does not mean that the magistrates were willing-
> ly perverting the facts in order to make out a case against the Mexicans or that they were prejudiced against the Mexicans. The

explanation is very much simpler; it lies in the domain of that psychological fact that the stranger is conspicuous and the conspicuous is remembered.[24]

Among the crimes singled out for special comment, the use of knives in assaults was the commonest, but this was treated as an almost inevitable outcome of the clash between the Mexican custom of carrying a knife, and the American code. "They live in a certain stage . . . where the community has not evoluted [sic] out of the stage of fighting with a knife to fighting with a gun."[25] To correct popular misconceptions, several other cultural peculiarities of the Mexicans were noted and explained, but there was no mention of the use of marijuana.

Southwest of San Antonio, in Dimmit County, a farming area of onions and spinach, investigators looked at charges against Mexicans in 1928–29. There, also, there was no indication of drug use. The single most frequent charge was card-playing. "The extent of law violations by Mexicans in Dimmit County is inconsequential."[26]

A survey by Paul S. Taylor, this one of the South Platte Valley in northeast Colorado (at the opposite end of the state from Alamosa), turned up no mention of marijuana in the criminal statistics for the 1925–27 period.[27] This was primarily a sugar beet area. Most arrests of Mexicans took place among the migratory workers during the growing season. Typical offenses were violating the liquor laws or disturbing the peace. After checking popular opinion about the "lawlessness" of Mexicans against the records, Taylor reported:

> The extent to which Mexicans violate our laws appears to be magnified unduly not only by the northeastern Colorado community but even by the officers who handle the Mexican offenders. Examination of the books of one officer who vigorously denounced the criminal quality of Mexicans showed only 40 percent of the proportion of Mexican arrests which he said emphatically his records would show. In another county the percentage shown by the records was only 16 percent of the *a priori* asserted proportion of cases.[28]

In California, 1923 was the last year that overall demand for farm labor exceeded the supply. Table 4–1 illustrates the movement of these forces from the end of World War I through 1930, when the effects of the Depression on labor supply were reflected in the largest surplus recorded for the period. By 1930 the state's agricultural employers were still insisting that an unrestricted flow of Mexican immigrants was es-

TABLE 4–1

Demand for and Supply of Farm Labor
in California, 1918–30 (as of April each year)[29]

| Year | Percent of Normal | | Percent of Supply to Demand | Year | Percent of Normal | | Percent of Supply to Demand |
	SUPPLY	DEMAND			SUPPLY	DEMAND	
1918	80	103	78	1925	103	88	117
1919	93	103	90	1926	100	94	106
1920	84	104	81	1927	101	94	107
1921	99	93	106	1928	104	91	114
1922	107	96	111	1929	102	91	112
1923	94	96	98	1930	105	87	121
1924	102	85	120				

sential to the continued development of the farming industry and to the stability of commodity prices.[30] The governor's Mexican fact-finding committee, reviewing labor needs for crop production, stated that the industry was dependent on Mexican labor and by implication ruled out any alternative course of economic development without that labor base. But if, as the Table shows, there was a surplus of labor, how could it be said that without *more* Mexicans the farmers would be ruined? What possible damage could have been done by limiting the inflow of Mexicans as proposed in the quota legislation? Evidently there was a "shortage" of labor in the eyes of farm employers whenever a large unemployed reserve did not exist—why?

The answer is that the profitability of California's *crops* did not really depend on the Mexicans and would hardly have been affected had none been available. The profitability of *investment* in agricultural *land* did, however, depend on the cheap labor supply the Mexicans offered and on their stocking a permanent reserve of unemployment. To explain this even partially, I must mention the state of farming in California if the class interests that formed around the Mexican issue and marijuana prohibition are to be understood.

The Mexicans were the unwitting and unfortunate instrument of large-scale, corporate agriculture and the land-owning (as distinct from the farming) interests of the state. Through the AFL, union labor was undoubtedly correct in seeing them as an economic threat but tragically shortsighted in missing the more fundamental danger. Corporate agriculture was using the imported labor force not just to depress rural wage levels and lower unit costs in the short run but to finish off those traditional American ideals, the owner-operated family farm and the community of small but independent landowners, ideals that were already in a precarious economic position before the Depression.

Many urban wage-earners in California at the time still aspired to buy into such farms. Consequently, for a while at least, they potentially shared a common interest with the small farmers in the effect of cheap labor upon the price and availability of farmland. But this was not consciously apparent to either side. Only with the intensification of unemployment and the business losses of the thirties did they make a concrete, concerted effort at self-protection. Only then it was the Mexicans who bore the brunt of their aggressive campaign, and by then it was too late to save the small farmers. Getting rid of the Mexicans was a hopeless panacea for the job-hungry urban and native labor force. The passion and race hatred that surfaced in the anti-Mexican campaign glossed over the unreality of their economic and social analysis, and at this point in the story, marijuana reappears.

Let us return to the California farmyard. Only twice since 1870, and then only for very brief periods, had California been without an abundant labor supply recruited from immigrants whose low standard of living at home made them available for seasonal employment at low wages. Although the farm operators did not, by and large, resist the exclusion of the Chinese in the period just before 1882, they later organized to stop expulsion of the Chinese already working in the state. But the number of Chinese gradually declined over the next decade, and the depression in nonagricultural industry in the 1890s released a white labor surplus to continue to serve the farmers' needs. This number, too, diminished as the general economy improved, and Japanese immigration was encouraged to fill the rural labor reserve again. Another labor emergency did not occur until World War I, when it became the turn of the Mexicans, and secondarily the Filipinos, to head it off.

Five decades of cheap labor had permitted land values to rise rapidly and speculatively on the expectation of the high profits to be earned as long as such a labor supply continued to be abundant. The high price of land discouraged the small operator from buying his own farm and stimulated the conditions for tenant farming, absentee ownership, and instability and a high turnover among the operators.

In the Imperial Valley, for example, which produced a variety of truck crops, melons, and cotton, Taylor found that tenancy had risen from 31.8 percent of farms cropped in 1910 to 46.7 percent in 1925 and was continuing to rise. In the same period tenancy throughout the state had declined from an overall 20.6 percent to 14.7 percent. These were some of the consequences:

> Loans on real estate are not made for more than three years, and generally for less, because of the unsettled water conditions. Much of the land of the valley is held by absentee owners who bought out the early settlers, and hold now for increase in values attendant upon settlement of these water questions; or who prefer the high cost rentals paid by the growers of truck crops to farming for themselves. Under these conditions a class of landowning, working farmers cannot arise. . . . The idea of making a stake and moving out seems to dominate not only growers and farmers and white farm laborers, but also much of the rest of the community.[31]

Such an economic structure was threatened particularly by wage-bargaining, stimulated either by farmers outbidding each other to attract work gangs in times of scarcity or by union organization among rural laborers themselves. To obviate the first possibility, growers' associations in the valley and throughout the state sought to fix and standardize wage rates each year. Though the practice could not be made to stick in the year of greatest labor shortage, 1923, it was quite firmly established thereafter.[32]

Equally threatening was pressure from the labor force to own land or conduct farming itself. A decade earlier, the Japanese had tended to desert contract laboring and establish their own farming enterprises, but this was blocked by legislation in 1913, prohibiting them from owning land or operating farms. These were threats because they promised both to reduce the size of the available labor reserve and to mobilize the Japanese element of this reserve in cooperative formations which did not share the interests of either the existing landowners or the growers.[33]

Mexicans were especially favored by farm employers in the early 1920s because they showed little inclination or capacity for independent farming operations. In 1927 Taylor found "no indication that Mexicans, old or young, are moving toward ownership of the land which they till"; "the movement toward ownership of town lots is not taken as an occasion for alarm, for the owners remain ranch laborers and tend to stabilize the labor supply rather than to enter the field as competing growers."[34]

Actually, the growers preferred the Mexicans to remain mobile and migratory, for this meant they had only a limited period of contact with them. If the Mexicans moved back across the border for the slack winter season or into one of the larger cities such as Los Angeles, so much the better. Communal responsibility for their welfare would fall elsewhere. It would also mean that the workers would bear a larger share of their own housing and upkeep during the harvest season and the growers a smaller share. A spokesman for the farm employer interests told a U.S. House of Representatives hearing in 1928 that if "we should be forced to maintain our labor when it is idle we would be forced out of business."[35]

So long as the Mexicans continued to pour across the border looking for work, so long as they accepted the wages offered by the growers and threatened neither the growers' interests by seeking farms for themselves nor the county budgets by spending the unemployed time of the year on the dole or as charity cases, they were little cause for concern in the farming areas. Crimes which they committed were not considered especially noteworthy. According to a survey of Imperial County in 1927, "the record of law observance among Mexicans . . . is distinctly favorable to them."[36] Also, as in the rural areas of Texas and Colorado, there was no mention of marijuana use.[37]

Clearly what threatened these areas a good deal more was anything that might disrupt the precarious stability of the tenant growers' economic position or the speculative prospects of the landowners. The most serious threat of this kind came from unionism. When incipient labor organizations among the Mexicans led to agitation and strikes, such activities were punished under California law as felonies.

Cooperative and mutual aid associations had been important in holding each of the rural labor forces together ever since the first Chinese laborers arrived in California. As labor organizations, they contained two very different tendencies. One was that the organization moved in the direction of enriching itself at the expense of its members; the other was that it sought to improve the price of labor in the market and thereby aimed at serving the welfare of the membership. Among the Chinese the second tendency was generally less common than the first. Although the record shows the existence of a number of union organizations—that is, labor groups recruited apart from the *tongs,* including one for agricultural workers formed in 1919—their numbers were small, and their efforts were successfully disrupted by police arrests and employer tactics.[38]

Among the Japanese there was an extensive network of associations which were typically of the trade guild rather than the union type. They existed to improve the market position of independent farm producers and fishermen. There is no record of unions among the rural laborers, although their wage position was somewhat protected by strong kin ties between the crew and their contractor or boss, who could be generally relied on to negotiate terms in the interest of the crew rather than his own profit.[39]

A number of factors reduced the amount of social cohesion among the Mexican laborers and inhibited the development of either this kind of labor unit, or the classic union.[40] Still, mutual aid societies did develop and quite early; the first was in the Imperial Valley, Sociedad Mutualista Benito Juarez, which was established in 1919. These confined themselves pretty much to providing medical insurance and a minimal level of social security. They did not acquire the capital for financing the business enterprises of their members, as the rotating credit associations among Chinese and Japanese were able to do.[41]

Out of the Benito Juarez Mutual Society, the first labor union in Imperial Valley—and one of the first in the state[42]—established itself just before the picking season for melons began in 1928. The immediate objectives were to raise the wages set by the growers and improve working conditions. A strike began, which led immediately to widespread arrests of Mexicans and retaliation by the growers. The local sheriff threatened the strikers with deportation, and it was widely circulated that the strike was the work of communist agitators from Mexico City.[43] The outcome was mixed. Some revisions were made in the picking contracts, but they did not nearly satisfy the strikers' demands; some growers decided to pay the 15 cents per standard crate demanded, but since others refused to deal with the union, the unity of the growers' wage policy was broken. Finally, a large number of the arrested laborers pleaded guilty to charges in return for suspended sentences, a couple of leaders were deported, and the remainder had their cases dismissed before trial.

These events revealed for the first time a potential for militancy and union discipline among the Mexicans, which had not been recognized before by the farm employers. Until 1928 the common opinion was this one, from a field man for a large cantaloupe- and lettuce-grower:

> Mexicans are very satisfactory, and they offer no disciplinary problem, but require constant supervision and driving. Mexican laborers do not possess initiative, but that's no criticism of them from our point of view. They do with good grace what we tell them to do, and we don't have to be too particular about the way we tell them.[44]

At this time, then, union organization, agitation, and strikes were evidently the real crimes in rural California and not the carrying of knives, fights, prohibition violations, nor, finally, the use of marijuana, of which we have found so little evidence so far. Wage-bargaining of any kind was tantamount to a crime because it was felt that a competitive situation would push both wages and rents up, increase output or decrease sales, and either way push commodity prices down. Although Fuller estimated that truck crop producers could withstand such destabilizing forces and still show a healthy return, the short-term orientation of the tenant growers was a strong inhibition to adjustment or change, the economics of which might not have been disadvantageous over the long run.[45] But they were not prepared to wait that long.

The landowners stood to gain neither soon nor in the distant future, for the value of their investment had been based on the profits from employing cheap labor in the past and on the expectation that this would continue. Neither tenants paying rents, figured on the same basis, nor owners having just bought in at artificially high prices, could afford to pay competitive wages. If they were successfully forced, there would have been a concomitant downward pressure on rents and a decapitalization of land values, which, of course, would be a potential catastrophe for the speculative investor.[46]

Local police and courts were highly responsive to the possibility of such threats from the Mexicans. It was not a labor surplus now that constituted the threat, as it was during the opium period in 1880. Quite the contrary, a surplus was just what the employers wanted. As the surplus increased in the late twenties (Table 4-1), the Mexicans became more convinced of the need for collective and militant action to protect themselves.

The 1928 cantaloupe strike in the Imperial Valley was followed by another a year later. In April 1930, as the Depression was felt in earnest, a series of police raids were made in the valley, netting 103 arrests "in anticipation of the coming opening of the cantaloupe season."[47] Altogether, 32 strikes or attempted strikes were initiated by the Cannery and Agricultural Workers' Industrial Union between 1932 and early 1934. The union itself had grown out of a strike of lettuce workers in the Imperial Valley in January 1930.

In each case the response of the growers and county authorities was much the same. A strike was criminal syndicalism. Preaching anarchism was an indictable offense. Anything that smacked of communism was grounds for arrest under a variety of state laws. I have already noted the arrest of laborers in anticipation of a strike. It was commonplace for the county sheriff to arrest union leaders at the beginning of an agitation or while negotiations with growers were still taking place. Growers frequently organized vigilante gangs to break up picket lines, which were sometimes deputized by the sheriffs. At least three Mexican strikers were shot dead, and more than 20 were wounded during one of the worst strikes, the San Joaquin cotton strike of 1933.

I mentioned above that during the 1928 strike the Mexicans were threatened with deportation. This threat was frequently used in the years following. With or without the connivance of federal immigration officials, notices were posted, advising the laborers that joining a union or striking were against the law and would result in deportation. But this was actually a bluff, for the growers never intended to support the mass repatriations of Mexicans that were soon put into practice by several cities and backed by the urban labor unions. The growers also continued to block any legislative efforts to impose a quota system on the immigrants.

In other words, the growers were content to maintain the surplus condition at the same time that they sought to remove the individual "communists" they considered responsible for the labor agitation. The growers' policy was to avoid an intensive, unrestricted campaign against the workers or against Mexican "criminality" of the kind that was common in the cities. Instead, they made a variety of threats—of deportation and violence—to bluff the labor reserve into docility, and ignored their "criminality" to the extent that it did not impinge on the economic conflict. It should be emphasized, therefore, that if the Mexican laborer used to smoke marijuana with his friends after a day's work in the fields, as had long been the custom in the rural provinces of Mexico, the California county authorities were either unaware of it or essentially unworried by it.

Such was not the case in a city like Los Angeles, where an altogether different pattern of economic and social conflict produced a markedly different policy toward use of the drug.

Los Angeles is the one American city in which arrests of Mexicans for smoking marijuana were strongly in evidence in the early thirties. Joseph F. Taylor, the city's chief of detectives, is reported to have said that "marihuana is probably the most dangerous of all our narcotic drugs." The reason, according to him, was that "in the past we have had officers of this department shot and killed by marihuana addicts and have traced the act of murder directly to the influence of marihuana, with no other motive."[48]

An early report from the Missionary Education Movement made the following claim:

The use of *marihuana* is not uncommon in the colonies of the lower class of Mexican immigrants. This is a native drug made from what is sometimes called the "crazy weed." The effects are high exhilaration and intoxication, followed by extreme depression and broken nerves. [Police] officers and Mexicans both ascribe many of the moral irregularities of Mexicans to the effect of marihuana.[49]

In 1931 a report on "the trend of drug addiction" by the California State Narcotic Committee published statistics on drug-related offenses for the state and for San Francisco and Los Angeles. It concluded that marijuana use was "widespread throughout southern California among the Mexican population there."[50] It was also reported that in addition to its being grown in the state itself, "recent seizures . . . at the seaboard indicate that it is being smuggled into California on fruit boats from South America."[51]

Table 4–2 indicates that the marijuana problem was relatively minor in San Francisco and the state as a whole, but that it was concentrated in Los Angeles. Table 4–3 confirms the preponderance of Mexicans among drug offenders in Los Angeles.

In 1930 Mexicans in Los Angeles numbered just over 97,000. This was the largest concentration in the state (26.4 percent of the total Mexican population in the state), although it still represented less than 8 percent of the city's total. The actual number of Mexican drug arrests was small, but, comparing their proportion to the relative size of the Mexican population as a whole, it is clear why it was popularly believed that marijuana was a Mexican problem.

Mexicans were especially visible in the city, for although during the 1920s Los Angeles had been the fastest-growing city in the country (115 percent total population growth), the Mexican increase was nearly twice that (226 percent).[52] Together with the Japanese, they held 9.5 percent of all occupations in the city in 1930, but they were visibly concentrated in unskilled construction work (38 percent) and menial service (47 percent). Consequently, their average wage rates were the lowest in the city (less than 50 cents an hour), their level of housing and sanitation extremely poor, and their standard of health much worse than the Anglo norm or the annual county averages.[53]

The diseases to which the Mexicans were most susceptible were respiratory ones. While between 1920 and 1929 the case rate for tuber-

TABLE 4-2
Drugs Involved in Arrests, California, 1930

Drug	January 1 to May 31, 1930			July 1 to September 30, 1930		
	SAN FRANCISCO (percent)	LOS ANGELES (percent)	STATEWIDE* (percent)	SAN FRANCISCO (percent)	LOS ANGELES (percent)	STATEWIDE* (percent)
Morphine	32.93	26.32	42.81	64.29	27.58	41.34
Opium	39.02	14.47	18.77	21.43	6.90	26.26
Heroin	—	2.63	0.59	—	—	1.67
Cocaine	12.20	—	4.10	1.78	3.45	5.03
Marijuana	15.85	56.58	33.73	12.50	62.07	25.70
No. of cases involved	82	76	341	56	29	331

*The number of cases involved during identical periods in the different columns do not conform, because of differences in record-keeping procedures.

From Taylor, *Crime and the Foreign Born: The Problem of the Mexican*, p. 204.

TABLE 4-3

Nationality of Persons Arrested for Drug-Related Offenses, San Francisco and Los Angeles, 1930

Nationality	January 1 to May 31, 1930		July 1 to September 30, 1930	
	SAN FRANCISCO (percent)	LOS ANGELES (percent)	SAN FRANCISCO (percent)	LOS ANGELES (percent)
Anglo-Saxons and Latins	53.59	40.14	70.24	49.33
Negroes	6.22	2.63	5.79	4.00
Chinese	37.50	8.55	17.36	8.00
Mexicans	2.69	48.68	6.61	38.67
No. of cases involved*	112	152	121	75

*These figures cannot be reconciled with those in Table 4-2, probably again because of differences in definition and bookkeeping.

From Taylor, *Crime and the Foreign Born: The Problem of the Mexican,* p. 206.

culosis in Los Angeles county fell by 4 percent, the rate for Mexicans rose sharply.[54] In 1929 they represented 20 percent of all deaths from the disease; in 1921 only 14.5 percent. A detailed study made in 1926 by the County Charities Department found Mexicans disproportionately represented on the relief rolls, and of the total tuberculosis cases handled by the agency, nearly 40 percent were Mexican.[55]

Influenza, diphtheria, and pneumonia were also common, as has come to be expected in a working-class environment. In 1924 the last of these reached epidemic proportions and required emergency assistance from other parts of the country.[56] As the evidence in Chapter 3 might lead us to anticipate, patent medicines may have been the only resort for the Mexicans. Indeed, McCombs indicates that "drugstores report very large sales of patent remedies which are taboo by most informed people."[57] That cannabis was an ingredient in traditional peasant cures and therefore was demanded by Mexicans in Los Angeles for medical remedies seems only reasonable.

These, then, were the elements of the "Mexican problem" as Los Angeles experienced it in the twenties. Table 4-4 provides a summary of the arrest statistics for Mexicans and all other nationalities for

TABLE 4-4

Arrests of Adult Prisoners, Los Angeles, 1926–27, by Nativity and Charge

Arrests Charging Offenses Against

	THE PERSON			CHASTITY AND FAMILY		
	No.	% of all arrests of nationality specified	% of all arrests on charge specified	No.	% of all arrests of nationality specified	% of all arrests on charge specified
Natives of						
Mexico	209	3.8	11.6	209	3.8	9.7
United States	1422	4.2	78.7	1,680	5.0	77.6
All nationalities	1806	3.9	100	2,165	4.6	100

	PROPERTY			MISCELLANEOUS		
	No.	% of all arrests of nationality specified	% of all arrests on charge specified	No.	% of all arrests of nationality specified	% of all arrests on charge specified
Natives of						
Mexico	555	10.1	11.1	112	2.0	6.3
United States	3,898	11.5	77.7	1,327	3.9	74.3
All nationalities	5,015	10.7	100	1,787	3.8	100

From Taylor, *Crime and the Foreign Born: The Problem of the Mexican,*
p. 213.

1926–27. It is clear that for most offense categories and for all arrests counted together, the Mexican proportion is somewhat larger than their proportion in the total urban population.

For several reasons this does not amount to an open-and-shut case for the distinctive criminality of the Mexicans. One is that the Mexican population was more concentrated in the 18–65 age range than was the total population. A more valid comparison is between the 11.8 percent Mexican arrests and the proportion of Mexicans to the the total population between these age limits. It is likely to have been larger than 7.8 percent, which represents the unadjusted population ratio.

Another reason is that the tabulations lump together all offenses in a single category. Thus there is no way of judging whether Detective Taylor's claim about the link between marijuana (and hence, Mexican nationality) and homicide was true. Homicides would be included

PUBLIC DECENCY AND GOOD MORALS			PUBLIC HEALTH			ADMINISTRATION OF GOVERNMENT		
No.	% of all arrests of nationality specified	% of all arrests on charge specified	No.	% of all arrests of nationality specified	% of all arrests on charge specified	No.	% of all arrests of nationality specified	% of all arrests on charge specified
3,597	65.3	12.5	769	14.0	11.3	27	0.5	14.2
20,475	60.6	71.3	4,646	13.7	68.3	102	0.3	53.7
28,697	61.3	100	6,798	14.5	100	190	0.4	100

NONCRIMINAL DETENTION			GRAND TOTAL		
No.	% of all arrests of nationality specified	% of all arrests on charge specified	No.	% of all arrests of nationality specified	% of all arrests
28	0.5	8.0	5506	100	11.8
276	0.8	78.8	33,826	100	72.3
350	0.8	100	46,808	100	100

among offenses against the person, but so would charges of assault with a deadly weapon; since Mexicans often carried knives, the latter charge was a common one.

The records of the Los Angeles County coroner indicate that the homicide rate (per 100,000 population) was in general *falling* during the 1920s. Although it never climbed back to the 1921 peak, there was a slight increase between 1928 and 1934.[58] There is no evidence on the race or place of birth of those charged or convicted of murder, except what was provided by officials to the nine-city survey carried out for the National Commission on Law Observance and Enforcement. This evidence was published before the 1930 census population estimates were available, so rates expressed as number of persons charged per 100,000 of population of the same class and 15 years or over exaggerated the situation, particularly for Mexicans and blacks whose numbers rapidly increased in the cities surveyed. Adjustment for these shifts brings the Mexican rate almost to the Italian one and significantly *under the black rate*. This applies to all nine cities together and is not specific to Los Angeles.

Recordkeeping for many offenses did not really begin in the city until 1931, but it is possible to determine that the burglary rate fell continuously from 1921 to 1929, when it started to rise again (although not steeply), and the robbery rate rose in the first half of the decade and fell in the second, beginning another rise in 1929.[59] Changes in racial and ethnic classifications applied to police records limit the comparisons that can be made for these and juvenile offenses. Compared with whites, including Mexicans, blacks showed the highest juvenile arrest rates for every year of the decade; however, for the one year in which a rate for Mexicans can be estimated, 1931, it appears to have been *lower* than that of whites, blacks, and all others.[60]

In short, the typical marijuana user in Los Angeles at the time was Mexican, although official action against him did not actually step up until late 1929. Any relationship between use of the drug and other crimes committed by Mexicans remains hypothetical, but drug-related homicide involving Mexicans could not have been more frequent than drug-free Anglo homicide, and was probably less common than black homicide, with or without drugs. Most offenses for which Mexicans were arrested were for disturbing the peace or vagrancy (65.3 percent). This was also true in Stockton and San Francisco, where recorded marijuana use was negligible.[61]

Of course, the figures we rely on are only of arrests. They indicate only what the police *did*, not what the Mexicans were doing or the extent to which this varied from the police interpretation of the law. The one group of offenses in Table 4-4 for which the Mexican percentage was greatest is called "offenses against the administration of government." These included "criminal syndicalism" and picketing, which were becoming more and more common by 1930. These were political crimes, in the sense that the offenders were challenging the legitimacy of the system under whose rules they were charged and convicted.

In Los Angeles the union movement among Mexicans made several notable organizational gains. The Confederacion de Uniones Obreras Mexicanas was founded there late in 1927 and rapidly built up a membership of 2,000 to 3,000. Strongly influenced in doctrine by IWW principles and committed to a vision of "class struggle in order to effect an economic and moral betterment of its conditions, and at last its complete freedom from capitalistic tyranny," the union leaders may well have been exposed to arrest from the beginning.[62]

Disturbing the peace was a catchall term for the Los Angeles police. Stockton police preferred to hold Mexicans for investigation without lodging charges, then release them after a day or two in jail.[63] Taylor concluded "that Mexicans in the United States, both aliens and citizens, are frequently subjected to severe and unequal treatment by those who administer the laws."[64] But racism and prejudice are not the end of the story, for the pattern of enforcement of the law against the Mexicans must be understood as an essential ingredient of public policy toward their very existence in the city.

Marijuana enforcement, like enforcement of the vagrancy laws, the antiunion provisions, or the virtual suspension of habeas corpus, began to gather momentum in the late 1920s, and intensified with the deterioration of economic conditions and the onset of the Depression. What is vagrancy if not the "crime" of being unemployed and without economic means? As the Depression hit the city's industry, Mexican unemployment was nearly twice the rate of the native whites, 13.1 percent as compared with 7.2 percent.[65]

The unemployed Anglos sought agricultural work, only to find themselves in competition with Mexicans whose numbers were continuing to increase. And, of course, few Anglos had ever worked at Mexican wage levels. Therefore it seemed to them that their only relief lay in getting rid of the Mexicans. This view found support in the county administration, though for other reasons. The county faced a major budgetary crisis in having to finance burgeoning numbers of unemployed seeking to enroll for relief payments. It was then discovered that shipping Mexicans across the border was much cheaper than maintaining them on welfare, so a plan for mass repatriations took shape. In addition to the support of the Anglo working class and the AFL, the repatriation plan was backed, for different reasons again, by the urban employer interests and many of the growers. Dr. George Clements, a spokesman for the Los Angeles Chamber of Commerce, asserted that "the Mexican on relief is being unionized and is being used to foment strikes among the few still loyal Mexican workers. The Mexican casual labor is lost to the Californian farmer unless immediate action is taken to get him off relief."[66]

At first, the vagrancy laws were used to break up urban concentrations of the unemployed, with jail sentences traded for removal to the fields. In an effort to break strikes, it was not unusual for county authorities in league with employers to threaten sending into strike areas batches of Mexicans on the welfare rolls.[67] In February 1931, however, the repatriation effort began on a large scale in Los Angeles, when the first trainload was dispatched to Mexico City. Similar shipments continued at a rate of about one a month for several years. Los Angeles alone repatriated 11,000 in 1932.[68] According to Mexican statistics, between 1931 and 1932 over 200,000 returned voluntarily or under duress from the United States.[69]

On a single trainload, it has been estimated, the Los Angeles County budget was saved nearly $350,000 in welfare costs.[70] To city officials this was more economical than earlier "work fare" expedients. It was also more effective than the policy of threat and intimidation carried out by law enforcement agencies. Ultimately, to the growers, it may not have seemed so effective, for the repatriation campaign did not reduce the level of union strife, which increased as the thirties wore on. On the other hand, it depleted the labor reserve which they had wanted all along to maintain. In one sense the campaign backfired, for, by reducing the total labor pool, it strengthened the bargaining hand of the organized labor that remained. (Their locals, incidentally, had for a long time advocated an incentive scheme for voluntary repatriation, as well as legal measures on the part of the Mexican government to "obstruct and discourage all further immigration of Mexicans into the United States.")[71]

The context in which the state marijuana laws were enforced in Los Angeles should now be clear. Jail on drug or other charges, or repatriation by force or choice—these were the methods adopted for reducing the Mexican labor surplus in the city where surplus, and not scarcity as in the rural areas, was the fundamental economic threat. The situation was thus similar to the opium and Chinese exclusion campaign 50 years earlier. Then as now, the use of a "narcotic" drug[72] was one of many personal and social vices of the target group; Mexicans were lazy, dirty, promiscuous, violent, subintelligent, criminal, anarchistic, communistic—and intoxicated with marijuana.

The intoxication with marijuana was important only insofar as it was part of the overall, hostile stereotype of the Mexicans. It reflected, at the same time it was designed to justify, a drawing of the lines of economic conflict. Where there was conflict between the classes, as in the agricultural counties, the marijuana issue was so marginal as to be almost unheard of. The growers focused on the anarchistic-communistic elements of the stereotype, but they did not need even these as arguments to mobilize the police and other agencies of state power for their own defense.

In Los Angeles, as in several northern cities, the lines of conflict over employment were drawn essentially along ethnic lines *within* the working class—between Mexicans and Italians, Mexicans and Poles (Chicago), or Irish and Greeks (New York, Detroit, etc.). This was a struggle for a diminishing number of jobs in the unskilled sector and at declining wage standards. Although some of the older, established ethnic groups were strongly represented in the police and even on the magistrates' bench and could implement a rough version of their feelings toward the Mexicans, for this to become public policy required a broader mobilization of community groups, one that carried authoritativeness and legitimacy in public opinion. What was needed was some sort of basis for a broad coalition of anti-Mexican forces, and the racial stereotype and ideology of marijuana provided exactly that.

As small a problem as the use of marijuana really was, it was immaterial beside the importance of the "Mexican problem." Once launched, the ideology of marijuana grew independently of the original concern in a way that produced several historical quirks. New Orleans is an interesting illustration of this and one that had an unusual bearing on national prohibition of the drug.

In the early 1930s, a number of New Orleans city officials were instrumental in producing several of the earliest "scientific" papers on the drug and its effects, references to which used to keep cropping up as the federal government launched its campaign to get the Marihuana Tax Act bill passed. One was written by the New Orleans prosecuting attorney who called it unambiguously, "Marihuana as a Developer of Criminals."[73] The article was cited in a 1933 Utah case, *State v. Navaro*, in which it was adopted as substantiation for the judgment that the drug produced crime and insanity. It appeared again among the references advanced by supporters of the Marihuana Tax Act bill during hearings on the measure.[74]

Another highly influential document represented a joint effort by a group including the county (parish) coroner, the district attorney, the commissioner of public safety, and the assistant city chemist.[75] This paper, written by a doctor in private practice and presented to the Louisiana State Medical Society, along with comments from the other group members, attempted to buttress the connection between drug use and crime with some neurological guesswork and a rather fanciful construction of social Darwinian ideas. According to the New Orleans coroner, Dr. George Roeling,

> this marihuana drug stimulates the cortical cerebral centers and inhibits the controlling sub-cortical centers of our mechanism which is responsible for . . . the bolstering up of their courage and the various phenomena which will eventually . . . lead them into the most crime-producing individuals that we have.[76]

Dr. Fossier supplied the framework, not only for identifying a racial or ethnic distinction in the use of drugs, but also for judging the race of people who used them as distinctly inferior to Americans:

> the debasing and baneful influence of hashish and opium is not restricted to individuals but has manifested itself in nations and races as well. The dominant race and most enlightened countries are alcoholic, whilst the races and nations addicted to hemp and opium, some of which once attained to heights of culture and civilization have deteriorated both mentally and physically.
>
> Whilst it is most unfortunate for humanity to be subjugated by intoxicants or narcotics of any kind, which at this state of our civilization seems to be a necessary evil, the possible substitution of alcohol for a greater evil [marihuana] should be considered the greatest possible calamity that can befall a nation. It is not confined to the criminal class.[77]

Most of the typical features of the ideology of opium have been taken over here holus-bolus. There is total obscurity as to what is meant by addiction and whether it differs as to marijuana, cocaine, and the other drugs. There is the hoary theory of victimization, "despite every precaution school children of tender age have been detected smoking muggles [marijuana]."[78] Finally, it is assumed that since adjudicated criminals smoke (are addicted to) marijuana, the drug causes them to act criminally. Only one of the discussants raised doubt about this; he was a doctor with experience in treating drug cases and not a city official:

> all such addicts that we have seen were young persons, under twenty-five, who were defective in brain and nervous structure before they began smoking this weed. . . . They give a history of being incorrigible at home and at school, and as they grow into manhood become criminally inclined. . . . From what we have seen these smokers are criminals before they become addicted to the weed.[79]

The coroner supplied data suggesting that out of 450 prisoners surveyed in the city prison, 125 were "confirmed marihuana addicts," and the district attorney produced figures claiming that in the year before, 1930, 17 out of 37 murderers and 21 out of 115 assault and robbery suspects were "addicts" of the drug. The police commissioner concluded that marijuana "should be put in the same class as heroin" and that only "gigantic enforcement (. . . that could only be accomplished by the [federal] Government)" would destroy the menace.[80] This view was incorporated in a resolution submitted to and passed by the Louisiana State Medical Society, requesting that marijuana be included under the terms of the Harrison Act and enforced by the Federal Bureau of Narcotics. The commissioner was later to write: "throughout the South, little addiction is found until you come to New Orleans."[81]

It is not clear why the New Orleans authorities felt they needed federal legislation and enforcement. Sale or possession of marijuana had been illegal under Louisiana law since 1924, and in 1928 the New Orleans police made 76 arrests on the charge (3.8 percent of all felony arrests). Three quarters of the offenders were native whites, nearly 16 percent were black, and 5.3 percent were listed as foreign-born whites.[82]

The effect of economic depression was generally to lift crime rates throughout the country.[83] The New Orleans authorities may have been conscious of the higher rates although blind to their structural causes. There is no telling how the figures quoted by Fossier were arrived at; today, few would be likely to blame marijuana use as producing the crime. Jesse Steiner, who surveyed crime in New Orleans for the National Commission on Law Observance and Enforcement, did not specifically mention marijuana, but reported that as far as violations of the prohibition and narcotic laws were concerned, "the New Orleans police give little attention to these types of offenders."[84]

That was between 1928 and mid-1930. The role of marijuana crime appears to have been something of a discovery late in 1930 or early in 1931. Ten years before, both the governor of Louisiana and Dr. Oscar Dowling, the state's most important medical officer, had urged the U.S. surgeon general and the Federal Prohibition Commissioner to do something about the drug, because of a couple of incidents in which its use had been linked to a crime.[85] By and large, however, crime, and especially homicide, were blamed on the Italians or blacks of New Orleans—on racial or ethnic characteristics—not on drugs.[86]

Steiner shows that neither the Italians nor the remainder of the city's foreign-born whites were responsible for the proportion of the criminal arrests (1 percent) comparable to their proportion in the city population (in 1920, 6.7 percent). "It can be stated with reasonable assurance," he concluded, "that the foreign-born whites are the least criminal of the New Orleans population and the colored the most criminal, with the native-born standing somewhere between the two extremes."[87]

As we have seen, marijuana was generally identified with Mexicans but rarely, at that time, with blacks. This does not mean that in New Orleans blacks did not in fact use the drug. Remember that here we are talking about the *ideology* of marijuana and not the truth about its prevalence. This ideology was stimulated by the New Orleans group who influenced the authors of papers in the next few years, including the one that characterized much medical and psychiatric opinion from then until quite recently.[88] Mexicans, however, were not explicitly mentioned by Fossier or his associates, although they may have been the ones meant in the reference to inferior races at the prealcohol stage of civilization.

The Mexicans were not a particularly visible group in New Orleans in 1931. A decade before, there had been 1,306, but unlike most of the places I have examined, this number *fell* in the 1930 census to 991. This was barely two-tenths of 1 percent of the city total. The number of Italians also dropped during the decade, and 25 percent of the statewide black population moved out, mostly to the North.[89]

So the propagation of racial or ethnic stereotypes to blame for crime or the deterioration of economic standards, which we have found to be common almost everywhere else in the country, was evidently too implausible to persuade the working class of New Orleans. Politically, blacks were no threat; they had been disenfranchised many years before. To working-class whites, the greater economic threat seemed to come from big business in the city and the plantation owners outside.

This was the period of the rise of Huey Long, whose major gubernatorial victory of 1928 reflected a sharp class antagonism toward the plantation interests, and a developing alliance between the urban working class and the poor farmers.[90] What Long offered them was a populist, protosocialist attack on the state's "vested interests," an ideology of "share our wealth" and "every man a king," and a largely egalitarian economic program. His election and takeover of state policies radically shifted the ideological climate in Louisiana leftward, with the result that there was little enthusiasm for the kind of interethnic or antiworking-class conflict that spawned the marijuana myths elsewhere. In New Orleans' terms, therefore, "the marijuana menace" was an anomaly, an idea no one but the city authorities and some doctors would buy and a campaign which never achieved popular support.

Ironically, on the national scene this small New Orleans group of doctors had an influence out of all proportion to the strength or value of its case, for very little that could be regarded as legitimate scientific evidence of the harmfulness of marijuana had emerged from the West and Southwest as newspapers and legislatures in the region attempted to rationalize what was more often than not an open campaign against Mexican farm laborers. Typical was the debate in the Montana legislature when a bill banning nonmedical use of the drug was quickly pushed through early in 1929:

> There was fun in the House Health Committee during the week when the Marihuana bill came up for consideration. Marihuana is Mexican opium, a plant used by Mexicans and cultivated for sale by Indians. "When some beet field peon takes a few rares of this stuff," explained Dr. Fred Fulsher of Mineral County, "he thinks he has just been elected president of Mexico so he starts out to execute all his political enemies. I understand that over in Butte where the Mexicans often go for the winter they stage imaginary bullfights in the "bower of Roses" or put on tournaments for the favor of "Spanish Rose" after a couple of whiffs of Marijuana.[91]

At the hearings on the Marihuana Tax Act bill, the Mexican connection persisted in spite of efforts by Anslinger and other Narcotics Bureau witnesses to depict the dangers of the drug as national in scope and pervasive among the young. Thus one witness from the West reiterated the older and limiting propaganda: "The Mexican laborers have brought seeds of this plant into Montana and it is fast becoming a terrible menace, particularly in the counties where sugarbeets are grown."[92]

The importance of the New Orleans papers was precisely that they initiated antimarijuana propaganda of a different source and type, no less credible on examination. They nevertheless added to the legitimacy and refinement of an ideology that came out of the West and Southwest too crudely formulated to justify federal action. In this manner they added to the political pressure on the federal government to enact new legislation over and above the existing provisions of state codes and of the Uniform Narcotic Drug Act passed three years before.

We see how a variety of conflicts, each in the local context the result of different alignments of social and economic forces, resulted in pressure, quantitatively roughly equal, to bring about a major policy change at the federal level. On the face of it, no one would guess that 507 Mexican laborers in Alamosa, Colorado or the price of land in Imperial County, California or the Long vote in the "Irish channel" of New Orleans could have had so radical an effect, but to the extent that the marijuana episode was part of the deeper and longer course of class conflict in Depression America, this was indeed how and why it happened.

Chapter 5.
Race or Class, 1949–1953

Today most narcotic addicts are thought to be black.[1] Most of them live in three Northern cities (New York, Chicago, Washington, D.C.) and Los Angeles. The majority of black people, however, continue to live in the South where the addict population is quite small and mostly white.[2] Race *by itself*, then, cannot account for the likelihood that blacks will use narcotics much more than whites. The question is: What factors do produce this, and are these the same as were operating in the earlier cases we have looked at?

The history of black narcotics use is actually quite a short and recent one. The earliest mention of the phenomenon was an article appearing in the *North Carolina Medical Journal* in 1885. The author, a medical practitioner named Roberts, reported that in all of his experience he had "heard of but three well authenticated cases of opium-eating in the negro." One of these had occurred in his own state, the others in South Carolina.[3]

Although it is quite likely that blacks consumed opiates in the patent medicines they bought at this time, there is no sign that this led to habitual use, as it supposedly did in the same region among whites. Roberts explained this in terms which fitted the Negro stereotype of the time but left narcotics use out of it:

> He [the Negro] has not the same delicate nervous organization and does not demand the form of stimulant conveyed in opium—a grosser stimulant sufficing. . . . [Since the opium habit is generally contracted] from the physician's prescription being too long continued [the Negro is less liable] first on account of his general ignorance, and next from his poverty, as well as from the less desire he has for this form of stimulant.[4]

Thirty years later in Georgia the picture seemed not to have changed. Only six drug cases involving blacks appeared in the records of the Georgia State Sanitarium between 1909 and 1914; two only were for the use of opium.[5] In 1913, in Jacksonville, Florida, a survey of prescription records required under a local ordinance turned up 541 opiate users in the city, of whom 134 were black (28.8 percent). Since over half of the city's total population was black, the survey confirmed that "the white race is more prone to use opium than the negro."[6] Two years later in Tennessee, where state law required a system of registration for regular opiate users, Brown found only 10 percent blacks in this group—significantly less than their proportion in the state overall.[7]

In the Southern states more generally, blacks were underrepresented among the narcotic users, although the region had a higher rate of addiction than the rest of the country.[8] Kolb and DuMez explained this high rate as due "to the known value of opiates in treating diarrheal diseases . . . but also for the discomforts arising from such diseases as hookworm and malaria, these diseases being much more prevalent in the states enumerated than in the remainder of the country."[9] Of course, if it had been simply this, blacks ought to have been as liable to narcotics addiction as they were exposed to the diseases, but this was not so.

Roberts had believed this might change among blacks migrating to the North, as their income rose, and Green, the author of the Georgia study, predicted that "in communities in which the negro is more prosperous, drug psychoses are often found."[10] We can see how far this proved correct in Figure 5–1, which illustrates the racial composition of the addict population in various cities and areas up to 1940, as provided by the available surveys.

Whites clearly predominated in every case, northern and southern alike, and the Jacksonville group amounted to the largest *proportion* of black addicts for nearly 30 years.

What the chart does not indicate are the major shifts in the black population from south to north, and the consequent change in the size of the black and white population from place to place. Since these will have affected the racial proportions of the addict group also, what we need to know is the *relative likelihood* of blacks becoming heavy narcotics users compared with whites over the same period. A simple way to express this is to take the ratio of black to white users for each area and divide it by the ratio of the black to white total population for the same place. At unity we can say that blacks were as likely to use narcotics as whites in that locality; for fractions, the smaller the score the

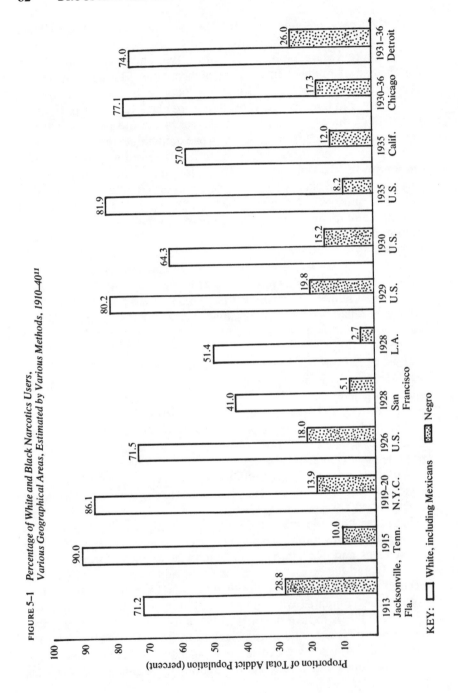

FIGURE 5-1   *Percentage of White and Black Narcotics Users,*
Various Geographical Areas, Estimated by Various Methods, 1910–40[11]

KEY: ☐ White, including Mexicans   ▨ Negro

more underrepresented blacks were among the users, and above unity, the larger the score, the more overrepresented and hence more likely they were to become users as compared with whites. (See Figure 5-2.)

Two things become clearer. Although the number of blacks among drug users was still small during the period, by 1929 they were more than twice as likely as whites to be among this group. Compared with Southerners, Northern black users were more likely to exceed their popular distribution.

The case of the New York City Narcotic Clinic is an interesting one. It will be recalled that the widespread rumors of a cocaine epidemic among blacks, in New York in particular, were largely groundless. Here is evidence, however, that the use of *opiates* was unusually widespread among the city's blacks—yet almost no public notice was taken of it at the time. The city health commissioner, reporting on the drug problem early in 1920, failed to mention the race of the clinic's patients; what struck him most was that the majority of them was under 25, "mere children"; and that there was "hardly a calling or occupation without representation. Apparently the evil is so widespread that it reaches every stratum of society and every nationality."[12] He reported that over two-thirds of these people were straight heroin users; only 10 percent admitted to mixing cocaine with morphine or heroin; and an insignificant number claimed to prefer the use of cocaine by itself. The clinic experienced almost no demand for it.[13] In other words, the drug which a generation of publicists and legislators had blamed on the blacks was relatively uncommon in 1920, while the heroin habit, which young blacks were developing at a faster rate than whites, was all but invisible.

A similar situation may have been the case in California where in 1935 a relatively small proportion of blacks was arrested on narcotics charges, although this amounted to more than ten times the popular distribution. This, too, was invisible, concealed by the public obsession with marijuana and the "Mexican problem."

It pays not to read too much into these statistics, for the sources and methods of collection vary widely between them; they are useful as rough indicators of the regional or racial distribution of narcotics users at static points of time, but they cannot reliably be used to point up changes over time. For this we need a continuous statistical series based on a constant method of measurement. The two commonest examples are the yearly enumerations issued by the Federal Bureau of Narcotics or its predecessor units since 1915; these list the number of people charged with criminal violations of the Harrison Act, and are

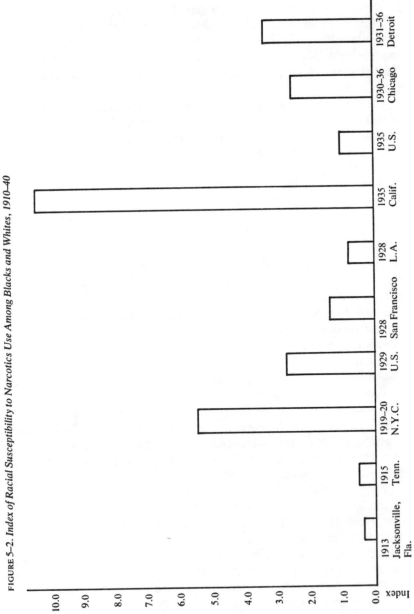

FIGURE 5–2. Index of Racial Susceptibility to Narcotics Use Among Blacks and Whites, 1910–40

separate from the enumeration of violators of the Marihuana Tax Act. The second series is the yearly enumeration of nonfederal narcotics prosecutions collected by the Federal Bureau of Investigation and published in the annual *Uniform Crime Reports*.[14] Figure 5-3 (below) indicates the overall trend for the two series between 1915 and 1962.

The FBI series differs from the FBN's by including marijuana cases; in 1953, for example, marijuana arrests amount to 12.4 percent of the annual total; the following year, this was up to 16.6 percent.[15]

This is not the only problem with interpreting the *Uniform Crime Reports*. For example, while the FBN series is essentially complete and comprehensive for the whole country, the FBI *Reports* are missing information (especially fingerprint records from which racial data are obtained), and frequent changes in the reporting system cast doubt on the accuracy of the figures available.

These have been variously interpreted to mean, on one hand, that there was a steady and deep decline in the number of addicts from the passage of the Harrison Act to around 1948, when narcotics use began to rise again. In particular, this was the view of Commissioner Anslinger. In the decade before 1948 he told a congressional committee that "addiction had reached an irreducible minimum."[16] Addiction in this context was synonymous with an arrest record on narcotics charges, no matter what the individual circumstances.

On the other hand, critics of this view have argued that since the average age of reported addicts kept falling during the same period, at the very least the group must have been reproducing itself, and since the time period was too short to permit the typical addict to "mature out" of his habit, it is likely the total number was on the rise.[17] Changes in enforcement practice, measurement error and a calculated "public relations effort" are said to be behind the Anslinger and official interpretation.[18]

A third possibility is that both of these things were happening at once. This was possible because large demographic changes and a gradual change in enforcement policy beginning in the middle of World War I, almost as soon as the Harrison Act came into force, produced a divergence in the geographic and racial composition of narcotics offenders, or addicts as of course they were officially known.

Compared to the North, the southern offense rate continued relatively high until 1948 when the sharp upturn in the national picture (Figure 5-3) was primarily a phenomenon of the northern cities and Los Angeles.

There is a problem with regional comparisons, however, because

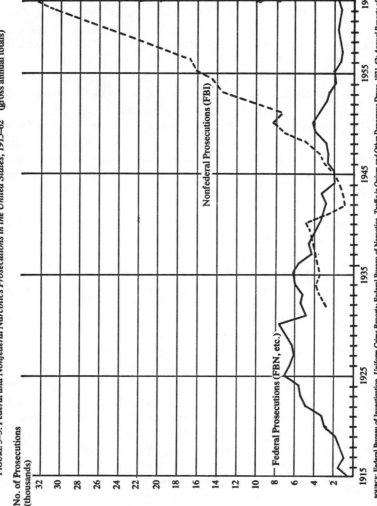

FIGURE 5-3. Federal and Nonfederal Narcotics Prosecutions in the United States, 1915-62   (gross annual totals)

No. of Prosecutions
(thousands)

SOURCE: Federal Bureau of Investigation, *Uniform Crime Reports*; Federal Bureau of Narcotics, *Traffic in Opium and Other Dangerous Drugs*, 1931-62; *Annual Reports of the Commissioner of Prohibition*, 1927-30; *Annual Reports of the Commissioner of Internal Revenue*, 1915-26. Figure reprinted from Alfred A. Lindesmith, *The Addict and the Law*, Bloomington: Indiana University Press (1965), p. 21.

marijuana and opiate offenses cannot be disaggregated from the FBI totals for each region. Since the marijuana campaign originated in the Southwest and West and was pursued most forcefully there, the figures for the states in these regions must be considered inflated as an indicator of opiate offenses.

The FBI reports nevertheless illustrate a parallel decline in drug arrests for all regions of the country through the late years of the Depression and during the Second World War. At the same time, however, the proportion of blacks arrested rose steadily. The figures on the racial characteristics of narcotics offenders show that all races reflected the central tendency, illustrated in Figure 5–3, of an overall decline between 1933 and the end of the war. Most of this was due, however, to the intervention of the war, and the large spurt in arrests between 1939 and 1940 and again between 1945 and 1946 suggest that there was no "natural" decline in addict numbers due, as Anslinger used to say, to the success of his bureau's enforcement efforts.

The ratio of blacks to whites among reported offenders shows an almost unbroken linear increase toward more and more blacks, fewer whites, until 1950 when the number of blacks became a majority for the first time. In all likelihood what this means is that Northern, urban blacks were steadily increasing their representation among narcotics offenders at the expense of the Southern whites who were dropping out of the habit or out of sight of the police. These were the older addicts; it was the steady influx of youthful black users which was pushing the mean age of the official addict population downwards.

Did the white addicts simply disappear? From the FBI records they did, and whether or not they continued using narcotics, all that can be said is that from the early thirties on, they were less and less likely to be arrested. In the same period a black's chance of being arrested increased, and, according to these statistics, it came close to two-and-a-half times greater than the white's.

A common explanation for the racial shift in arrest rates is that the police enforced the law differently on racial grounds alone, at the same time as fewer people of both races were being arrested on narcotic charges. Black jazz musicians and the clubs where they played, for example, seem to have been singled out by the authorities for close and constant surveillance. "Practically all the outstanding players of bop were arrested during this period."[19]

This was probably characteristic of enforcement policy in the North rather than the South (I say probably because the FBI figures are not further broken down to reflect race by region for the same offense), although it remains to be settled whether the actual prevalence of narcotics use among urban blacks was disproportionately greater than among whites and arrests simply reflected it, or else whether the police used the narcotic laws to attack blacks arriving from the South in the same way as we saw the marijuana laws used against the Mexicans.

Writing about Chicago in 1919 Tuttle found common stereotypes about blacks to include that "they consistently sold their votes, carried razors, habitually shot craps, and had one front tooth filled with gold with their first earnings"[20]—no mention of drugs. At exactly the same time in New York, as noted before, opiates were circulating quite widely in the black community although unnoticed by whites. Katzman, who has published a history of the Detroit ghetto, has evidence that drugs were commonly available in saloons patronized by blacks in the late war years, but that this was ignored by the authorities for as long as the practice was confined to a limited quarter, usually the "red light" district of the city.[21]

A number of factors combined to drive this more into the open. During the war a nationwide campaign to protect soldiers from contracting venereal diseases, enforced by directives from the Secretary of War, led to the break-up of many of the established urban vice areas, but this only encouraged the dispersion of the trade into previously "respectable" areas of the city. This increased the visibility of drug use, which in turn stimulated greater enforcement efforts. The steady flow of black migrants into the cities during the twenties, and the expansion of the black residential areas increased this visibility in general, while Prohibition may have increased the marginal advantage of drugs over alcohol to consumers on low incomes.

It does not really matter whether the FBI figures represented accurately the prevalence of narcotics use from the early thirties on, for even if they do not, they still reflect an important change in the focus of official concern regarding the potential threat of the narcotic problem— who was (and who was not) susceptible to addiction and the circumstances in which new measures might be required to deal with the problem. Either way, we learn that the *potential* for a distinctive black narcotics problem was in evidence soon after the First World War, at least in New York, that it was concentrated in the urban North and West, and that it continued to grow through the thirties despite a decline in the overall number of reported users.

This potential could have been expected to manifest itself concretely as the black share of the inner-city population steadily increased; the 1940 figures were an indication of what was to come immediately after

TABLE 5–1

Average Annual Number of Arrests and Arrest Rates,
Nonfederal Narcotic Violators, by Race, 1934–41

Race	ANNUAL AVERAGE GROSS TOTAL	RATE PER 100,000 PEOPLE (based on 1930 Census)
Black	413.8	3.5
Mexican	282.9	19.9
Chinese	525.5	514.4
White	1,548.9	1.4

the war was over. However, to the authorities the drug problem was all but forgotten—except for the Mexicans and marijuana. Table 5–1 provides the arrest statistics for 1934–41, the eight years when, as we have seen, the agitation over the "Mexican problem" reached its peak and during which the FBI reported Mexicans as a separate racial category.

In light of the widespread publicity given to the Mexicans and the intense public concern for the dangers of marijuana at this time, it is surprising to find that the average number of Mexicans arrested annually on drug charges was smaller than the number of any one of the other races. In simple numerical terms the major drug problem at the time was a white one, but Anslinger and his agents treated this as residual and inoffensive. If racial concentration of drug use gave this problem its popular visibility, then it was not the Mexicans on whom everyone should have fixed their attention, but the Chinese instead. Their offense rate was higher than the highest rate of addiction ever estimated for the country as a whole, and yet nationally it was almost completely ignored at the time.

Why this was so will take time to explain adequately. For the moment it is important to emphasize the lack of any relationship between the true dimension of the narcotics problem and the nature of official and public concern about it. The Mexican problem was a small one relatively speaking, yet it created a national furor; the black and Chinese problems were larger but were totally ignored.

Immediately after World War II the number of narcotics prosecutions began to rise (Figure 5–3) and the rate of increase among blacks was three times faster than that among whites. Although this number has continued to rise steadily ever since, 1951 was what was officially described as a peak year because in that year the number of offenders under 21, and hence the most recent recruits to the drug, reached the highest proportion to be recorded until nearly 20 years later.[22]

From then on, the statistics show a steady pattern of aging among the offender or addict population, as the proportion of new and younger offenders declined and the proportion of older and repeat offenders grew.[23] The number of new offenders never dried up altogether, but we can reliably treat the period between 1949 and 1953 as a distinct episode in our overall story.

Officially this was the period of an adolescent epidemic in drug addiction. For example, the Kefauver Committee Report on organized crime stated in 1951 that it was "this phase of the narcotic problem [which] is a matter of acute public interest and widespread alarm,"[24] despite the fact that offenders under 21 never made up more than a quarter of the total at the peak of the period in the city most affected— New York. This distortion helped obscure the fact that the *majority* of so-called addicts uncovered in the "epidemic" postwar years had begun using narcotics before the war or during it, and that consequently the sharp rise which precipitated public concern between 1949 and 1953 was largely the result of a gradual but steady rise in the years before. This was one way that the narcotics enforcement agencies avoided policy dilemmas of their own making, at the same time as they helped stimulate the very problem they were supposed to suppress by encouraging the substitution of heroin for marijuana among the drug-using population.

According to the Bureau of Narcotics, the greatest concentration of offenders was in three cities, New York, Chicago, and Los Angeles.[25] What we can learn about this episode is most readily gathered from focusing on the first two.

In New York several agencies reported on the number of narcotics users entering their overlapping, sometimes separate jurisdictions. Table 5-2 summarizes these reports at the same time as it reveals a number of discrepancies and inconsistencies that typically exist between sources.[26]

Since these are, strictly speaking, tabulations of arrests, not of individuals, and only of those individuals falling into the hands of the law, estimates of the number of addicts in New York at this time differ both from these figures and even more widely from each other. Between 1952 and 1955, Police Commissioner Kennedy told the Daniel Hearings, there were 10,638 known addicts in the city, 87 percent of them (9,255) heroin addicts.[27] Inspector Joseph L. Coyle of the Narcotics Squad estimated that between 1952 and 1958 there were 22,909 "drug addicts," but he did not distinguish heroin-users from marijuana- or cocaine-users, and included an unidentified number of people convicted of selling drugs, though known not to be users themselves.[28] Anslinger reported from FBN statistics that between 1953 and 1954 there were 7,937 addicts in New York.[29] Yet another estimate was provided by Peter Terranova drawing on the register of addicts maintained by the State Board of Health after 1951. According to this source, there were 14,196 addicts in the state between 1952 and late 1955, of whom 18.2 percent were under 21.[30] Rough reliability for this is suggested by the finding of Chein and his associates who carried out a most extensive search of institutional records in New York City between 1949 and 1955. They identified 3,457 new cases of boys (only) in the 16–20 age group who were discovered to be involved with narcotics in that period. About 500 of these youths were caught each year; the peak year was 1951 when over 800 new cases were presented in the courts or hospitals of the city.[31]

According to the State Board of Health, 57.9 percent of the addicts were black, 24.1 percent white, 14.9 percent Puerto Rican, and just over 3 percent Chinese. In 88 percent of all cases, heroin was the drug involved. Curiously, Chein never presented a simple tabulation of the race or ethnic origin of the youthful offenders he was able to identify, although a breakdown of the boroughs and census tracts in which the offenders lived showed a very high concentration of drug use in predominantly black and Puerto Rican areas—Harlem, the Morrisania section of the Bronx, and scattered sections of Brooklyn, notably Bedford-Stuyvesant. Altogether, across the city, 15 percent of the tracts, containing 29 percent of the 16–20 year old boys, contributed 83 percent of all cases on record.[32] The concentration of black and Puerto Rican population significantly marked off the areas where drug use had reached "epidemic" proportions from those areas where its prevalence was low.

At the beginning of the period surveyed by Chein (1949) more than half the drug offenders were using marijuana, with only a small proportion using it together with heroin, cocaine, or something else. Within a year this had changed and by 1952 heroin completely dominated consumption patterns.

Superficially it looks as if high rates of drug use and high rates of juvenile delinquency in general (apart from drug use) went closely together. It was a common belief that the former led to the latter as

TABLE 5–2

Narcotics Offenders Reported in New York City, 1946–54

Year	Javits TOTAL ARRESTS	Javits Number (minors)	Javits Percent (minors)	Kennedy TOTAL ARRESTS	Kennedy Number (minors)	Kennedy Percent (minors)	Terranova TOTAL ARRESTS	Terranova Number (minors)	Terranova Percent (minors)	Hogan Number of Addicted Youth Arrested	Davidson Number of Addicted Youth Arrested
1946	712	33	4.6	—	—	—	—	—	—	—	—
1947	1,014	78	7.7	—	—	—	—	—	—	—	—
1948	1,305	130	10.0	—	—	—	—	—	—	45	—
1949	1,410	175	12.4	—	—	—	—	—	—	60	—
1950	2,482	521	21.0	—	—	—	—	—	—	196	—
1951	3,647	788	21.6	3,661	782	21.4	3,661	802	21.9	353	—
1952	2,969	533	18.0	2,967	560	18.9	5,297	260	4.9	219	560
1953	3,605	573	15.9	3,605	573	15.9	3,605	573	15.9	231	573
1954	4,316	749	17.4	4,316	749	17.4	4,316	749	17.4	242	749

SOURCES:

Javits—*Narcotic Addiction in New York—1955, A Continuing Problem*, Report of Jacob K. Javits, Attorney General to the Legislature of the State of New York, reprinted as Exhibit No. 19, *Daniel Hearings*, p. 1,900.

Kennedy—Testimony of New York City Police Commissioner, Stephen Kennedy, *Daniel Hearings*, p. 1,643.

Terranova—Testimony of Peter E. Terranova, Head (retired), New York Police Department Narcotics Squad, in *Treatment and Rehabilitation of Juvenile Drug Addicts*, Hearings before the Subcommittee to Investigate Juvenile Delinquency of the Committee of the Judiciary, U.S. Senate, 84th Congress, 2nd Sess., December 17–18, 1956, p. 81.

Hogan—Testimony of Frank S. Hogan, District Attorney, New York County, *Daniel Hearings*, p. 658. Figures are for the county only.

Davidson—Testimony of Congressman Irwin D. Davidson, *Daniel Hearings*, p. 671.

TABLE 5–3

Multiple Correlations* of Selected Combinations
of Variables with Drug Rates in High-Use Areas of New York, 1949–55[34]

Variables	MANHATTAN	BRONX	BROOKLYN
Percentage less than $2,000 income p.a., percentage in low occupations	0.68 (46)	0.69 (48)	0.50 (25)
Percentage Negro, percentage less than $2,000, percentage in low occupations	.79 (62)	0.69 (48)	0.50 (25)
Percentage Negro, percentage less than $2,000, percentage in low occupations, percentage without TV, percentage of crowded dwelling units	0.81 (66)	0.75 (54)	0.52 (27)
All but percentage Negro and percentage Puerto Rican	0.82 (67)	0.83 (69)	0.63 (40)
All but percentage Puerto Rican	0.86 (74)	0.83 (69)	0.63 (40)

*The percentages of variance in the drug rate accounted for by the given combination of variables are given in parentheses next to each correlation coefficient. Table reprinted from *The Road to H: Narcotics, Delinquency and Social Policy*, Isidor Chein (New York: Basic Books, 1964), p. 21.

drug users were forced to resort to crime to finance expensive habits. Actually Chein found that the total amount of delinquency was independent of drug use, and that the reported rise in other than drug offenses reflected increased activity on the part of the *police.* Areas with high drug use did not reflect a rise in delinquency which was significantly more marked than the rise in areas where drug use was low, although the types of offenses committed did vary along these lines. High drug-use areas showed a greater concentration on income-producing crimes such as robbery, burglary, jostling, shoplifting, etc. The delinquency of the low drug-use areas tended to be more violent and antipersonal in nature—assault, disorderly conduct, nonrape sex offenses, and auto theft were more common. These findings suggested to Chein that there were two quite distinct patterns of delinquency in the city—one drug use, and the other, the delinquency of gangs and fighting.[33]

Both kinds of delinquency were concentrated in the same parts of the city, even though within a section there was differentiation between groups of delinquent drug users and delinquent nonusers. We can get a good idea of what these areas were like by examining those combinations of variables which had the highest correlation with drug rates in each of the boroughs.

In plain language this means that around 1950 you were highly likely to become involved in drugs—or at least to get caught at it—if you lived in a neighborhood of New York in which household incomes averaged less than $2,000 annually, in which the men who worked had jobs which were low in demand, low in skill and productivity, and low in wages— what economists call the secondary labor market. Lack of income also meant a neighborhood with relatively few television sets and a lot of crowding in tenements. Or else you were highly likely to be reported as a drug offender if you were black or Puerto Rican.

These conditions do not by any means explain why people became drug users between 1946 and 1953, but the correlations are high enough for us to say that they do identify the kinds of people who did.

In Chicago the picture was similar. In 1955 the Chicago Police Department estimated that there was a total of 3,500 heroin addicts in the city.[35] Kobrin and Finestone, who searched the institutional records for the period 1947–53, claimed that there were about 5,000 habitual drug users in Chicago at the end of that time, but they did not divide the heroin users from the rest. In general they found that "of those persons with official records as drug users, approximately 90 percent used heroin."[36] In 1950, however, the psychiatrist in charge at the municipal court remarked that there had been an increase in drug use in the 17–25 age group, but that this was mostly confined to marijuana.[37] The arrest records for 1954, the one year in which the specific drug used was reported, show, however, that of over a thousand cases of sale or possession of drugs, 26 percent involved marijuana.[38]

It is worthwhile to clarify where possible the exact nature of the offense charged. The Chicago police, for example, typically used to pick up people known or suspected to be drug users and charge them under a disorderly conduct provision of the municipal code, which had been amended early in 1951 to include drug-users. These arrests were generally for the purpose of getting information on the drug trade or of forcing a trade of detention time and harassment in exchange for names and other incriminatory evidence. Just as we saw similar statutes used by California police to drive Mexicans out of the local area in the 1930s, so these tactics of selective and arbitrary arrest were used in Chicago against the predominantly young and black population of the early fifties.

Charges under this provision were never fewer than 50 percent of all narcotics charges. For the years between 1951 and 1955 they made up 52 percent, 70 percent, 72 percent, 70 percent, and 69 percent, respectively. In effect, drugs were a pretext; barely half of the arrests resulted in convictions. The system was admittedly an illegal one, the state's attorney for Cook County told the Daniel subcommittee, but "you have to go along with a certain amount of the fringe violation, if you see what I mean. . . . [We cannot] get too excited if a known addict has been unlawfully arrested and then discharged, knowing that because he is a known addict the police have to take little extra measures."[39] The fact was that the numbers of arrests far exceeded the true number of known heroin addicts, and that as many as a quarter of those charged used marijuana and were not addicts in this sense at all. Since the age at which drug use started was typically around 16, and since a quarter of those arrested in 1951 were close to this age, the police could not have known who or what these people were when they were arrested—except, of course, that they were black teenagers. The operation, in other words, was a dragnet aimed at a whole section of the urban population, and the only justification for it, that "in order to catch a dope peddler, you must have an addict,"[40] was an ex post facto rationalization of the operation itself.

The numbers of adolescents using heroin did nevertheless rise in this period. The best evidence for this is not police figures but rather data on first admissions from the Chicago area to the federal narcotics treatment facility in Lexington, Kentucky. These show that between 1947 and 1951 a total of 357 under-21 year olds were admitted as compared with only four between 1937 and 1941. As a proportion of the total Chicago admissions this group was over 24 percent in the later period, 1.4 percent in the earlier one. The numbers and percentages are still small, small enough to justify dismissing claims that this was *primarily* an adolescent phenomenon. In any case the number of new offenders of any age rapidly trailed off after 1951, and by 1954 the police reported 85 percent of their narcotics arrests were repeats.[41]

The geographical concentration of police activity and of reported drug use was quite as evident in Chicago as it was in New York. The police identified four sections on the city's South Side as the hub of the narcotics traffic: these, Prairie, Wabash, Hyde Park and Woodlawn, were mostly black.[42] In all, 91 percent of the Narcotics Bureau cases lived in fifteen community areas containing only 25 percent of Chicago's total population. Since blacks made up only 14.1 percent of that total (1950 Census), but nearly 90 percent of the drug offenders, they were many more times more likely than whites to be involved. (See Table 5–4.)

Chicago's drug users were not newcomers to the city. Most of the new and young ones had been born in Chicago or had spent their adolescence there,[43] and most had been born in the middle years of the Depression to parents who had migrated at that time from the South. A similar pattern was true also of the younger New York users.[44]

Kobrin and Finestone were not in a position to investigate patterns of delinquency and crime apart from narcotics use in area by area of the city, although they did find that adolescent heroin users had probably "engaged in delinquency in a group-supported [read *gang*] and habitual form either prior to their use of drugs or simultaneously with their developing interest in drugs."[45] Both Senator Daniel and his witness, the sheriff of Cook County, agreed that in general, addicts had a history of crime prior to their using drugs.[46] The onset of addiction increased the frequency with which crimes were committed, however, and altered their pattern somewhat. Street-fighting and gang assaults, Kobrin and Finestone observed, died down when gang members began taking heroin, and after addiction they became more specialized in the kinds of crimes they would commit. In general they would not engage in more serious (more antipersonal and violent) crimes than those committed before addiction.[47]

These then were the main features of the narcotics situation as it existed around 1951 when public concern stimulated the first official reactions, and vice versa.

Several already familiar themes were drawn together in 1950, during the life of Senator Kefauver's Special Committee to Investigate Organized Crime. "There can be no doubt," the committee concluded in its final report, "that the narcotic traffic is highly organized crime."[48] The shape of the organization, the identity of its members and the power that its money could buy were the subjects of the committee's hearings, held in 14 cities and televised around the country. These launched the specter of the Mafia and such Italian masterminds as Frank Costello, Lucky Luciano, and Tony Accardo, together with Jewish confederates such as Meyer Lansky and Mickey Cohen who had reportedly introduced to the world of crime such basics of the legitimate economy as market concentration, lateral and vertical integration, and the division of labor.

"It would be most unfortunate," the committee warned, "if any inferences were erroneously drawn in any way derogatory to the vast majority of law-abiding citizens of Sicilian and Italian extraction."[49] Nevertheless, the foreignness of the criminal gangs was a recurrent point in the testimony and was used to bolster the image of a nationwide, indeed international syndicate, linked by organic ties of kinship and ethnic loyalty and disciplined by an age-old Sicilian code of secrecy, which had subverted vast segments of native American life. The nativism of this approach, however, produced a paradoxical account of the narcotics traffic in the immediately preceding period.

Thus while testimony obtained by the Kefauver Committee brought to light the rise of drug offenses following the war, other testimony contradicted the official Bureau of Narcotics line that the traffic in drugs had largely been suppressed from the mid-thirties on. A powerful New York gang was identified as having successfully smuggled narcotics from China until around 1940; New Orleans was reported as having been a center for incoming marijuana and opium grown in Mexico during the war; a Mafia group operating in Kansas City and supplying narcotics throughout the Midwest was apparently able to maintain an uninterrupted flow of drugs from Havana, also during the war years.[50] Either these activities should have been reflected in the arrest statistics for those years or else, if the latter figures are to be believed, the Mafia was nowhere near as powerful in the drug traffic as was claimed.

The rise in drug addiction after the war was again largely supplied by gang sources, according to Kefauver. Cocaine was introduced from Peru in 1948 but reportedly was suppressed by the Bureau of Narcotics a year later. There was a "tremendous flow" of marijuana from Mexico under the direction of "some of the most astute, wily and desperate criminals who operate interstatewise"[51]; the influx of heroin immediately after the war was largely credited to Lucky Luciano, who had been deported to Italy early in 1946, and who was alleged to have funneled drug shipments both from there and from Cuba the following year.[52]

At the opening of a new round of hearings, in April 1951, the chairman, Congressman Boggs said:

I first became interested in this legislation about a year and a half ago when I received a letter from a member of a Federal grand jury. This juror said that about 50 or 75 percent of the time of the Federal grand jury in New Orleans was being consumed by second, third, and fourth offenders; maybe more than that, of the narcotics law, so it became quite obvious, after I took it up with the [Federal] Bureau [of Narcotics], that one of the greatest difficulties in enforcement was the fact that the penalties were not severe enough.[53]

At the time the records of the United States Fifth Circuit Court indicated that narcotics violators in New Orleans were in fact being convicted and imprisoned in significantly greater proportions than the national average, and the typical sentence was longer.[54]

Boggs had been convinced, however, that the city was the center of a Mafia-run narcotics traffic. This was the view at least of the FBN agent in charge at New Orleans, Thomas McGuire, who had testified to that effect at the Kefauver Committee hearing in New Orleans late in January 1951. The evidence for this was, in fact, slim; the only notable seizure of drugs mentioned was a small one—$21,000 by police estimate; and no evidence was introduced that heroin use in the city had increased at all. It appears, moreover, that what the Kefauver Committee referred to as narcotics was in fact marijuana, smuggled in from Mexico.[55] The reputed kingpin of the city's drug traffic, Carlos Marcello, had a long criminal record but the only evidence of his involvement in drugs pointed to marijuana and nothing else. [56]

The peculiar sensitiveness of New Orleans officials to this drug was noted before; the original political context for their concern had been an anti-working-class one at the time Huey Long was building a successful populist alliance against planters and the business interests of the city. It had also carried undertones of hostility toward the Italians of New Orleans who had been the whipping boys of the city's political machine since the late nineteenth century.

In 1951 a similar constellation of political forces was organizing in an effort to overthrow Earl Long, Huey's brother and the governor of the state since 1948. The opposition was largely based on support from the rural planters and urban business groups, whose attacks on the corruption and mismanagement of the state by the Long administration found a strong echo in the Kefauver Committee's exposé of criminal racketeering in the city and elsewhere in the state. Charges of bribery and of official complicity in the rackets, made in the hearings, helped structure the shape of the gubernatorial campaign for the following year.

One of the candidates was to be Congressman Boggs whose political task was a difficult one. In fact, he was a Long candidate and owed his political debts to both the governor and his son, U. S. Senator Russell Long. His district in New Orleans, however, was a middle-class one which showed every indication of voting for the anti-Long candidate in the gubernatorial primary. What Boggs had to do was to gain popular visibility, maintain for himself the working-class votes which traditionally went for the Long candidate, and at the same time somehow capture the middle-class vote for efficient government, law, and order.[57]

The Kefauver hearings offered the basic campaign ingredients and

had resurrected that classic device for cutting across class politics—
the ethnic scapegoat. In New Orleans terms the Mafia had existed all
along, ever since there had been Italians, and the Kefauver Committee's final report went along by identifying the city as the virtual origin
of the organization in America.[58] What Boggs was to do in his hearings
was to pinpoint the one racket in New Orleans which involved the
smallest number of people, had the least public support (as compared,
say, with gambling which was very popular), and was as innocuous as
marijuana use had always been in the city—and introduce it as a national problem of epidemic proportions. This was how Boggs discovered the narcotics problem and began running for governor.[59]

"Gentlemen," one of the witnesses told the hearing committee,
"somewhere right at this minute a little boy like yours, or a little girl
like mine, is getting a first taste of the needle; it is going into their
bloodstreams. Their bloodstreams are coursing the drug that will soon
destroy them."[60] As the testimony presented the problem, it was primarily one involving juveniles, but one which cut across class lines to
occur in almost any social environment:

> The most terrifying thing about the drug disease among the youth
> to parents and citizens who are worried about its rapid spread is
> that it happens to normal and average children—not only to sub-
> normal children but to normal and average children as well.[61]

Mrs. Wright, from the General Federation of Women's Clubs, added
similar sentiments:

> We feel that these rats who peddle drugs are more of a menace
> than even a potential murderer. They kill the very souls of those
> with whom they traffic; they rob them of all moral values; they
> take their health away; they drag our boys and girls into some cir-
> cle of Hades where those who love them are unable to reach to
> help.[62]

The clear implication was that the drug was heroin, although no evidence at all was presented to indicate the relative prevalence of heroin,
cocaine, and marijuana use. Had this existed, though, and even supposing marijuana had been the most common one, the hearings developed the view that one drug inevitably led to the other. Anslinger, for
example: "The danger is this: over 50 percent of those young (heroin)
addicts started on marijuana smoking. They started there and graduated to heroin; they took the needle when the thrill of marijuana was
gone."[63]

The theory of drug use was essentially that the young were victims of an unscrupulous network of smugglers, dealers, and pushers who seduced the innocent and unwary into addiction by stages—first marijuana or perhaps cocaine and then heroin.

There was no doubt about the identity of the network. "Is it a fact," Boggs queried Congressman James Donovan of New York, "that Lucky Luciano is now the principal exporter from Italy?"[64] "Have you found any connection with the racketeer Luciano there [in Italy]?" he asked Deputy Narcotics Commissioner Cunningham.[65] And again, this time in an exchange with Anslinger:

> MR. BOGGS. And you have to strike at the center of the octopus really to wipe it out?
>
> MR. ANSLINGER. And at the big fellows, and the big fellows are not being sent away. . . .
>
> MR. BOGGS. Under the Harrison Narcotics Act—this may be an elementary question and possibly I should know the answer to it, but I will preface my remarks by putting it this way—I understand quite a few aliens are involved in the dope traffic.
>
> MR. ANSLINGER. Yes, sir.[66]

If the identity of the sources of the drug traffic was never in doubt, what about the consumers? Did Mrs. Higgins, Congressman Yates, or Mrs. Wright mean Harlem or the South Side of Chicago when they referred to "a little boy like yours" or "normal average children"?

The answer is no, which is the strange thing about the Boggs hearings: in testimony of more than 15 witnesses, running to over 200 pages, there is virtually no record of the fact that most narcotics users, young or old at the time, were black, poor and concentrated in just three cities.[67] Of course, the witnesses may have been afraid that drug use would spread out of these areas, but such a fear belied almost total ignorance of the social characteristics of the susceptible population. No evidence existed then, before or since, that narcotics (heroin) have ever spread beyond a fairly narrow segment of the urban working class.

Blindness to the real situation, then, made it possible for the Boggs subcommittee to uncover a variety of spurious relationships between the prevalence of drug use and enforcement policy. In Southern states, for example, such as Tennessee where, as I reported earlier, blacks had been underrepresented among the addict population, the low arrest rate was thought to be a consequence of a policy of heavy prison sentences for offenders.[68] (A year later, according to the FBI reports, the rate shot up in spite of this policy.)

The subcommittee was told that inadequate enforcement was responsible for the new situation in the drug traffic after World War II. There was a paradox in this, however, and something of a dilemma for enforcement officials. For according to the FBN, a relatively small enforcement effort had been able to reduce the addict population to an "irreducible minimum" around 1948. Between then and 1955, on the heels of the epidemic, the federal field force was increased slightly, and enormous expansions were made in city narcotics squads. In 1950 there were 10 men on the New York Police Department squad and seven on the Chicago squad; in 1955 these had jumped to 200 and 96, respectively.[69]

This increased enforcement did not reduce the drug traffic, however; the reverse occurred. More police meant a higher volume of arrests, which continued to grow throughout the 1950s (Figure 5–3). As a measure of the addiction problem, a rising index justified further demands for larger forces, although eventually it would become evident that there was a self-sustaining, vicious cycle here. The policy dilemma was that the police agencies could not for their own sake afford to be successful, for as the Bureau of Narcotics had discovered, a falling index, the goal of enforcement effort, had led in the forties to a withering away of agency budget and strength.[70] The newly expanded bureaucracy of enforcement which came into being after 1950, was thus bound to fail in the strict interpretation, but it could not *appear* to be doing so.

The buck had to be passed on, and the Boggs subcommittee accepted the idea that it was a feeble court system which was to blame. It was not only a case of inadequate sentencing, which the Boggs bill's minimum sentence provisions were designed to remedy; there was an underlying ideological current to the criticism of the courts, and also to the explanation of where the drug epidemic had come from. Congressman Harrison, a member of the investigating subcommittee, declared:

> I just do not know how you can, by legislation, supply some of these Federal judges with the spine that they do not have. There are a very great many fine men on the Federal bench today, but there are just too many political touts and parlor pinks utterly incapable of understanding the danger of organized crime and organized subversion.[71]

Organized subversion? This was a theme with many different elements in it. The Kefauver Committee had claimed, for instance, that the Chinese *tongs*, vilified 60 and 70 years before in San Francisco, were behind narcotics distribution in some parts of the country.[72] They operated exactly like the Mafia; they even had a supply connection with Lucky Luciano.[73] But their principal source of supply was China, which, in 1951, meant Communist China.

The possibility that the narcotics epidemic was some form of Communist plot was introduced tentatively in the Boggs hearings. Anslinger spoke of Communist China as a definite point of origin for heroin, and reported the arrest in Japan of "two or three Communist leaders" for involvement in the traffic.[74] Chicago Police Commissioner Prendergast was quoted as warning that "there are certain people in our country who want to destroy our Government, and we don't know whether that element is sponsoring the advancement of the use of narcotics or not."[75]

Three years later, before the United Nations Commission on Narcotic Drugs, Anslinger formally charged the Chinese Communist regime with "distributing drugs abroad and . . . selling heroin and opium in large quantities to the free countries of the world." The opium crop was grown in Yunnan, transported by land into Thailand or Burma, and transhipped to Hong Kong, from which processed heroin was distributed to Japan, the United States, and all over the world. The commissioner claimed, moreover, that "millions of dollars obtained through the sale of opium and other narcotics are used by the Communist regime . . . for political purposes and to finance agents who have been found actively engaged."[76]

In the course of the 1955 Daniel hearings, reviewing the narcotics traffic for the whole postwar period, a parade of well-known public officials repeated Anslinger's claims—Frank Berry, an Assistant Secretary of Defense, James Ryan, the Bureau of Narcotics chief in New York, Jacob Javits, and Governor Harriman.[77] Senator Daniel expanded on this testimony by suggesting that the Chinese employed heroin to subvert U. S. Army personnel fighting in Korea and to try to demoralize the free nations of the world in the context of the cold war struggle.[78] A year later a further congressional committee was being lectured by a witness on the "pattern of Communist narcotic aggression":

Drug addiction in the free nations is a subtle and diabolical form of conquest in which the victims pay for their own enslave-

ment. . . . The export of narcotics brings about mass self-
destruction among peoples marked for slavery by the Red im-
perialist. . . . That this conspiracy also has had its effect upon
America cannot be doubted.[79]

The truth of the matter was that it was not the other side in the cold
war but *our side* which was responsible for the heroin traffic in Southeast Asia. Specifically, it was not the Communist Chinese but the Nationalists who were involved in both the cultivation and first-stage
refining of opium as a profitable sideline to their guerrilla campaign on
the Burmese and Thai sides of the border with China. There is additional evidence that in almost all the Southeast Asian states allied with
the United States or France after the war, opium cultivation not only
flourished—it was directly encouraged by American military and intelligence units as a counterweight to the growth of popular liberation
movements.[80] In France, also, it appears that the American commitment to stopping the Communists led to CIA partnership with the Corsican crime syndicates of Marseilles in the period of labor strife from
1947 to 1950. After 1951 the same syndicates began to operate the heroin laboratories which have been the principal source of supply for
American consumers ever since.[81]

The Mafia and the Reds, a criminal conspiracy and political one—
congressional investigators produced numerous permutations and
combinations of these elements to account for a rising narcotic problem that seemed impervious even to the rapidly growing powers of
enforcement.[82] Of course, as explanations of the drug phenomenon,
these were concentrated wholly on the supply side of the traffic. On the
demand side I have already pointed out the manner in which official
reaction and public concern were blind to the real characteristics of
drug-users; this persisted more or less without change or criticism
throughout the Daniel hearings in 1955 and the further series of hearings conducted by Congressman Boggs and by Senator Kefauver later
in 1956.[83]

Now even if we make allowances for the statistical inflation due to
changing enforcement policy and increased manpower, there is no
doubt that there was an increased aggregate demand for heroin between 1947 and 1953. Why should it have happened then?

The conventional answer has been to regard the drug as so attractive
at first, so compelling afterward, that increased supply, whatever the
reason for it, would automatically translate itself into increased demand. Why, then, was the geographical distribution of demand so lim-

ited? The efficiency with which the supply networks were thought to operate all over the country should have resulted in the reticulation of drug use far beyond the major ports of entry and distributing points—at least as widespread as the slot machines and gambling houses which preoccupied the Kefauver Committee's attention. If Meyer Lansky and Joe Adonis dominated the rackets of Miami, in league with Luciano and Santo Trafficante, who managed vast narcotics smuggling operations from Havana and used Florida as an entry port, why was the offense rate for the Florida area one of the lowest in the country? The answer, that narcotics which entered Florida were destined for New York, does not explain why the supply created a demand in the latter but not the former place.

There was obviously more to the picture than supply factors. Not only was the increased aggregate demand for narcotics concentrated geographically in the three largest cities in the country. Within these cities the demand was sharply differentiated by race and was characteristic of only the poorest sections, where the black population lived. This was one problem which did not have to be officially accounted for because officially it was barely acknowledged. Nevertheless, why them?

I have pointed out that blacks had been overrepresented among the numbers of heroin users in the North since the end of the First World War. In all likelihood they were young men at the onset of addiction, which was and has remained the typical pattern for most narcotic addicts. In 1916, 18.9 percent of the drug offenders appearing in the New York Court of Special Sessions were under 21. Later in 1919, of the first 3,000 patients admitted to the New York City Narcotic Clinic, 27.8 percent were under 20, and well over 90 percent of the total reported that they had been using drugs for two years or more.[84]

The blacks attending the clinic were probably not recent immigrants to the city, but had either been born there to immigrant parents or had moved from the South quite early in their childhood. Likewise, the whites were mostly (69 percent) American-born, though of immigrant parents, with a disproportionately large number of Jews among them.[85]

The jump over time in the proportion of black drug-users is perfectly obvious, but so is the rise of the black population as a proportion of the total one. Had the rate of increase been the same in both cases, the number of black users would have risen, but the index would have remained constant, unless, of course, the susceptibility of blacks to drug use, as measured by the index, also increased.

The table shows that between 1920 and 1950 this is what happened,

TABLE 5–4

Comparison of Black and White Drug Users and General Populations, New York City and Chicago

	NEW YORK		CHICAGO	
	1919–20	1952–55	1930–36	1951–54
Percent black users	13.9	57.9	17.3	86.7
Percent white users	86.1	39.0	77.1	13.3
Percent nonwhite population	2.9	9.8	7.7	14.1
Percent white population	97.1	90.2	92.3	85.9
Index of susceptibility	5.3	13.5	2.8	40.7

SOURCES: Figure 5–1, Table 5–2, and Census figures.

although to differing degrees in the two cities. This certainly makes it appear there was something about being black as a racial characteristic which determined whether a person would use narcotics. However, we cannot really tell whether this is so from the Table because it ignores some very important historical changes and economic differences which were occurring among the white population as a whole.

The Hubbard report on the New York Clinic, which, of course, operated legally and was open to anyone, indicates that fewer than 7 percent of the patients could be classed as professionals, managers, or proprietors—the majority of these, in fact, were actors or actresses. Of the rest, most were unskilled or semiskilled manual workers (the two commonest occupations listed were driver and laborer) followed by skilled tradesmen and, last by clerks and salesmen (10 percent).[86]

This suggests that the addicts of the time were economically members of the working class rather than the middle class and tended to be concentrated in the bottom of that class, in jobs with the lowest pay and greatest insecurity. This did not change between 1920 and 1950, as Chein's correlations indicate (Table 5–3).

By measuring change in the susceptibility of blacks and whites to drug use in terms of *gross* population movements, we obscure the class and ethnic characteristics among whites, which have historically made all the difference between drug use and not. If Jews, for example, were big heroin-users in New York in 1914 and unheard of in 1951, perhaps their social, economic, and occupational mobility had something to do with the change. If class, therefore, is related to drug use, then change in the aggregate demand for narcotics between blacks and whites may be related to shifts in the relative blackness or whiteness of the working class or that bottom segment of it in the urban, industrial North. Simple but important demographic changes will help settle this question of race or class.

World War I effectively halted the flow of European immigrants into the United States and the swelling of New York's population from Europe. Unemployment, inflation, and general economic conditions were so severe after the war that when foreign immigration began to regain its old momentum, the federal government decided to limit the inflow by fixing a quota on each nationality. At first the effect was to stabilize the size of the foreign-born population and then, over the decade, to diminish the totals of certain ethnic groups (foreign-born generation). Between 1920 and 1930 the numbers of Russian-born people had fallen nearly 16 percent; the Irish dropped by 11 percent; both Germans and Greeks registered slight declines. Italians, however, increased their numbers by just over 11 percent. Counting all foreign-born whites in 1920 and again in 1950, we find an overall decline of 25 percent.[87]

All the while blacks continued to move north, especially to New York and Chicago, and the jobs they took were the ones the European immigrants had traditionally taken. By any criterion they were the worst jobs. In the slaughterhouses and meatpacking plants in Chicago, for example, this was the picture in 1909. Foreign-born white workers outnumbered the native-born whites and blacks by nearly four to one; blacks were only 3 percent. The largest ethnic group was the Polish (27.7 percent); the Lithuanians came next (12 percent), followed by the Germans (10.4 percent) and the Czechoslovaks (9.6 percent). In 1928 the situation was quite different. Blacks were now the largest group (29.5 percent) and native-born whites came after them (27.3 percent). The number of Polish-born had dropped to a third of what it had been (11.9 percent), Lithuanians were down to 7.8 percent, Germans to 2.9 percent, and Czechoslovaks to 2.1 percent.[88]

In steel in the Calumet region between 1912 and 1928 much the same thing occurred. Blacks went from being 1.5 percent of the work force to 12.3 percent, while the Poles fell from 25.7 percent to 14.1, the Slovaks from 6.2 percent to 3.8, and the Croatians from 9.4 percent to 3.9.[89]

Fairly quickly blacks became concentrated in the jobs at the bottom of the occupational structure, and the foreign-born ethnics who had been there before them moved out. In part this reflected some real gains which the white working class made through union organization and agitation,[90] gains made at the expense of the black work force which was excluded from union membership and shut out of the wage bargains the union was able to achieve. In part, it also reflected broader obstacles of racism and prejudice which stopped blacks getting the education or skill enhancement needed to justify higher wages or jobs in industries with relatively high technological development, expanding productivity, and stability of employment.

Blacks entered the Northern and urban labor market, having been lured there from the stagnation and poverty of the South by offers of higher wages. They were almost totally ignorant of the real value of these wages and were thus induced to sell their labor relatively cheaply. They were without effective labor organization to change the terms of this sale—indeed, the first generation of black community organizations commonly had been set up by the major employers of blacks, such as the meatpackers, to contain and pacify any stirring of industrial discontent.[91]

Since blacks were frequently recruited as strike-breakers for management to throw against militant white workers, they were in no position to gain white allies in a struggle to improve their own wages, and compared to Southern conditions, these were, after all, not too bad.

Here we have several of the classic conditions of what economists call a split labor market—a market in which at least two groups of workers are channeled into different and more or less watertight compartments of industrial work. One, called the primary labor market, has all the good jobs; it is characterized by high wages, productivity, stability, and rates of technical progress. The other, called the secondary labor market, is characterized by low wages, productivity, and security, as well as low rates of technological development.[92] Economists have shown that, once started, such a system not only maintains itself but steadily *increases* the gap between the conditions of work and workers in each of the segmented markets.[93] This has probably been more true in times of general prosperity and/or inflation than in periods of depression.[94]

Over the period 1920–50 this split labor market not only evolved into a distinct pattern of occupational segregation, it was paralleled also by changes in the working-class residential pattern across the face of the city. Areas which had initially been racially mixed were rapidly filled up by thousands of Southern immigrants. This kind of pressure on housing supply naturally forced rents up, but in the case of the black ghetto there was nowhere else for blacks to go to seek lower-cost housing. They were hedged into a few areas like Harlem, Bedford-Stuyvesant, or the South Side of Chicago where racial borderlines were effectively policed by the combined hostility of the law and the white gangs.

The European immigrants had never been hedged in this way. Residential segregation in their case was based on low rents, the proximity of the factories and work, and the willingness of the existing community to help the newcomers out. Nevertheless, the advancing population pressure pushed their rents up also, as did the competition of industry for the same land. Eventually, with changes in the zoning of the center-city immigrant neighborhoods and the opening up of outer-city tract developments, the white working class began to move out.

The blacks were not in that position. Their areas were further away from the plants and sweatshops, and after 1920 the housing scarcity within the ghetto was much greater than had been felt in the white areas. Land costs went up steeply but the potential productivity of black labor living on the land, locked into the secondary market as it was, failed to match this rise.

There were two consequences. From the businessman's point of view the price of land in the ghetto (per unit of his capital) was higher and rising faster than land further out of the city. The gains to be made from high-productivity employment were not available by hiring ghetto labor, and so industry too shifted location further and further away from the ghetto.

This left poor people and poor business in racial enclaves from which there was and would be no escape. Rents rose relative to the returns on the employment of labor or capital, which meant that most of the investment in the areas stayed in residential housing. Scarcity of housing, high rents, low wages, and overcrowding resulted in the common situation in which blacks paid more of their income to the landlord than the rest of the working class, and he provided less and less housing services, since keeping the tenements in good condition did not affect his rent, but would only increase his costs and lower his profits.[95]

In this manner the effects of occupational and residential segregation historically accelerated the displacement of whites by blacks in the heart of the Northern cities, producing the kinds of concentrations familiar today. It was in these concentrations that narcotics were to be found between 1949 and 1953. The fact that institutional racism in the economy and society produced the ghetto explains why narcotics users living in those areas were black. It does not explain why they chose to use drugs in the first place. But I want to emphasize that in the period just before the urban labor and housing markets were so forcibly split down the middle, when the Lower East Side of New York was a working-class Jewish area and Little Italy south and west of it was similar in economic characteristics, narcotics use was to be found there, too. By displacement I mean exactly that: blacks literally took the place of Jews and Italians in the bottom half of the working class, and black drug-users took the place of Jews and Italians in the addict population reported by the police.

A number of other demographic factors were bound to increase the number of these users over time, especially in the immediate postwar period, and make them more visible. One of these was the age structure of the black urban population. The birth rate among blacks arriving in the North during the thirties remained higher than among whites, notwithstanding a significant fall-off owing to the Depression. Both fell, but the black rate fell less steeply.

The effect was to widen the disparity between the two birth rates. Thus in 1920 the nonwhite rate was 35 (live births per 1,000 population), just over 30 percent higher than the white (26.9). In 1936, however, the year when rates for both racial groups reached their lowest point in recorded history, the black rate was nearly 43 percent higher than the white (25.1, 17.6). In 1934 the gap had been even greater—45.3 percent.

A person born in 1934 turned 16 in 1950. This meant that, compared with earlier years, the numerical gap between blacks and whites reached a maximum from 1949 to 1951 and that there were then bound to be relatively more blacks aged 16 than whites of the same age—the age, remember, at which heroin addiction usually starts.

The demography of the urban working class between 1920 and 1950 can help explain two things once we accept that narcotics use was and is a permanent feature of the condition of working-class life. It helps to explain why the addict population was blacker in 1950 than in 1920 and why this seemed to have happened so suddenly between 1949 and 1953.

I have shown that public concern about narcotics and the intensity of law enforcement were functions of a surplus condition in the labor market. I should qualify that now by saying that it has never been the overall market which counted but rather the secondary one. In other words, in times of scarcity when *unskilled* labor was hard to come by, popular anxiety about and police arrests of drug-users who came from this segment of the market used to fall to a minimum. This occurred again during World War II when unemployment rates touched bottom and labor force participation rates reached record highs.[96]

But times of labor surplus, the late 1870s in California, the early and late teens of the century in New York, and the thirties across the country, were times of industrial unrest, working-class agitation and militancy, and sharpened political conflict. To these manifestations, increased law enforcement has been the typical response of the State—a term which here covers every public authority from municipal police to federal narcotic agents. Repression is the simple word for it.

Of course, public officials with this purpose do not announce it as such, like a gang of blackshirts. Instead, drug enforcement became one of the ways a basically repressive policy directed at an entire class of the American people has been carried out—by all appearances legally and under the pretext of meeting a new and vicious threat. First, prohibition of liquor and then prohibition of drugs were the testing grounds of the constitutional guarantees of personal freedom in such cases, but the courts allowed the expansion of police power to override the guarantees and virtually handed over the role of determining what public welfare required and what threats to it were genuine and serious, to popular usage, prevailing morality, or strong and preponderant opinion—the words were those of Supreme Court Justice Oliver Wendell Holmes.[97] This police power gave legitimacy to anti-working-class politics at the same time that it provided a method for splitting and factionalizing the class against itself, by identifying ethnic or racial minorities as scapegoats for larger and more fundamental social ills.

In 1950 drugs were not the only threat to society. The Communists and the Mafia were feared from within and without, and purportedly the traffic in drugs was carried on by both. This was the ideology of the time, but what about labor conditions? How did they affect the black dope addict of this episode?

Teenage employment is a sensitive indicator of changes in the broad labor market. Being unskilled and inexperienced, teenagers are usually the last group to get hired in prosperity and the first to be fired when things turn around.[98] Economists think that the more teenagers there are in the population, the lower their wage rate falls. Since this widens the gap between teenage and adult wages, employers get an inducement thereby to hire the cheaper teenaged labor. The effect is not necessarily to increase teenage participation in the labor force, because when wage rates are too low, there is a tendency for teenagers to stay on in school. This, in turn, cuts teenage unemployment on a technicality, but it explains why it happens that, even in a strong economy, teenage labor force participation can be low, at the same time as their unemployment is low. They simply give up looking for jobs.[99]

When the size of the teenage population is falling, however, supply and demand factors keep wage rates up, and labor force participation rises. This is invariably true for whites, but for blacks the situation is markedly different. As teenagers they find it hardest of all to find jobs, and so, when their share of the total teenage population increases, general teenage unemployment rises, along with teenage/adult wage ratios, while labor force participation rates decline.[100]

Table 5–5 illustrates the basic demographic picture between 1920 and 1970. Two important things were happening. One was that the nonwhite (or black) share of the total *teenage* population rose by nearly ten percent between 1940 and 1950. (The same thing happened again between 1960 and 1970, before the most recent narcotics episode.) This was despite the second population shift, which resulted in the teenage share of the general population (blacks and whites) going down by 25 percent. This amounted also to a decline in the total number of teenagers of 1.7 million.

According to the economic theory, the second decline should have produced a *rise* in aggregate teenage employment and a contraction of unemployment. The decennial census figures bear this out. For 14–19 year olds the 1940 labor force participation rate was 34.4 percent (males) and 19.0 percent (females). This had risen in 1950 to 39.3 percent and 22.6 percent, respectively.[101]

But the theory also says that if the proportion of blacks to whites among the teenage population goes up, so does unemployment, as discriminatory hiring practices reject blacks and push them to the very end of the hiring line. Did this also happen?

The record shows that both things happened. For the teenage group as a whole, there was a significant increase (14 percent) in the numbers entering the job market. But this increase was entirely absorbed by whites (rise of 17 percent males, 26 percent females). Black labor force participation actually fell during the decade and among males continued falling through 1970. This is the first sign that a deteriorating labor market was directly connected to the narcotics epidemic.[102] There are several others.

When a 16 year old who wants to leave school and get a job cannot find one, he can decide to stay on in school, continue looking for a job and then go on welfare,[103] or join the *hustler pool*. This is the group of people who are neither enrolled in school nor at work. When this num-

TABLE 5-5

Teenage Share of the Total Population, 15–19-Year-Olds, by Race and Sex, 1920–70 (in percent)

Year	Teenage Share of Total Population			White Teenage Share of White Population			Nonwhite Teenage Share of Nonwhite Population			Nonwhite Teenage Share of Total Teenage Population		
	Total	MALE	FEMALE	Total	MALE	FEMALE	Total	MALE	FEMALE	Total	MALE	FEMALE
1920	8.9	8.7	9.2	8.8	8.6	9.0	10.2	9.7	10.7	12.0	11.6	12.4
1930	9.4	9.3	9.6	9.3	9.2	9.4	10.4	10.0	10.8	11.5	11.1	11.9
1940	9.4	9.4	9.4	9.3	9.3	9.3	10.2	10.1	10.4	11.4	11.0	11.8
1950	7.1	7.1	7.0	6.9	7.0	6.8	8.2	8.1	8.3	12.4	12.1	12.8
1960	7.4	7.5	7.2	7.3	7.4	7.2	7.9	8.0	7.7	12.2	12.0	12.4
1970	9.4	9.7	9.0	9.2	9.6	8.9	10.1	11.0	10.2	14.2	13.9	14.4

SOURCE: *1970 Census of Population, General Population Characteristics, U.S. Summary,* PC(1)–B1, Table 56, p. 1–276/77.

TABLE 5–6

Ratio of School Nonattenders to Attenders,
Male 14–19-Year-Olds, by Race, New York 1940–60

Race	1940	1950	1960
Black	0.41	0.47	0.47
White	0.45	0.38	0.27

SOURCE: Census figures.

ber expands you can expect narcotics use—as well as every other kind of crime and juvenile delinquency—to increase. But I want to illustrate how the demographic factors I have mentioned, together with labor market forces, produced the potential numbers for a larger hustler pool, and hence addict population, between 1947 and 1953.

The fall in labor force participation among black teenagers just observed might have led to more people staying in school, only this is not what happened.

Since 1940 white teenagers have increasingly taken advantage of longer periods of schooling and consequently the ratio for them has shown a consistent decline. Between 1940 and 1950, however, black teenagers, blocked from entering the job market, did not stay in school, and in fact the relative number of dropouts increased. Put another way, we find 67.7 percent of the black boys in this age group in school in 1950, and 72.4 percent of the whites. The difference in ratios meant that there were nearly 2,000 more black teenagers out of school and needing a job than would have been the case if the ratios had been the same.

Among the (male) nonattenders now, how many found a paying job? This is a hard question to answer, both because teenage school dropouts slip out of sight of the Census taker and because Census tables for 1940 and 1950 are not exactly comparable. Table 5–7 provides a clue at any rate.

It is safe to say that, as far as finding employment, blacks were worse off than whites in 1950, just as they had been in 1940. Table 5–7 also suggests that the relative severity of unemployment for blacks grew in the decade, because the ratio of black to white unemployment rates ran from 1.2 to 1.7—the latter figure covers the whole of the United States; in New York or Chicago the ratio was probably closer to 2.0.[104] Unemployment itself reached a peak between 1949 and

TABLE 5–7

Employment Among Male
14–19-Year-Olds, by Race, 1940–50

Year/Area	Race	Labor Force	Employed (except on emergency relief)	Percent Employed	Seeking Work	Percent Seeking Work
1940 New York	Nonwhite	5,122	1,707	33.3	2,549	49.8
	White	98,958	53,073	53.6	39,611	40.0
1950 U.S.	Nonwhite	123,990	95,810	77.3	28,180	22.7
Summary Urban	White	1,044,585	901,900	86.3	142,685	13.7

SOURCE: Census figures.

1950, after the period of wartime labor scarcity. From then on, it has seesawed between high and moderately high rates.[105] Relatively speaking then, let's say, blacks were more in need of a paying job than whites in 1950 and hence more likely than whites to end up in crime to provide income.

Even those in legitimate jobs can be shown to have earned substantially less than working whites.[106] In addition, in black families this income was more urgently needed. Although relatively few teenagers actually contribute to their family's resources 24 percent or more of its annual income, twice as many blacks as whites typically do so.[107]

The range of economic pressures on black youth was therefore particularly broad and intense in the postwar period, when there were relatively more of them to feel it. This was the situation which led the police virtually to declare war on all black adolescents and when public concern about narcotics was whipped up to provide the justification for it.

There is no denying that black teenagers used narcotics, but why they did is less of a historical question than a social-psychological one—one which has not differed much from generation to generation.

However, this was not the first time black youth had used heroin, although it was the first episode in which it was noticed. It was also the first occasion that public concern, however reluctantly to begin with, identified addicts as disproportionately black. This fact did nothing to alter the working-class nature of the phenomenon, and demographic shifts explain most of the color change.[108]

Race and racism are central features of the way in which the labor market operates. To the extent that blackness condemns a person to working his life out in the secondary labor force and bars almost all occupational mobility (upwards), it also determines the particular black susceptibility to drug use which this chapter has recorded.

But this can change, just as the conditions of working-class life have changed and as the membership of that class varies. These are the things that make the ideology of drugs an antiworking-class ideology and that determine the recruitment of new drug-users. By 1967 a new labor surplus, especially among the young, was imminent once more, and again there were signs of a new heroin epidemic. This time, however, the Vietnam War had a unique impact. The effect was to introduce large numbers of white working-class young men, veterans of the war and the military, into the addict population for the first time in almost half a century.

Chapter 6.
Vietnam

The outcome of the Boggs Subcommittee hearings in 1951 was an Act of Congress which substantially stiffened the penalties for drug offenses and compelled judges to sentence offenders for at least two, five, and ten years for the first and subsequent convictions. It also did away with suspension, probation, or parole for repeaters. This was the backbone legislators aimed to give a spineless court system, as one witness had called it, which was blamed for the dope problem.

Four years later Boggs reconvened his committee and held a new set of hearings to establish how well he had done in the first place. Commissioner Anslinger declared: "without that Act we would not have been able to hold the fort."[1] Across the country state legislatures, most of them with small numbers of drug offenders to deal with, had followed the federal lead with "little Boggs acts." Several enacted devices making known offenders or addicts subject to arrest simply for being an addict. This was an innovation since being an addict (whatever that was) had never before been an offense on the statute book, and such measures virtually ensured that no first-time offender, certainly not a Negro living in a high-drug use area, could escape the label and the persistent police harassment which was its consequence.[2]

The Bureau of Narcotics presented table after table of evidence to show that since 1950 the average sentence for drug offenders had gone up. For instance, for federal prisoners received from court on both marijuana and narcotics charges, the average went from 21.2 months in 1950 to 43.6 in 1954.[3] In the judicial district covering New York City there was a similar increase (narcotics offenses only) from 18.7 months to 35.4; in Chicago, 20.5 to 43.6; and in Los Angeles, 22.2 to 43.3.[4] Among federal prisoners the proportion with previous commitments on narcotics charges fluctuated with narrow limits between 1949 (67.7

percent) and 1955 (63.8 percent)—except for 1952, when the relative number of first-timers reached a peak (43.4 percent).[5] The statistics on parole also showed the effect of the Boggs Act, although it did not last for long. In 1950, 23.5 percent of drug offenders were released on parole from federal prisons. This rose in 1951 to 28.1 percent and then fell by more than half the following year (12.8 percent). By 1955, however, parolees numbered nearly a third of the releases (31.6 percent)—the highest proportion in seven years.[6] This indicates that the mandatory minimum sentences had exactly the opposite effect to the one intended, for they *increased* the likelihood that offenders would be paroled within a relatively short time.

This interpretation was not one of the ones offered by the Bureau representatives at the hearings. Instead, a parade of witnesses from many jurisdictions came to the witness table to testify to a decline in the drug problem. This, they swore, was the work of the Boggs Act: ". . . you are advised that it is our opinion that the Boggs Act has been effective in this district" [Boston]. "The Boggs Act has been a strong factor in causing a material decrease in the overall picture of the narcotic traffic in the judicial district of Connecticut" [Hartford]. "In my opinion, the Boggs Act is a good and necessary law. However, it has one glaring weakness. Sentences for first offenders are not severe enough" [New York]. "It is the opinion in this district [San Francisco] that the Boggs Act has very definitely put a brake on the narcotic traffic." And so it went, almost without exception.

The one skeptical voice came from a narcotic agent in Washington itself: "it cannot be said, in my opinion, that it has diminished the trafficking in narcotic drugs to a detectable degree," he reported to his superiors,[7] and the evidence bears this out. As can be seen from Figure 5–3, there was a noticeable drop in the number of nonfederal arrests on narcotics charges in 1951, although this total sprang back the following year. Similar brief declines and then rebounds are reported for New York and Chicago. Although it then took nearly 10 years after the Boggs Act for the numbers to return to the 1951 peak, it was only four years before the 1949 level was reached, seven before the 1950 figure.

However, once the old peak was reached, the arrests did not stop but kept increasing steadily. From 1957 the total more than tripled itself every five years in spite of a battery of new punitive measures voted into law after the second series of Boggs hearings was completed (The Narcotics Control Act of 1956).[8] Table 6–1 reports the yearly totals between 1957 and 1972.

Of course, one element behind the continuous rise in arrests was the

Table 6–1

Nonfederal Narcotics Arrests, by Race and Age, 1957–71

Year	TOTAL	Percent under 18	WHITE	Percent under 18	BLACK	Percent under 18	INDIAN	Percent under 18	CHINESE	Percent under 18	OTHER RACES (INCLUDING RACE UNKNOWN)	Percent under 18	Number of Agencies Reporting
1957	7,277	3.0	3,092	—	4,108	—	18	—	13	—	46	—	1,473
1958	9,863	3.8	3,807	—	5,740	—	17	—	34	—	265	—	1,586
1959	10,562	4.3	4,626	—	5,767	—	19	—	52	—	98	—	1,789
1960	16,370	4.1	8,506	—	7,570	—	16	—	54	—	194	—	2,446
1961	18,419	7.0	11,371	—	6,742	—	78	—	69	—	159	—	2,759
1962	21,147	8.6	11,956	—	8,794	—	68	—	37	—	292	—	?,917
1963	20,760	6.4	13,003	—	7,485	—	56	—	29	—	187	—	3,951
1964	23,730	10.2	14,135	12.7	9,277	6.4	69	5.8	13	7.7	236	13.1	3,940
1965	31,294	12.8	18,530	15.4	12,069	8.3	80	18.8	29	13.8	586	26.1	4,043
1966	44,204	15.7	27,846	17.8	15,562	11.2	106	39.6	22	22.7	668	26.5	4,021
1967	81,454	22.8	57,146	25.9	22,848	14.6	187	32.1	46	23.9	1,227	26.0	4,508
1968	137,598	28.3	105,886	31.6	29,608	16.4	270	40.0	70	18.6	1,764	27.9	4,758
1969	193,743	26.1	148,556	29.2	42,397	15.1	469	33.9	74	28.4	2,247	29.0	4,627
1970	291,600	23.1	226,779	26.0	61,223	11.7	710	42.4	167	24.0	2,721	32.8	5,208
1971	354,783	21.8	273,733	25.0	76,652	10.2	1,230	38.6	208	18.3	2,960	27.3	5,610
1972	402,265	23.5	313,237	26.8	84,413	11.2	1,072	35.1	297	12.8	3,246	21.9	6,114

SOURCE: FBI, *Uniform Crime Reports* (since 1959, also known as *Crime in the United States*).

parallel increase in the number of agencies reporting statistics to the Uniform Crime Report section of the FBI. This is not as important as it looks simply because the overwhelming proportion of arrests was made in the big cities, where police departments were among the earliest to join the FBI system. Thus, the fourfold rise in reporting units would probably account for very little of the nearly-fiftyfold increase in the total number of arrests.

The table does reveal two important trends in the period. One of them is that there were relatively more white offenders than black with each successive year, reversing the 50-year-old trend described in Chapter 5.

In 1951 the ratio of black to white offenders was 1:14, reflecting a numerical majority of blacks. In that year also, in Chicago, blacks added up to 90 percent of all those charged for drug offenses. Yet at no time during the most recent period did blacks ever constitute more than a minority of the total arrested, and according to the index of racial susceptibility, which can be figured for the three census years, 1950, 1960, and 1970, their likelihood of being arrested relative to whites fell by a factor of four. In 1950 the index stood at 9.7; in 1960 it had dropped to 7.4; and in 1970 it was 2.1.

The second important trend has to do with the aging of the offender population. The table indicates that this was growing younger and younger until 1968, when the proportion of arrests under 18 reached a peak of just over 28 percent. This compares with a maximum of 24.7 percent under-21 year olds arrested in Chicago in 1951 and 21.6 percent the same year in New York. In other words, the typical drug offender between 1967 and 1971 was significantly younger than his counterpart of 20 years before, and the proportion of the young was nearly twice as high among the white offenders as among the black.

This was a gradual development, meaning that there was a slow but steadily increasing recruitment of neophytes throughout the period. However, by 1970 this total had grown so large that narcotics use was once again identified publicly as having reached epidemic proportions.

"The heroin addiction crisis has reached threatening proportions," Congressman Pepper declared at the opening of special hearings by his Select Committee on Crime. "Our cities are besieged. Our suburban areas have become infected. Even our rural areas are now feeling the shocking effect of this malady . . . our citizens are properly asking whether their Government is helpless, or corrupt, or even worse, totally incapable or unwilling to deal with a public health epidemic."[9]

It is important to notice, however, that the proportion of the youngest age group among arrestees began to decline after 1968, just as had happened after the epidemic year of 1951. Had the total number of offenders also stabilized at the same time, it would be reasonable to guess that the flow of new recruits had slowed down or stopped and that most arrests were of repeaters. This did not happen; instead, the total shot up by 150 percent, reinforcing the idea of an epidemic, although this was no longer primarily a juvenile phenomenon. New users were appearing in police records but they were increasingly 20 or over.

Let's be clear that drug offenders were still disproportionately black and young in relation to the racial and age distribution of the general population and the distribution of the drug offenders during the 1950 episode. The same basic configuration of demographic and labor market conditions which had operated during the late 1940s were active again to increase both the total numbers of teenagers, especially blacks (Table 6–1), and sharpen the disparities in labor market participation, unemployment, and wage rates between black and white youth.

The first of these has already been illustrated. Regarding the second, for 16- to 19-year-olds, the black unemployment rate was consistently twice the white rate from 1966 on, and the teenage rate was roughly five times the rate in the work force over 25, black and white, separately or together.[10] The period 1966–72 was the worst for teenage unemployment in recent history; the total (all races) rate did not stop rising until the first quarter of 1972 when it hit 17.5 percent.[11] In Harlem, Bedford-Stuyvesant, and those parts of New York included in the federal poverty area survey of 1970, 41.9 percent of black teenagers out of school were counted as unemployed, and the actual proportion was probably higher. By contrast, white teenagers living in the same areas had an exceptionally high rate of unemployment, but at 35.5 percent still significantly lower than the black.[12]

The same survey showed that for all 51 urban areas covered across the country, the median hourly earnings of a black youth were almost invariably lower than those of a white youth, no matter how much schooling had been received or the extent of job training obtained after leaving school.[13] At the same time, the inflationary crunch on wages actually *reduced* the real earnings of inner-city black workers from their 1959 level, thereby making even more desperate the black family's need for more income and better-paying jobs. The concentration of black workers in the secondary labor market intensified, as did the population density of the ghetto areas.[14]

The statistical litany is getting to be a familiar one. Since these things are correlated with narcotics use, it can be expected that as the former got much worse, so would the latter, which also helps to explain why the narcotics problem in 1970 was so much greater than in 1960 or in that year over 1950. The consistency of the change over time, however, belies the claim that the "epidemic" of 1970 was a sudden departure from normal, whatever that was, although the pressures building up from the structural changes I have mentioned do not account for all the change in the number and characteristics of drug offenders.

One of these changes, the increasing proportion of whites, looks as if it contradicts the typical pattern of concentration among the poor and racially isolated elements of the urban working class, which I have identified in every episode so far—especially so if the white offenders were the suburban, middle-class types which congressional witnesses and the press claimed them to be.

There is no doubt that heroin has been used in the middle-class suburbs of the country. Only one case of an "epidemic" in such places has actually been verified, and there, in Grosse Pointe, Michigan, the numbers involved, while large maybe in the local context, were insignificant in the state aggregate or by comparison with the number of drug users estimated for a big city like Detroit.[15] But this is the point: in the *aggregate* of narcotic offenders or addicts, is the suburban or middle-class representation anything but a small minority of the cases?

If it was happening, it ought to have occurred in New York State which by popular and expert estimation contains the majority of the country's narcotics users.[16] There has been very little sign of it, however. In 1968, at the beginning of the national "epidemic," over 90 percent of the drug offenders committed to the state's Narcotic Addiction Control Commission (under the civil commitment laws) came from New York City alone, and 92 percent of them were from the three boroughs, Manhattan (33 percent), Brooklyn (26 percent), and the Bronx (32 percent).[17] Three years later, 86 percent were from the city and 87 percent from the same boroughs.[18]

In the one available survey of the state for drug use taken in 1970, not a single upper- or upper-middle-class heroin user could be found. The class measurement was made on a neighborhood basis by professional interviewers, and according to the author, the methodology used favored discovery of the stable and higher-class drug user. Still, the proportion of middle-class heroin users identifying themselves (15 percent) was less than half their distribution in the general population, and the lower-middle-class or lower-class users (84.4 percent) were significantly more numerous than the normal distribution.[19]

On the other hand, drugs disproportionately used by the upper-middle class included legal narcotics (pain-killers like Demerol, Dilaudid, and Dolophine), hallucinogens (peyote, psilocybin), marijuana, and diet pills. The middle-class drug users disproportionately preferred LSD, the pain-killers, and relaxants and tranquilizers such as Valium, Librium, Miltown, and Equanil. These forms of drug use may have amounted to an epidemic, but in one crucial respect this differed from the heroin problem—it was legal in most cases.

There is one nagging question about this remaining to be answered, and that is: Can there be or have there been a significant group of middle-class opiate users who remain out of the hands of the law and and consequently out of sight altogether?

This would be the case, for instance, if the middle-class consumer were able to pay for his supply of drugs out of his income or assets, without resorting to crime. Or if he were able to regulate his consumption and consequently the cost by putting it on an occasional basis, rather like the common pattern of social drinking; or, again, if even after apprehension by the police, he could avoid jail and obtain some form of private psychiatric treatment instead.

To take the last of these first, it will be recalled that in the twenties Dr. Alexander Lambert had specifically identified morphine users, whom he thought to be predominantly middle-class in background, as most susceptible to the medical cure for addiction and least deserving of a stretch in prison. However, even while the New York Clinic remained open dispensing a legal supply of drugs, the number of its patients from white-collar, let alone professional occupations, was minuscule.[20]

Recent investigations have revealed fairly sharp differences in the social class of drug users who are known to the police and those who are not but appear in public psychiatric records. There is no doubt that middle-class narcotics consumers, where they exist, are far more likely than working-class consumers, black or white, to conceal their behavior with impunity. This has been confirmed in a study involving drug use statistics in the Maryland Psychiatric Case Register, a cumulative record of admissions and discharges of all individuals entering a psychiatric institution in the state since 1961. These records were compared with records from the Baltimore and Maryland county police departments, as well as with the list of names from the Federal Bureau of Narcotics' register of active narcotics users from Maryland.[21]

When drug-users (all drugs) were counted together in the period between 1966 and 1967, it was found that more than 56 percent of those recorded in the psychiatric register were unknown in the police records, and clear demographic and social differences were indicated between the two groups. Females were much less likely to be known to the police than males. The same was true of whites compared with blacks, those who lived in the suburban and rural counties compared with those who lived in Baltimore, and predictably (when postal zones were isolated), the suburbanites of Baltimore compared with the residents of the inner city. In more specific class terms, college-educated drug-users had a greater probability of remaining unknown to the police than those with less education; of the occupations involved, 21 percent of those with professional, technical and managerial backgrounds had police records, while 79 percent were unknown to the police. This was in sharp contrast to those employed in construction work of whom 69 percent were known to the police, and only 31 percent unknown.

It should be emphasized that these comparisons cover individuals using all types of drugs, not just the narcotics, and when the specific drug is introduced into the comparison, it is immediately obvious that police records cover narcotics users much more effectively and thoroughly than those using other drugs. When only narcotics are considered, differences do remain; females, for instance, are nearly twice as likely to avoid the police as males. But racial differences are slight and there is no evident trend for blacks to be better known to the police than whites. In fact, within the city of Baltimore, they are somewhat less likely to have been apprehended than whites.

What the investigation points up, however, is that notwithstanding the difference social class makes among drug users, those who are not known reflect the conventional drug preferences of their class, as Chambers' findings in New York State reveal them to be. Most of the hidden middle-class drug use in Maryland involves barbiturates, amphetamines, and the hallucinogenic drugs. In short, there are next to no hidden narcotics-users among the middle class.

If the white drug offenders newly arriving on the scene in 1970 were neither suburban nor middle-class, who were they and where did they come from?

Again, the best source is New York, but since the police there do not release racial or other background information on the people they arrest, the only alternative is to look at the much smaller group of drug offenders who landed in the registers of the Narcotic Addiction Control Commission (NACC) or the Prisons Department or Board of Health.

In 1971 it is evident that blacks outnumbered whites and Puerto Ricans who, combined, added up to 45.5 percent of the total. In earlier years though, the combined group was in the majority; the 1968 figures, for instance, showed 26.9 percent whites, 34.1 percent Puerto Ricans, and 38.8 percent blacks.[22] According to the Chambers survey, in 1970 there were 11,000 regular heroin users who were white (34.4 percent), and 9,000 Puerto Ricans (28.1 percent), making a total of 62.5 percent, together with 12,000 or 37.5 percent blacks.[23]

Now the FBI counts Puerto Rican drug offenders as either white or black so that we can immediately say a large part of the increased white percentage is made up of individuals in this group. How much of a part is not exactly clear because the Puerto Ricans figure primarily in the New York arrest totals and little elsewhere and because it is impossible to estimate how many Puerto Rican offenders are white, how many black. In Puerto Rico itself, Von Eckhardt has reported 73 percent of the drug offenders are white, 27 percent black or dark-skinned.[24] According to NACC, the black percentage among Puerto Rican admissions has been much less—6 percent black to 94 percent white.[25]

The condition of the Puerto Ricans in New York is identical to or worse than that of the blacks, and a similar set of demographic and labor market forces were working during the sixties in association with their apparent take-off in drug use and narcotics offenses. Heavy migration plus high birth rates have produced a large bulge in the population distribution aged 16 to 24 and low educational attainment, little prior work experience and concentration in unskilled manufacturing work, a sector with sharply declining employments needs, have produced the classic split labor market phenomena of low wages and high unemployment, especially for teenagers.[26] According to the Census, poverty area survey of New York in 1970, more than 40 percent of the 16- to-19-year-old Puerto Ricans (males) who had left school were unemployed.[27]

It will be useful to refer to the NAAC register to see what level of education the non-Puerto Rican whites had achieved. This is another way, although a far from perfect one, of telling the social class of the white drug offender represented in the FBI figures, assuming of course, that class is associated in linear fashion with educational attainment—the higher the class, the higher the attainment, and vice versa. Almost two-thirds of the group had not graduated from high school, which strongly suggests working-class origins for most of the group, and economic circumstances which did not differ too much from that of the blacks and Puerto Ricans. It is unlikely that the white heroin users reflected in the Chambers sample were concentrated in the high school student population any more than the other groups. Since this amounted to only a third of the total—53.1 percent in a job of some sort and 12.5 percent unemployed—the educational level probably reflects stable class background rather than mere coincidence in the timing of the survey interviews with the onset of drug use in school.[28]

Thus, even if increasing whiteness of the narcotics offender population during this episode was a novel phenomenon, it does not appear that among the whites the typical pattern of class and economic conditions, which were the operative ones in every episode before, had changed one iota.

One change which is still puzzling, however, is the aging of the offender population after 1968 parallel with the recruitment of older drug users aged 20 or over. Who were they?

The answer is that in all likelihood they were veterans of military service, most probably veterans of the Vietnam War. A number of different studies point to the same conclusion by exposing the relatively large number of veterans among institutionalized offenders. Statistics for a variety of drug-care facilities indicate about one veteran for every five drug-users in New York City. Veteran enrollment in therapeutic programs ranged from 9 to 30 percent in early 1971; in the city's Health Services Administration program as of June, the same year, the percentage was 20.2.[29] Through March 1972 the ambulatory detoxification clinics identified an average of just over 19 percent veterans,[30] and among prisoners in the Manhattan House of Detention, 15 percent of those requesting detoxification were veterans.[31] A comparable study of the inmates of the District of Columbia Jail found one-quarter of the identifiable addicts claimed military service.[32]

In Boston, according to a study of Vietnam veterans and veteran drug-users which was made there, approximately 10 percent of all admissions to city treatment programs during 1972 were veterans.[33] When the total number admitted to separate Veterans' Administration facilities was added in, their proportion of the general addict population rose to between 24 and 33 percent.[34] This represented a sharp rise from the year earlier when the proportion in the Boston city drug treatment program was only 5 percent.[35]

Moreover, it seems that most veteran heroin users are white, with blacks possibly underrepresented in this population. Surveys taken in Vietnam differ somewhat on this. A Defense Department information release has claimed that 68 percent of GIs using heroin were white; 32 percent black and other races.[36] An unpublished Army survey of support units located in and around Long Binh late in 1971 found "no correlation between [black] race and drug abuse in Vietnam." Among those admitting to heroin use (8.3 percent of the sample), 72 percent were white, 13 percent black, 6 percent Mexican-American, and no Puerto Ricans. These figures compared with the following distributions in the full test population: 73 percent white, 19 percent black, 3 percent Mexican-American, and 2 percent Puerto Rican. In other words, black soldiers were significantly *under*represented in the drug-using group.[37]

Among veteran heroin users, two sources point to a relatively low number of blacks: Patch in Boston identified 90.5 percent white, 9.5 percent black; and a Veterans' Administration patient census in mid-1971 indicated 71.5 percent white, 26.1 percent black.[38] A third source found that race was not significantly related to drug use, although black users were more likely to be *detected* as such. Incidentally, this source reported a much smaller number and proportion of veterans on heroin than had been estimated by anyone before.[39]

With this kind of variability in estimates, it is practically impossible to say what proportion of the veteran drug offenders found their way into the FBI's count of whites and blacks. The least we can say is that veterans may amount to as many as a third of all narcotics offenders, more likely about a fifth of them; and that the majority, probably 70 percent, are represented in the white total.

Other things being equal, this would help account for the relative increase of white offenders over black, and it may also explain the origin of the new 20- to 25-year-old offenders appearing in police records after 1968. If veterans, we would expect the new offenders to be concentrated in this age group, since 68.6 percent of all veterans (75.8 percent of Vietnam theater veterans) left the service in this age group.[40] We would also anticipate the fastest growth in this group of offenders after 1969 when large-scale heroin use really began in Vietnam and throughout the military. Table 6–2 illustrates that this is roughly what happened.

How did these men begin using heroin? Did it occur before they joined up, their tour of duty merely postponing what would have shown up in the official records at an earlier age and time had they remained civilians? Or was the drug habit a consequence in some way of the war itself, conditions in Vietnam and military policy towards drug use? Finally, was the military (then veteran) narcotics user any different in educational or social class background from the typical working-class pattern I have already described?

In order to answer these questions, let me first describe something

TABLE 6–2

Nonfederal Narcotics Arrests, by Age, 1968–71

Year	Age			
	15 or less	16–19	20–24	25–29
1968	8.6%	38.7%	28.1%	10.9%
1969	8.0	37.6	30.7	11.4
1970	6.9	35.9	33.8	11.6
1971	7.1	34.7	34.9	11.8

SOURCE: *Uniform Crime Reports.*

of the history of military drug use, for a drug problem so-called can be found in every one of the wars the United States has been in before Vietnam.

Any schoolboy who reads war adventure comicbooks knows that our Asian adversaries in World War II and the Korean War attacked only after they had been thoroughly hyped up by a heavy dose of opium. The logic behind this, I suppose, since there has never been any evidence for it,[41] was that the only way you could get soldiers to undertake missions so hazardous that their chances of survival were close to zero, was to make them insensible to the risks by giving them drugs.

In fact, this logic has been a feature of military policy—*our* military policy—from earliest times. Of course, the drug has varied.

One account of the Revolutionary War indicates that the American and the British sides depended on some 35,000 gallons of rum shipped from New Hampshire for fighting rations, although reputedly the Americans consumed less per man than did the British.[42]

During the Civil War a mixture of narcotics and alcohol known as Hosteller's Bitters did double duty as a remedy for dysentery and a disinhibiting agent or relaxant on official issue to the troops before a battle. It was a variant of the traditional double-or-triple rations of spirits issued to soldiers and sailors before a fight, at least through World War I.

Morphine was also widely used during the Civil War to treat the wounded. This followed the first application of morphine by hypodermic injection in 1856. Terry and Pellens mention a couple of sources to support their claim that "following the Civil War the increase in opiate use was so marked among ex-soldiers as to give rise to the term 'army disease,' and today in more than one old soldier's home are cases of chronic intoxication which date from this period."[43] If the aggregate demand had been large, it ought to have been reflected in the import figures for crude opium and morphine during and immediately after the war. Indeed, there was a sharp rise in morphine imports during 1865, with ups and downs in opium supplies in the years before that. But this was followed by a decline and then an unstable pattern of rises and falls until the early 1870s, when the pattern firmed into a slow but fairly steady increase.[44] It is inconclusive either way.

Following the Spanish-American War of 1898, in particular the campaign in the Philippines, there were reports that opium smoking had caught on in the Army and Navy. Here is one:

> The number of men using opium in the army has greatly increased since the occupation of the Philippines, many "Opium smokers" acquiring the habit there from Chinese or natives. . . . Quite a number of enlisted men have been discharged from both army and navy during the last five years than for any ten years previous. . . . Not a single case of drug habit coming from the prescription of an opiate by a medical officer can be recalled, opium and allied drugs being very guardedly and carefully used by army and navy medical officers.[45]

Heroin use was first reported in 1913 among army personnel in Boston. Its prevalence was apparently quite widespread involving several companies, and the supplies (in pill form) were obtained by a couple of soldier-dealers who bought them from a local drugstore and prescriptions from a Chinese doctor. Captain Blanchard was apparently caught completely unaware of the situation: "This practice among soldiery is, so far as I know, unprecedented and exists nowhere in the U.S. Army, nor had I ever heard of this derivative of morphine being used in this fashion."[46]

A year later—1914—"cocainism" was discovered in the army, this time on the Mexican border. Predictably the Mexicans were blamed for peddling the drug by some officers,[47] but the first to identify the cocaine problem, Lieutenant W. B. Meister, identified association with prostitutes as the source of contagion. In particular he referred to a prostitute operating in El Paso who bought from wholesale chemists in New York and retailed to soldiers in several forts in the surrounding area. The incidence of drug use was "alarmingly on the increase. . . . If a soldier is reported as being 'queer,' too talkative, or too morose, unbearably egotistical, oblivious to duty, prone to argue with superiors, suspect him of cocainism."[48]

Meister's report was unique in another respect in that he was probably the pioneer of what is today known as urinalysis testing for drug traces. Like the present generation of military policymakers, Meister was convinced that the horrors and dangers of cocaine were so great as to override the legal and constitutional problems involved in compelling a soldier to give up his urine or blood for possible evidence of drug "possession." The method he devised was based on the assumption that cocaine traces would be retained by the body for some time after consumption, and that by testing urine samples with an iodine reagent, the sign and size of a cocaine dose recently taken could be determined. This, in turn, he intended to be used as a screening device for troops, with immediate isolation and discharge for those drug users caught out.

Not unexpectedly, Meister could not raise an experimental sample by calling for volunteers and was forced to resort to using a dog instead. In the end no trace of several sizable doses fed to the animal could be found, so the idea was dropped.

In Chapter 1 I mentioned several of the reports dealing with heroin use in the military in the years just before American entry into the war. Leaky found evidence of the habit among naval enlisted men in 1915–16. King, the only officer to have attempted to estimate a prevalence rate, found that more than 4 percent of general military prisoners had been drug users while in service, and that maybe one percent of total enlisted strength could be so identified.[49]

In the Allied Expeditionary Force itself, there seems to have been relatively little drug use—at least in France and at the front. A summary report issued in 1920 testified that among neuropsychiatric cases handled by the medical corps, little more than 5 percent were classified as inebriety by reason of either drugs or alcohol. "Probably no army ever was so temperate"—this was an exaggeration to be sure, although it is more than likely that the flow of heroin to the trenches in France was severely diminished. If supply and not demand conditions explained this, Bailey's conclusion about the relatively low prevalence of drug use (in both the military and the veteran-civilian environments) was misleading.[50]

Going back a little to 1916, the first mention was made in official channels of marijuana being used by troops, in this case within the regiment based in Puerto Rico.[51] From there attention shifted in the early twenties to American units in Panama. Possession of the drug was prohibited in 1923, but a conference of medical and command officers not long after found that "there is no evidence that mariajuana [sic] as grown here is a 'habit-forming' drug . . . or that it has any apparently deleterious influence on individuals who use it."[52] The regulations were therefore rescinded and the Republic of Panama repealed its antimarijuana law in 1928.

Lower-ranking unit officers continued to blame the drug for whatever trouble they experienced in command, and a further study was initiated by the Panama Department between 1928 and 1929. Once again, the finding came up "that the use of the drug is not widespread and that its effects upon military efficiency and upon discipline are not great."[53]

In spite of this, new regulations were promulgated late in 1930, around the time when the civilian drive against Mexican marijuana users was picking up momentum in California and the Southwest. Use of the drug became an offense but a further study committee was convened in 1931 and this reported to the commanding general in Panama that "no recommendations for further legislative action to prevent the sale or use of marijuana in the Canal Zone, Panama are deemed advisable under existing conditions."[54] In short, it left the regulations on the books although it considered use of the drug more or less insignificant and harmless.

Each of the eight major army installations in the Canal Zone was surveyed for prevalence of marijuana use, which varied from 0.6 percent in one to 20 percent in another; the average was 5 percent. In addition, a group of 34 users was interviewed intensively and put through several tests to see if deprivation of the drug led to withdrawal symptoms. It did not. No data on race or educational background were provided; the mean age of the group was 23, and social class can be inferred from the low "mental status" assigned to the majority.[55] "Sixty-two percent were constitutional psychopaths and 23 percent were morons. . . . Morons and psychopaths are believed to constitute the large majority of habitual smokers."[56]

This may have been a spurious explanation, in that it reflected a range of social and other factors predisposing low-ranking lower-class soldiers to deviant and rebellious behavior without this having anything to do with their so-called mental status. But precisely because Colonel Siler, the Chief Health Officer in the Canal Zone Army, believed in it, he was able to see the spuriousness of the popular belief that it was the drug, marijuana, which was to blame for delinquent behavior. Those who thought this, he wrote, disregarded "the fact that a large proportion of the delinquents are morons or psychopaths, which conditions of themselves would serve to account for delinquency." He warned also that "delinquencies due to marijuana smoking which result in trial are negligible in number when compared with delinquencies resulting from the use of alcoholic drinks."[57]

The use of quasi-diagnoses and psychiatric labels like these has been a tricky matter in military psychiatry. Although the labels have changed over time—in present procedure psychopaths are usually labeled more specifically (schizophrenia, assaultive tendencies, affective disorders, etc.), and the term *moron* has been replaced by intelligence test grades—their meaning and function have remained just as ambiguous as they always were. In the case of marijuana users, the key issue in the thirties and then during World War II was whether drug use was ipso facto evidence of mental disorder. If so, then was the drug offender a case of *medical* treatment, with return to his unit the ultimate goal, or was he a straight *disciplinary* problem to be court-martialed and either jailed or discharged or both? On top of this, if drug use was correlated with psychopathology or defective mental status, as Siler had argued, it followed that the best way to deal with the problem was not within the service but rather outside of it—to raise the mental standards for entry into the service and screen out the defectives, whether or not they used drugs or had any offense on their record.

To a degree disputes on these policy issues within the military paralleled the broad civilian controversy over medical versus police approaches to drug use. More or less consistently the medical corps refused to sanction the punitive approach throughout the war. In 1943 the semiofficial journal, *Military Surgeon,* dismissed concern about marijuana as groundless and stated that the drug was no more harmful than tobacco and relatively trivial in its effects. "It is hoped," an editorialist wrote, "that no witch hunt will be instituted in the military services over a problem that does not exist."[58]

A nonexistent problem? To unit commanders this seemed obviously untrue. The use of narcotics—marijuana was generally treated as such—turned up often enough by itself and in the context of other offenses against regulations to appear to justify harsh punishment. The psychiatrists who got to the drug users once they were in the stockade reiterated their claim that it was the personality structure of the individual, and not the drug or its effects, that produced the disciplinary problem. Freedman and Rockmore, for example, could find no evidence to "support condemning the use of the drug [marijuana] although the use is not to be recommended."[59] Marcovitz and Meyers went even further to emphasize (for the first time in military annals and probably in the psychiatric record, too) that the personality problems of marijuana users in the army stemmed from the social environment from which they came:

In their actual situations one finds marihuana users unable to endure frustration, deprivation or discipline from any authority. . . . This frustration in terms of objective reality has been due in large part to extremely adverse socioeconomic factors of class and caste.[60]

This meant, in short, that military drug users were typically working class in origin, but unlike the heroin users of World War I, they were black. Davis and his colleagues studied one hundred AWOL cases at Richmond Army Air Base Hospital and found 64 percent chronic alcoholics and 24 percent drug-users (usually marijuana). The men were mostly between 19 and 25, their average educational attainment was eighth grade, and 43 percent reported their background as poor.[61] Another study, this one of a thousand prisoners in a naval stockade, found 9.6 percent alcoholics, among whom several had used narcotics. Again, social class was low; the average school grade completed was 8.8.[62] The Freedman and Rockmore study examined 310 enlisted men in detention who were known marijuana users. There were 88 percent blacks, 12 percent whites. The former averaged 5.7 years of school, the latter 8.8. Two-thirds of the total group were from city areas and marginal unskilled work and unemployment had been common before enlistment. Most of them had begun using the drug as teenagers before the war, and the chief reason given for drug use was to escape the strain of military duty.[63] Marcovitz' and Meyers' sample was much smaller—only 35 men at an army air force regional hospital—but again blacks were in the majority, 97 to 3 percent. The average age was 23 and the background was the familiar one of low education, no jobs, urban poverty, delinquency, and crime.

The evidence shows two things. First, the use of marijuana (and to a much lesser extent the opiates) was, if not common, at least recognized as a significant disciplinary problem during World War II, although most users did not begin with drugs in the service. Second, the military authorities who made drug policy pursued exactly the kind of witch hunt against drugs which the medical corps had advised against, and upheld the theory of drug-inspired delinquency which an earlier series of studies had exposed as phony. While military psychiatry wrestled with its labels and diagnoses, seeking to obtain institutional legitimacy for them and to break free from being an adjunct to the straight disciplinary process, the punitive policy reinforced the class and racial pattern of offenses, a pattern that was even more sharply defined during the Korean War.

Table 6–3 reports the number of army personnel admitted as drug addicts (no specification of the drugs involved) to medical service facilities, expressed as a rate per 1,000 mean strength per year. As absolute

TABLE 6–3

Admission for Drug Addiction—United States Army Personnel,
Total Army by Year, 1947–53, and Selected Areas by Year, 1950–53

					Number per 1,000 mean strength per year				
	1942–45	1946	1947	1948	1949	1950	1951	1952	1953
Total, Army	0.05	0.06	0.04	0.06	0.11	0.23	0.31	0.17	0.12
CONUS*	—	—	—	—	—	0.13	0.22	0.11	0.10
Total, outside CONUS	—	—	—	—	—	0.38	0.46	0.25	0.14
Far East and West Pacific	—	—	—	—	—	0.74	0.79	0.42	0.25

*Army stationed within the continental United States.

SOURCE: Data supplied by Major General S.B. Hays, Surgeon General, published in testimony of Dr. Frank B. Berry, Assistant Secretary of Defense for Health and Medical, *Daniel Hearings*, p. 220.

measures of the incidence of drug use the figures barely cover the tip of the iceberg, since medical treatment for drug users, once discovered, was the least likely outcome in military procedure. Court-martial and confinement were far more common, and then, of course, there were all those who were never caught.

The table is useful, however, in pointing out the relative increase in incidence which began in 1948 and peaked in 1951. The incidence rates were highest among troops stationed in Korea or elsewhere in the Far East; other figures for 1953–54 indicate that 68 percent of the military drug offenders were picked up in Japan and 31 percent in Korea.[64] Over three-quarters were army personnel. Just under one-third were aged 18 to 21, and 51 percent were between 22 and 25. Whites amounted to 28 percent, blacks 72 percent.[65] The incidence rate among black troops, according to another estimate, was 20 times the rate among whites. The drug used was generally heroin.

To what extent was this problem simply the carryover of the civilian epidemic of the same time? Predictably, perhaps, military officials have said that service experience itself had little to do with the incidence of drug use. They claimed that many, if not most, of the military users, would have become so had they never entered the service. During the Korean War, however, surveys of convicted offenders found only 19 percent who had used narcotics in civilian life before joining up, plus another 5 percent who first used drugs while still stationed in the United States. In the remainder, 40 percent began in Japan and 33 percent in Korea.[66] Later, in 1955, a survey covering the armed forces worldwide found a smaller number of so-called addicts than had been identified before. Of these, 56 percent had begun drug use before entering the service.[67]

These figures do not necessarily imply that without their military experience the group which began on drugs in the Far East would not have done so in civilian society. To a degree they shared some of the demographic characteristics of the civilian drug offenders. For one thing, they were black, although compared to the New York and Chicago groups (Tables 5-2 and 5-4) they were somewhat younger. Offense rates, at least at the height of the war period, were roughly the same between the military and civilian sectors.[68] The military offenders typically had a background of disciplinary trouble in the military, and most (70 percent) had served for two years or more.

These bits and pieces really cannot settle the question of whether or how military life and military policy stimulated a novel pattern of drug use which was not occurring at home. Military authorities tended to explain the phenomenon in supply terms as an overwhelming temptation for the naive and the gullible (again the role of prostitutes as the agents of temptation was stressed), and a number of civil officials saw in it evidence of a Chinese Communist plot to subvert our armed forces. This was denied by officers like General Maglin, the Army provost general.[69] Since incidence never approached the levels which were to be achieved in the Vietnam War, nor threatened command policy with anything like the rebellious intensity of the troops of the later period, it occurred to no one to approach the phenomenon from the demand side, let alone seek evidence that drug use reflected a deep alienation from the military system and its objectives in prosecuting the war. This, as we will now see, is what happened to make the Vietnam period unique in this history.

Opium isn't grown in South Vietnam, but the trade in it has been a key element in the political economy of the region ever since the French colonial administration built up a monopoly of imports, refineries, licensed dens, and retail shops which footed most of the bill for the colony's administration, just as the British had done in Bengal a century earlier.[70]

The opium which is cultivated in Laos, Burma and Thailand has in the last 30 years variously financed French counterinsurgency efforts against the Viet Minh, most political regimes in Saigon, covert political parties, the Saigon police, Corsican gangsters operating between Marseilles and the Far East, anti-Communist guerrilla groups working with the CIA, as well as irregular armies operating in Laos (the Meo) and along the China–Burma border (the Chinese Nationalists).

The trade itself has many requirements: armies to protect land caravans transporting the opium or morphine base, or else aircraft and high-speed boats for frontier hopping; laboratories and technicians for refining the morphine base into heroin, and high skills to obtain the No. 4 grade of heroin which is favored by consumers for its potency and by retailers for the ease with which it can be diluted or cut.[71] A multilevel organization for marketing, distribution and retail sale provides an elaborate network to provide security, oversee payment and insure failsafe conduits for the banking of the profits. These are enormous. In 1938 opium profits provided 15 percent of all colonial tax revenues for French Indochina. In 1971 the GI demand for the drug alone was said to produce $88 million a year for the trade, not to mention the value of international exports.[72]

By contrast to a business as complex as this, almost any Vietnamese farmer can produce marijuana, and selling either in bulk or packaged as cigarettes, the trade is localized, rudimentary and low in both technical needs and capital. Prices are low and so are profits. As competing enterprises, the opium-heroin industry is bound to win any contest of economic strength, to dominate organizationally and politically, and to supplant marijuana on the market, if not drive it off altogether.

At the beginning of 1970 this is almost what happened in Vietnam, and the political-economic forces of the trade operating at the time go a long way to explaining what took place—the largest rate of incidence of heroin use among Americans ever recorded.

Marijuana use rose steadily with each new year of the war; Table 6–4 illustrates developments between 1967 and 1971 for all the major drugs in use.

It is evident from these sources that the largest number of soldiers smoked marijuana but because such a significant portion of them had used the drug in the United States before assignment to Vietnam, the increase in true incidence for the drug in Vietnam was small when compared with the increase in barbiturate use, hallucinogenic drugs (although the evidence is contradictory on these), and, of course, heroin and morphine. In terms of the impact Vietnam itself had on drug use before 1970, only opium use showed really large gains, which suggests that even before the heroin market established itself, there was a strong demand for opiate-type drugs among the GI population, at least for smoking. Until 1970 what reported heroin and morphine use there was probably involved mainlining rather than smoking, was supplied around major base areas such as Saigon, Long Binh, and Da Nang, and concentrated among medics and their friends. There was a strong inhibition among the troops at large against the needle, which persisted through the war.

Then in May 1970—all of a sudden, it appeared to most observers— high-potency No. 4 heroin was available the length and breadth of the war zone, and GIs started to consume it. Almost a year later, in March 1971, an Army survey of men returning from Vietnam found that nearly 23 percent admitted to using heroin or morphine at some time during their tour of duty, and 16 percent had been using it within 30 days of their departure from Vietnam. The percentages for opium use were high, but not quite as high as these.

In April another Army survey, this time of support command troops based at Long Binh, identified 10.5 percent heroin, morphine, or opium users.[73] Estimates published in May ranged between 10 and 15 percent of the enlisted men serving in Vietnam, or 25,000 to 37,000 in total numbers.[74] In the fall a Defense Department contractor surveyed over 36,000 men in all services and found 11.7 percent who reported having used narcotics at least once in the past year. The proportion for the Army men altogether was 20.1 percent and for those in Vietnam, 28.5 percent. Of these, about 20 percent used heroin every day.[75] In September another Defense Department contractor found that among 13,000 Army returnees from Vietnam, 35 percent altogether said they had tried heroin, and one in five reported having felt "strung out" on the drug.[76]

What happened to transform the minuscule 2 percent of heroin morphine users of late 1969 into 10 or more times that proportion in two years? And what made May 1970 the turning point?[77]

Most accounts tailor the explanation to an a priori point of view. Official military sources tended to see the phenomenon as generated on the supply side rather than by demand. The North Vietnamese were blamed, as the Chinese had been during the Korean War, for using drugs to sap our fighting strength, and on occasion reports have circulated that the Chinese were again involved. The Army command in Saigon itself denied these claims.[78]

McCoy's account, which in other respects has nothing in common with the point of view of the authorities, also points to supply factors

TABLE 6–4

Comparison of Drug-Use Patterns
Among Enlisted Returnees from Vietnam, by Year

DRUG AND USAGE	1967	1969	1971
Marijuana			
light (1–19 times)	21.6%	20.50%	24.75%
heavy (20+ times)	7.4	29.60	34.09
total users	29.0	50.10	58.80
Amphetamines			
light	—	11.00%	12.52%
heavy	—	5.20	3.85
total users	—	16.20	16.40
Barbiturates			
light	—	7.80%	10.80%
heavy	—	3.80	4.58
total users	—	11.60	15.46
Hallucinogenics			
light	—	3.20%	14.31%
heavy	—	2.10	0.30
total users	—	5.30	14.61
Heroin/Morphine			
light	—	1.40%	10.27%
heavy	—	0.80	12.33
total users	—	2.20	22.68
Opium			
light	—	9.80%	13.12%
heavy	—	7.60	6.36
total users	—	17.40	19.59

SOURCE: *1967*—R.A. Roffman and E. Sapol, "Marihuana in Vietnam: A Survey of Use among Army Enlisted Men in the Two Southern Corps," *International Journal of the Addictions*, 5, no. 1 (1970), pp. 1–42. *1969*—Morris D. Stanton, "Drug Use in Vietnam: A Survey among Army Personnel in the Two Northern Corps," *Archives of General Psychiatry*, 26 (March 1972), pp. 279–86. *1971*—K. Eric Nelson and Jacob Panzarella, "Prevalence of Drug Use, Enlisted Vietnam Returnees Processing for ETS Separation, Oakland Overseas Processing Center," manuscript (March 1971).

but makes it clear that it was the South Vietnamese, abetted by the CIA in some cases, who were behind the trade. They were grouped in several factions—elements of the South Vietnamese air force, particularly the air transport wing controlled by former Premier Nguyen Cao Ky, which reportedly flew processed heroin out of Laos, Phnom Penh, or points in Pleiku Province to which the drug was transshipped by the Laotians; the police and customs sections of the civil administration in Saigon, dominated by Premier Khiem, which conspired with smugglers using the major air and sea ports; and, finally, elements of the army (ARVN), navy and National Assembly which have owed their positions and power to President Thieu.[79]

McCoy suggests that it was the Cambodian invasion in May 1970 that changed the character of the drug trade in Vietnam and led to the heroin epidemic among GIs.[80] It opened up the Mekong River to the South Vietnamese Navy all the way to Phnom Penh, and, in turn, opened that city to the drug exporters of Southern Laos. A number of high-ranking Vietnamese naval officers are named by McCoy as having organized the smuggling from Cambodia into the Cholon district of Saigon. There the shipments were broken down, packaged and distributed throughout the country, principally to networks of dealers and pushers operated or protected by Vietnamese army personnel; from them to GI consumers whose numbers and demand grew, and in this fashion the trade cycle was completed.

A popular alternative theory, though still oriented to supply factors, has been that American military policy itself stimulated the switch from marijuana consumption, which reputedly would have continued to suffice for most GIs, to heroin consumption when the crackdown on marijuana made this too risky to carry or smoke. The intensive campaign of personnel searches and sharp enforcement of drug prohibition followed a period in which enforcement practice had been relaxed as the numbers of marijuana users had grown too large to handle or deter. Under the kind of pressure initiated after the end of 1969 marijuana was replaced by heroin, which was more easily concealed and virtually impossible to detect by sniffing the way marijuana could be.[81] Just the same, marijuana never appears to have been in short supply at any time; most soldiers questioned have indicated that even where the popular choice in their units was heroin, marijuana was generally available for sale, and had not been driven off the local markets.[82]

There is no telling now what the volume of heroin trade was which moved down the Mekong, nor the relative size and returns of the trade in marijuana as compared with heroin. In any case, neither volume per se, nor the saturation marketing system for heroin which had established itself early in 1971 can explain the *readiness* of American soldiers to switch to the drug, and supply factors should not obscure the evident fact that around that time there was a change of drug *preference* among GIs.

It is to misunderstand the situation to ask GIs, as a great number of surveys have done, why they liked marijuana or heroin, for the answers no more explain why the preference changed from the former to the latter—typical reasons given fit both drugs equally well[83]—than they explain why drugs like these were chosen in the first place over, say, alcohol, which was clearly the preference of many GIs but not, as it turned out, of those who used drugs. Efforts at producing psychological theory to explain the patterns of behavior have suffered the same fault where they have concentrated on soldiers' remarks about drug effects.[84] When instead they involved casting back in time to find the predispositions to drug use which had existed before the soldier had entered the military, let alone reached Vietnam, the kind of profile research has produced is in fact characteristically the profile of *all* working-class soldiers in what was an unusually working-class army.[85]

The major official study of Vietnam drug use—outlined in the two reports by Lee Robins, whose work was supported by the Department of Defense, the Veterans Administration, the Special Action Office for Drug Abuse Prevention and other Washington agencies—managed to spell out such a profile, or the factors best predicting drug use in Vietnam, without ever observing that they were characteristic of the working-class soldier in general. Equally, the study failed to point to the distinction that even in the condition of widespread narcotics use as there was in Vietnam, the difference of class among GIs made a great deal of difference to the pattern of their drug use.

The strongest predictor of drug use in Vietnam, according to Robins, was drug use prior to service, and this was commonly associated with relatively low educational attainment, delinquency, urban residence, police record, alcoholism and marital problems among parents—a pretty conventional litany of working-class life. Where narcotics had been used before service—and this was rare among GIs—it had generally been codeine, not heroin, and again the evidence indicates this to have been a working-class adolescent practice, especially in Italian or Irish neighborhoods in the Northeast.[86] The next best predictor of drug use in the war was service status, with enlistees much more likely than draftees to have become users. Again, class is pertinent, for the latter were significantly better educated and from more middle-class homes than the former.[87] Truancy from school and unemployment at the time of induction also helped ultimately to distinguish the drug-users from the nonusers, and the same general observation of class applies. Additional survey evidence reinforces this.[88] The historic pattern of working-class narcotics use is thus repeated once more, with the one variation that this time working-class *white* soldiers appear to have been more common among heroin users, in relation to their total unit numbers, than working-class blacks.[89]

To Pentagon officials this became evidence for the claim that the prevalence of narcotics among GIs in Vietnam was a direct carryover from the civilian society in which drug use had gotten started. Neither military institutions nor the war were held responsible one way or the other, except for the possibility that Army programs to combat drug use had succeeded, where civilian policy had failed, to reduce the incidence rates among soldiers to a level below that of comparable civilian groups. Dr. Richard Wilbur, the Assistant Secretary of Defense for Health and Environment, made these points in testimony given to a House of Representatives subcommittee hearing in mid-1973,[90] and they have become part of a more general case, argued both within the military and among civil administrators, for the application of coercive quarantine and urinalysis testing of possible drug-users, as practised in the Army, to the so-called high-risk areas of the civil society, with a concomitant deemphasis of methadone and other maintenance programs in effect in those areas.

This represents a particularly manipulative and misleading use of the Robins' results, and Lee Robins dissociated herself in particular from the Assistant Secretary's publicized interpretations.[91] What her results showed in common with those of the only other comprehensive study of the situation[92] was that previous drug use affected only the initial *trying* of narcotics in Vietnam: "the degree of use once [the GI] decided to try them was not predictable from his Army record or from the background factors we asked about in interview."[93]

The Robins' finding was little more than that soldiers from working-class backgrounds were more likely than those from middle-class ones to try narcotics in the war zone; her report treated the incidence of regular heroin use as having no particular cause at all. This, however, ignored the vital role played by protest and revolt against the war and the groups of soldiers which organized it. How this occurred is spelled out in detail in my *Bringing the War Home*, but the essence is this: as soldiers arrived in Vietnam, they aligned themselves very quickly with one of two major groups which were active in virtually every company unit. One, nicknamed *juicers*, used alcohol heavily but avoided drugs (although most juicers conceivably had once tried marijuana or heroin); the other, known as the *heads*, avoided alcohol and used marijuana and then opium and heroin on a regular, often daily, basis. The juicers were for the war and conformed in opinion and behavior to command policy and orders, while the heads opposed continuation of the war, rejected government and command policy, and actively disobeyed orders to the extent, in some cases, of mutiny and killing officers.

The point about this ideological split is that the choice for alcohol versus drugs was the way it first started, signifying group identification immediately and remaining throughout the tour of duty the most important badge of group membership and allegiance. The finding that "both alcohol and drug use before service were related to drug use in Vietnam but that heavy use of alcohol while in Vietnam seemed to protect men against drug use"[94] struck Robins as "paradoxical,"[95] but in the context of the working-class soldier's resistance to fighting the war, it is perfectly explicable, and indeed helps confirm the conclusions of the other study.[96] Far from signifying previous experience with drugs, then, the use of heroin in Vietnam was the unique innovation of American troops, one in every three, who after 1969 refused to believe either that the war could be won or that the attempt was worth the risk to their lives.

It is understandable perhaps that the military authorities would not readily admit as much, although the ferocity with which drug detection and control programs were pursued is a fair intimation that they understood the *ideological and political* character of the drug danger; whether they acknowledged it or not, regular heroin consumption had virtually no adverse effect by itself on the performance and efficiency of soldiers on duty.[97]

It took nearly two years (after 1970) for senior Pentagon spokesmen even to admit to the high prevalence of heroin in Vietnam; they have continued to resist reports from the press, research results, and even, most recently, from the Veterans Administration,[98] that the war and the military services released a large number of veterans who continued using heroin on the same regular basis as before. *Study Confirms That Vietnam Veteran Drug Abuse at Low Levels* was the headline of Secretary Wilbur's news release when the first Robins report was issued.

The final report indicated that there had been a substantial fall-off in the number of veterans continuing narcotics use at home after departure from Vietnam and discharge from the Army. In all, 10 percent of a general sample of returning veterans indicated that they had used narcotics on some occasion in the eight to twelve months between release in late 1971 and the time of the interview. Only 1.3 percent reported that they had felt addicted at any time during the same period.

At his news conference Wilbur extrapolated from this last statistic to claim that of more than 310,000 Army enlisted men who had served in Vietnam between 1970 and 1972, less than 4,000 were likely to have remained addicts in the United States. This, he added, was virtually the same as the rate of narcotics abuse identified among civilian young men examined at induction stations around the country at the same time, so that once again it could be said neither the war nor the military had done anything to accentuate the domestic narcotics problem. Several other conclusions appeared logically to follow:

> In-service and Veterans Administration rehabilitation programs are succeeding beyond our highest expectations. Who would have predicted two years ago that almost all drug abusers and drug dependents could have been restored to a drug free existence in our society?
>
> A drug dependent person can apparently withdraw from narcotics use without assistance as witnessed by the fact that one half of all those who reported heroin dependency in Vietnam had withdrawn on their own and were not identified at the time of their departure.
>
> Urinalysis for drug abuse is a socially acceptable medical measure within high risk populations contrary to popular belief.
>
> The treatment opportunities which exist in the Veterans Administration and civilian agencies are presently adequate to meet the needs of Vietnam veterans.
>
> We now know that recovery from heroin dependence is not impossible; and that in the case of young, healthy, well-disciplined men in the armed services, rehabilitation will be successful in the majority of cases.[99]

The conflict in the evidence is obvious. Figures reported early in this chapter indicate that military veterans (a larger group, of course, than Vietnam veterans) constituted anything from 10 percent of the institutionalized addict population to approximately 33 percent, depending on the city, year, season, type of institution and enforcement policy operating at the time. Counting veterans in Veterans Administration drug programs, other state institutions, and estimating for veteran users on the street, I calculated the total for the state of Massachusetts alone in 1971 to be just over 2,300, or nearly as many as Wilbur claimed for the whole country.[100] A conservative estimate, assuming that veterans at the time amounted to 15 percent of the total addict population, was 45,000,[101] and expressing this in terms of the total of Army war veterans indicates that as many as 15 percent of the returnees continued regular drug use.

There can be no satisfactory end to juggling these figures; it is clear for example that narcotics use was not confined to Vietnam and by 1972 was rising fast in the Army in Europe. On top of that must be added additional numbers of Navy and Air Force personnel, also serving in Southeast Asia and likely to have picked up narcotics as had the Army ranks. From the Robins' sample of 43 narcotics users after Vietnam, none had begun with heroin after returning from the war zone—all were carryovers from Vietnam, 30 percent were carryovers from heroin use before Vietnam.[102] In my sample of 30, drawn from the general addict population in the New England area, only 3 percent had used heroin before Vietnam and 47 percent carried over from the war. Fifty percent, however, *began* heroin use *after* leaving the war zone. These, of course, would not have been detectable in the urinalysis screen at the departure point and were much more likely than Robins' subjects, so long as they remained undetected, to choose to avoid contact with a Pentagon-sponsored study such as hers. Since her sample *under*represented men from the New England and Mid-Atlantic states[103]—where heroin addiction was most concentrated in general—it is more than likely that these "new addicts" are completely missing from the official count.

Contrary to Wilbur's claim, urinalysis testing was notoriously faulty for identifying active heroin users. Evidence presented at hearings of a unit of the Senate Armed Services Committee in 1972 indicated that military laboratories had a record of 45 percent overall accuracy and civilian laboratories somewhat better at 61 percent, but with a sizable margin still of unaccounted-for error.[104] Robins herself admitted that the urinalysis taken as men left Vietnam failed to detect or deter men who continued using heroin after they left Vietnam; it missed 13 percent of men who were active drug users at the time of the test, and labelled another 3 percent with false positives.[105]

Dr. Wilbur's claim that military treatment programs had been particularly successful at rehabilitation was pure invention, and Robins' final report was unambiguous on this score: "we have not been able to show much in the way of evidence for the effectiveness of treatment in the Army, either in Vietnam or since."[106] No evidence either way was offered in the report on the Veterans Administration programs, but other sources indicate widespread dissatisfaction.[107] The claim that the existing treatment facilities were adequate for the numbers of veteran addicts was repudiated by VA officials themselves.[108]

One clue to the discrepancy between the Pentagon's extrapolations and most other estimates of veteran heroin users, which never shrank to less than 10 times the Pentagon number, is the use of the term *addict* in the Robins report. This referred only to an interviewee's subjective report, that he *felt* addicted or strung out though the duration was unasked for and unspecified. Frequent narcotics use was defined in the report as for more than weekly for more than a month.[109] To publicly minimize the size of the problem Pentagon officials along with leading members of the White House Special Action Office chose to operate with the smallest percentage, 1.3 percent feeling addicted since Vietnam, although Robins had also identified 3 percent frequent narcotic use, and 10 percent any use at all.[110] As far as the law, the police and the FBI crimes index are concerned, distinctions between the three types of behavior are mere niceties, once they have been detected, and the term addiction has traditionally been applied to cover all three. That being the case, between 1970 and 1972 no less than 31,000 army returnees were continuing heroin addicts, or liable at least to be regarded by the law in that light. Adding in all Vietnam theater returnees for just one year, 1971, increases the likely total to 56,000,[111] which is much closer to the estimates used by Senator Cranston and VA officials. It is still substantially lower than has been indicated by some veterans groups and by the evidence presented in *Bringing the War Home.*

Ultimately, in the longer-term history of narcotics, it is not the exact numbers here which count but the proportions of military veterans in the total population of drug users; on this score there can be no doubt about the uniquely important impact which the war and the army had upon the working-class young men who served and fought—unwillingly. Historically the pattern is of one piece with the past, yet not in any of the public debate or research on the current heroin episode has it ever been noted as such. By the same token, the deceptions with which military authorities have attempted to cover up the true extent of narcotics use have functioned to perpetuate the very same ideology of opium which Dr. Wilbur's predecessors at the American Medical Association and in the government[112] applied at the beginning of national prohibition of the drug. Ultimately they have functioned to strengthen and extend the hand of police power over every aspect of working-class life in America.

Chapter 7.
Drugs and Class Conflict

The history may not be complete, nor the reader satisfied, if no place is made for the *character* of the individuals whose passing has been noted here, more often than not in the movement of large aggregate numbers responding to indexical shifts in the business cycle, labor supply, wages, unemployment, and so on.

In the days before psychological testing, drug users themselves were particularly mute or else their characteristic articulateness, with whatever clue that might have given to the question, Why did *they* become addicts? was typically arrested in a frozen moment of terror or grotesquerie or death. Hear them screaming, then:

> About 11 o'clock Tuesday forenoon, David C. Hodge, a resident of 'Hardscrabble,' took a large dose of morphine which resulted in his death about 12 o'clock that night. . . . The deceased left a note saying that no one but himself was to blame for the act. He leaves a wife and 4 little girls in destitute circumstances. He was a sober and industrious workman, quite well known and generally respected.[1]

> A young man, who has not been identified, went insane from cocaine poisoning in Battery Park last evening and ran about like a madman. He seized several women who were taking the air on the benches and soon the park resounded with their screams.[2]

> He repeated the story he had told the Sidney Chief of Police regarding his addiction to marihuana saying that his supply of the weed had become exhausted several days before the killing and his nerves were unstrung.[3]

> "The monkey's never dead, Fixer," Frankie told him knowingly.

146

Louie glanced at Frankie slyly. "You know that already, Dealer? You know how he don't die? It's what they say awright, the monkey never dies. When you kick him off he just hops onto somebody else's back." Behind the film of glaze that always veiled Louie's eyes Frankie saw the twisted look. "*You* got my monkey, Dealer? You take my nice old monkey away from me? Is that my monkey ridin' your back these days, Dealer?"

The color had returned to Frankie's cheeks, he felt he could make it almost any minute now. "No more for me, Fixer," he assured Louis confidently. "Somebody else got to take your monkey. I had the Holy Jumped-up-Jesus Horrors for real this time—'n I'm one guy knows when he got enough. I learned my lesson but *good*. Fixer—you just give the boy with the golden arms his very lastest fix."[4]

One day a squad of guys was unloading a truck-load of mortar shells. It was in my first month, I think. Anyway, one of these things rolls out of someone's hand, hits the ground and blows up, setting off all the other shells. Thirty guys were killed. They gave me the job of collecting the body parts and putting the,—you know, two legs, two arms, into body bags. I spent the whole day doing it. I'd never seen death, then [in Vietnam] I'd seen it ten or fifteen times every day—nothing was worth all of that. It wasn't political—I began to get no sleep, had nightmares, and was afraid of flying. . . . They took me off flight duty, and sent me up to Xuan Loc to work as a corpsman but I couldn't take that, so they sent me to Tay Ninh to work in a morgue—tag the bodies, bag them, put them in the freezer—type out the death certificates. They gave me downs [barbiturates] but I was into dope so I didn't take it.[5]

To be sure, these were the extreme moments, extreme because they were the terminus to which narcotics use has been thought inevitably to lead; the moments when the monkey on the man's back drove him beyond all hope of recovery, and beyond reason and sanity as well. But although the desperation, irrationality and madness have always been, and remain still,[6] standard elements of the image of the dope fiend or the junkie—they used to get a vigilance committee good and worked up for a raid on Chinatown, or a lynch mob after blacks— they hardly amount to a psychology of narcotics addiction. And if the drug user can be distinguished by his character, a connection which has been part of the legal philosophy of prohibition for almost the full century,[7] or if the character can be interpreted to explain and predict who is headed for the perpetual oriental somnolence, or else who will end up choked to death on some stoop or washroom floor somewhere—then there must be such a psychology of addiction and no doubt or ambiguity to it either.

The characteristic traits of users or addicts vary with the psychological theory involved, so there is overlapping and contradictoriness in enumeration, but the list will still be long. In the technical literature they have been described as introverted, sensitive, quiet, passive, submissive, and lacking in strong masculine identification.[8] Also, emotionally limited, manipulative, irresponsible, unsociable, dependent, destructive and derogatory of self.[9] Also, suspicious, paranoid, manic, depressive, psychotic.[10] Also, defective in superego functioning, weak in ego structure, unrealistic in future orientation, and distrustful of major social institutions.[11]

These characteristics reportedly develop from initial psychological abnormalities, including poor and distorted family experiences. The addict's mother, for instance, has been regarded in a number of studies as being unusually dominant, overpowering, overprotective, guilt ridden, aggressive or overambitious toward the child,[12] with the effect that the scope and direction for psychological development are unusually limited and frustrated, and a predisposition to drug use exhibited as a result.[13]

There is one problem, though, with these psychological findings and with the character type which has been constructed out of them. This is simply that they are *underspecific*. They may describe narcotics users or addicts faithfully enough, but they also describe barbiturate users who never touch narcotics, car thieves and muggers who have no experience with any drugs, delinquents for any cause, youthful alcoholics, potential or actual suicides, other psychiatrically disturbed youth, or indeed most any contemporary urban-dwelling, working-class youth between the ages of 15 and 25.

Levine, for instance, discovered that if addicted adolescents were compared to nonaddicted ones of the same class, no differences were to be found at either the conscious or subconscious level in subjective identifications with either mother or father figure.[14] Leeds found, in his own words, that "while the results obtained for the mothers of the addicted adolescent group are quite consistent with portions of the literature, these same personality factors and concomitant modes of behavior characterized the personality organization of the mothers of the delinquent nonaddicted adolescent group. The implication of this may be that the mothers of the two antisocial groups are basically the same in personality structure and organization."[15] Jackson compared drug-addicted prisoners with nonaddicted prisoners, and found that in personality traits they shared more in common as prisoners of working-class, particularly black origins, than they differed on account of their pattern of drug use.[16] Finally, McGrath, in what is perhaps the most thorough-going research of all, compared heroin users with other boys brought to court (in the Newark, New Jersey, area) for assault offenses, auto theft and barbiturate use.

The findings were that the heroin users were not more introverted and withdrawn than the others, probably less; nor more passive. They scored higher on ego strength than the others. On most other psychological measures there was no difference at all between them, so long as social class remained the same. The problems of broken families and supposed mother dominance are disposed of as characteristic of delinquents in general, blacks in particular—not at all peculiar to heroin users.[17] The conclusion: "no real evidence was found that psychological predisposition theories are any more correct than sociological theories as to why one becomes a drug addict."[18] And again: "if any group's behavior is due more to psychological problems than to social location it is the assaulters."[19]

The message should be clear. At minimum, there is no clear outline to the character of the addict free of ambiguity or serious doubt. But in all likelihood, there is not and never has been such a character—certainly no psychological evidence to establish outright that for reasons other than the drug use per se, the addict is or was a danger to himself or to others, and no evidence that addiction by itself produces such dangers, psychologically conceived.

It is strange indeed that so much of the contrary evidence referred to is contained in unpublished form, buried it might almost be said, without any record or notice of its existence surviving except through the most exhaustive search, for the implications of the hidden literature are radical indeed.

By attacking the theory of an addiction-prone character, it undermines the notion that there are character disorders to be treated, which is the rationale, of course, of virtually all medically oriented, reformist policy. Not that the "dope fiend" does not or cannot have existed in the past. It is just that what the underground literature makes plain is that the drug-user wasn't the only one who fitted the psychological description. The description was nothing less than the image of a typical working-class man, perhaps militant, perhaps not, depending on the economic conditions, and the characterology which grew up around the drug problem was and continues to be no less of a trap to catch him than the more sociological myths already accounted for.

And what of the prohibitionists? Public deception requires deceit, does it not, and lies liars to tell them? Perhaps there is a place for pathological character in this story among them. If the reader could only catch a glimpse of the personal diaries, were they to have existed and survived, of Dr. Hamilton Wright, the founding father of narcotics prohibition. Perhaps then it would be clear whether he was calculatedly lying about the prevalence of cocaine among Southern blacks, and would explain why if that were so. Set beside the pathological traits which have purportedly characterized and motivated the addict's behavior, what model of psychological health would such personal evidence about Wright testify to in his otherwise evident political ambition, his obsessiveness and fanaticism?

The first New York campaign for narcotics prohibition, which resulted in the passage of the Boylan Law, just a few months before the Harrison Bill was enacted in 1914, is said to have been initiated in the following way. Dr. Jackson Campbell, a physician employed at the Department of Corrections, told a Mr. Coulter at Christmas 1913 that there were 15,000 cocaine and morphine addicts in the city, that one-third of all crime was due to them, and that at any one time 40 percent of all inmates in the Tombs, the city prison, were habitual cocaine users.

Coulter, it happened, was personal attorney for the leading New York socialite, Ann Vanderbilt, and what he had heard he passed on to her.[20] This was early in January 1914, already, by that time, well into the city's social season. Some say that Mrs. Vanderbilt had been doing poorly for press notices thus far and was especially miffed by the relatively greater attention captured by Mrs. Astor and a number of others.[21] The consequence was that she decided on Coulter's advice to make a personal cause out of the drug issue, and to that end launched an extensive campaign which returned her to the newspapers on January 21. Ten days later she was back again, on this occasion on page eight of the *Times,* following a city-wide conference she had called on drugs. Three months after this, the legislation which the conference had called for came into operation, to limit for the first time the illicit trade in opium and other drugs by confining them to medical prescription and the registered retail druggists.

To be sure, the chain of circumstances leading to this outcome was a highly anomalous one. Had Dr. Campbell's misinformation not reached the apparently egomaniacal, aggressive, and manipulative Mrs. Vanderbilt, or, to stretch the details some, had it reached her at the end of the season when she was on her way to Newport for the summer, it is unlikely that so effective a press campaign and mobilization of medicos, lawyers, and politicians on so objectively thin a case would have resulted in the prohibition edict of the Boylan Law. Or would it?

Similar was the case referred to in Chapter 5, of how Congressman Boggs of Louisiana came to initiate his (1951) act for dealing with the narcotics episode which had begun in 1949. "I just became interested in this legislation," he said, "when I received a letter from a member of a Federal grand jury." This had been interpreted for him by the Bureau of Narcotics, whose agent in charge in New Orleans adapted for Boggs' benefit a longtime city myth, that an Italian criminal syndicate was responsible for running narcotics from the Caribbean and Mexico into New Orleans, which served a vast hinterland as the Mafia's entrepôt and trading point.

This was quite false—disinformation, strictly speaking, since it was a falsehood which would be readily believed, coming, as it did, on the authority of the Bureau of Narcotics. Was Boggs the dupe, then, of the Bureau? Or was the truth immaterial, once the political possibilities of the drug issue in promoting Boggs' gubernatorial candidacy had become clear to him? His campaign required a diversionary issue for, to put his situation precisely, he needed a liberal, anti-Long, clean government, law and order policy to capture middle-class votes, but he depended and would still do so for election on appearing the pro-Long populist, and on maintaining his solid working-class backing. The congressional hearings catalyzed Boggs' political chances, as well as underwrote a further stage of narcotics prohibition. Shall the latter be explained in terms of the former as a public deception, practised on a grand scale, for private gain? Boggs failed to get elected, but Senator Price Daniel, who launched a similar set of hearings years later as he prepared to run in the Texas gubernatorial race, was much more successful. Does the evidence of private manipulation and deceit in these cases warrant regarding them as psychologically deficient?

And those who gained from drug prohibition—Wright, Vanderbilt, Boggs, or Dr. Lambert of the AMA, the editor of the Alamosa county newspaper, Dr. Fossier and his associates of New Orleans, Assistant Secretary of Defense Richard Wilbur, or Harry J. Anslinger, the first and model narcotics enforcer, or in the present episode, having initiated the most repressive system of deterrence yet enacted, Vice President Nelson Rockefeller—did they believe the reasons they offered in public for what they proposed to be done, and did? And what was their gain thereby?

It has to be said in their defense that the mythology of narcotics, once initiated and embodied in legislation, and integrated with that authority into the routine of enforcement, police administration, and court precedent, establishes the standards and limits of belief, so that if there is and was deception, it isn't necessarily explicable as conscious or motivated deceit. Just the same, each episode of the development of the mythology, and the public policy which it underwrote, has revealed particular innovations and individual initiatives. Not that well-meaning and honest people have not been reasonably persuaded that the drugs had the pernicious effects which were claimed, but it required, as I have illustrated in each chapter, a radical downturn in the business cycle, the operation of a split labor market, and a sharp deterioration of the expectations of all classes regarding their economic welfare, in order to make it urgent and likely that action on drugs would be taken, and that it was. In the event, the particular gains secured by narcotics prohibition have been so varied for those who initiated it that in themselves they add little to our interpretation of the fundamental causes of what happened.

Gains there had to be for the individuals involved to act—career, self-advertisement, election advantage, bureaucratic aggrandizement are evident ones. By arresting the history of the use of narcotics and prohibition policy at these moments of individual initiative, it is possible to see exactly what the initiative consisted of and the relationship it bore to the existing mythology. It is also possible to gauge something of the psychology of those responsible for public policy formation— these zealots for normalcy, Machiavellian manipulators, megalomaniacs, obsessives, neurotic liars. The labels are crudely impressionistic, for the subjects will hardly volunteer for psychiatric examination and cannot be compelled, as can drug offenders. But, then, if psychologically there is nothing in particular which predisposes the offender to narcotics use or addiction and indeed, if in general psychiatric terms, there is nothing at all to distinguish the user or addict from anyone else of his class, then there is *nothing but his class* to identify him,[22] and the psychological theory is no more useful to account for there being individuals who "need" the drugs than it can be to account for there being individuals, who no less idiosyncratically "need" to prohibit narcotics, and punish offenders with a maximum of violence and severity. Again the facts of class will identify who they have been, or rather whose interests have been served by their actions. For it is the dynamics of class conflict rather than the payoffs to a particular conspiracy or mental aberration which have determined the long-term course and character of narcotics policy.

There never was an episode, a time, or an agency for that matter, which could not command enough scientific or expert evidence to back or at the very same time reject particular policy proposals. The medical and epidemiological testimony given by Sir William Roberts to the British Parliamentary Royal Commission on Opium, 1895,[23] would do almost as well as the protocol and technical papers supplied by the Vera Institute of Justice in proposing a trial legalization of heroin,[24] just as the testimony of other witnesses before that inquiry eighty years ago differs scarcely at all from the modern advocacy of strict deterrence—concretely now, under the Rockefeller legislation, that of mandatory life sentences for offenders.

These happen to be current issues in the present policy debate; they change from episode to episode, more in technical detail than in consequence, and they are no more likely to be settled now than they were in 1949, at the beginning of the last cycle, or earlier, or than they are likely to be settled twenty years from now perhaps, at the beginning of the next cycle. To arrest the history of narcotics, then, at the level of scientific argument and the conflict of theory[25]—let alone make it appear that the consequence of the history of drug prohibition has been progressive enlightenment—is just as misleading as it is to conceive of the course of events in individual or psychological terms.

Return again to class we must, where public policy is the stratagem of class conflict and law enforcement the weapon, as sharp as the exclusion campaigns against Chinese and Mexicans, or the repression of ghetto blacks and the American army in Vietnam. Not science but mythology potentiates this history and the social forces whose movement it records. If the monkey on the man's back were only the drug, he would still be a free man.

Notes

CHAPTER 1. THE VICE'S CYCLE

1. See the pioneering report by Norman E. Zinberg and Richard C. Jacobson, *The Social Basis of Drug Abuse Prevention,* Washington, D. C.: The Drug Abuse Council, 1974.
2. Throughout the past century both terms, *narcotics* and *addiction,* have been used very loosely, so that, as I indicated, narcotic drugs will include not only the opiates but cocaine and marijuana, which are, of course, quite different, both in their pharmacological characteristics and their physiological effects. Also, *addict* and *addiction* will cover every pattern of drug use, from intermittent to constant. To avoid confusion I will use the specific names of drugs where it is appropriate and consider a narcotic addict one who is under the influence of the drug for more time than he is not. At the same time, the terms will appear in their indiscriminate sense whenever that is the meaning I must report.
3. Over the years each new control system or agency has issued its own code of accepted science on the narcotics problem. For SAODAP see Richard H. Blum, ed., "Origins of Drug Use and Drug Problems: Fact, Theory and Implications for Public Action," Washington, D. C.: SAODAP, 1973.
4. Address of Richard G. Kleindienst, 79th Annual Conference of the International Association of Chiefs of Police, Salt Lake City, Oct. 17, 1972, pp. 7–8.
5. H. H. Kane, *Opium Smoking in America and China,* New York: G. P. Putnam's, 1882, p. 8.
6. Testimony of Dr. Lin Bun Keng, of Singapore, quoted in *Use of Opium and Traffic Therein,* Report of the Committee Appointed by the Philippine Commission, 59th Congress, 1st Sess., 1906, Senate Doc. #265, p. 106.
7. Emphasis in original. Captain Edgar King, "The Use of Habit-Forming Drugs (Cocaine, Opium and Its Derivatives) by Enlisted Men: A Report Based on the Work Done at the United States Disciplinary Barracks," *Military Surgeon,* 39 (1916), 380.
8. My emphasis. James Q. Wilson et al., "The Problem of Heroin," *Public Interest,* no. 29 (Fall 1972), 7.
9. For example, William F. Wieland and Michael Yunger, "Sexual Effects and Side Effects of Heroin and Methadone," *Proceedings: 3rd National*

Conference on Methadone Treatment, National Institute of Mental Health, Washington, D. C., Nov. 14–16, 1970, pp. 51–53.

10.   Wilson et al, p. 9.

11.   Former President Nixon appears to have held this view. The touchstone for him was "permissiveness," a condition of individual morality which is sufficient in itself to lead to both drug use and crime:

> *We have passed through a very great spiritual crisis in this country— during the late 60's . . . many lost faith in many of our institutions. For example, the enormous movement toward permissiveness which led to the escalation in crime, the escalation in drugs in this country, all this came as a result of those of us who basically have a responsibility of leadership not recognizing that above everything else you must not weaken a people's character. . . . The average American is just like the child in the family. You give him some responsibility and he is going to amount to something. . . . If, on the other hand, you make him completely dependent, and pamper him and cater to him too much, you are going to make him soft, spoiled and eventually a very weak individual.*

From the transcript of a preelection interview granted Garnett D. Horner and published in the *New York Times,* Nov. 10, 1972, p. 20.

12.   *Use of Opium and Traffic Therein,* p. 80.

13.   *Report on the International Opium Commission and on the Opium Problem as Seen Within the United States and Its Possessions,* published as *Message from the President of the United States of America,* 61st Congress., 2nd Sess., 1910, Senate Doc. #377, p. 51.

14.   King, p. 277.

15.   Wilson et al., p. 14.

16.   Kane, p. 4.

17.   *Some Reasons for Chinese Exclusion: Meat vs. Rice; American Manhood Against Asiatic Coolieism; Which Shall Survive?,* published by the American Federation of Labor, 57th Congress., 1st Sess., 1902, Senate Doc. 137, p. 22.
      In the case of the Chinese, the "quarantine" proposed was a combination of stopping further Chinese from entering the country and sending those already here home.

18.   King, pp. 278, 380.

19.   From a speech to a conference, "The Problems of Adolescent Drug Addiction—Prevention Through Education," quoted by James W. Hughes, "The American Medical Profession and the Narcotics Policy Controversy," Ph. D. diss., Department of Sociology, Indiana Univ., 1967, p. 131.

20.   Wilson et al., pp. 10, 22.

21.   Quoted by Hughes, p. 20.

22.   King, p. 275.

23. Quoted by Hughes, p. 134.

24. Ira Reiss, "Social Class and Pre-marital Sexual Permissiveness: A Reexamination," *American Sociological Review* 30, no. 3, 1964, 747–56.

25. Fred Strodtbeck and James F. Short, Jr., "Aleatory Risks Versus Short-Run Hedonism in Explanation of Gang Action," *Social Problems* 12, no. 1 (1964), 127–40.

26. Walter Miller, "Lower Class Culture as a Generating Milieu of Gang Delinquency," *Journal of Social Issues* 14, no. 1 (1958), 3–14.

27. Seymour M. Lipset, "Democracy and Working-Class Authoritarianism," *American Sociological Review* 24, no. 4 (August 1959), 482–501.

CHAPTER 2. THE CHINESE OPIUM CRUSADE

1. A useful, if incomplete, review of the economics of this arrangement is David Edward Owen, *British Opium Policy in China and India,* New Haven: Yale Univ. Press, 1934.

2. "Say's law"; Jean-Baptiste Say, *A Treatise on Political Economy,* C. R. Prinsep trans., London: Longman, 1821.

3. *Use of Opium and Traffic Therein,* p. 81 (testimony of Mr. Chao, Shanghai merchant), pp. 87 and 213 (extract of article by Dr. Dudgeon, a sometime medical resident).

4. Estimates from the San Francisco Customs Office listed the following arrival numbers by year:

1849	325
1850	450
1851	2,700
1852	20,000

From Ping Chiu, *Chinese Labor in California, An Economic Study, 1850-1880,* Madison: Univ. of Wisconsin, 1963, pp. 13, 142. This relatively unknown work is one of the best available sociological analyses of the beginnings of Chinese life in America.

5. Chiu, p. 24.

6. H. H. Kane, *Opium-Smoking in America and China,* New York: G. P. Putnam's, 1882, p. 8. Wright, p. 37. See also George F. Seward, *Chinese Immigration, Its Social and Economic Aspects,* New York: Scribner's, 1881, p. 212; Gunther P. Barth, *Bitter Strength: A History of the Chinese in the United States, 1850–1870,* Cambridge: Harvard Univ. Press, 1964, pp. 196–97; Rose Hum Lee, *The Chinese in the United States of America,* Hong Kong: Cathay Press, 1960, p. 23; Ivan H. Light, "From Vice District to Tourist Attraction: The Moral Career of American Chinatowns, 1880–1940," *Pacific Historical Review* (1974) 367–94.

7. Chiu, p. 61.

8. *Ibid.*, p. 136.
9. For a review of these arguments see Seward, *Chinese Immigration*, esp. pp. 160ff.
10. One of the reasons went to the heart of the "sojourner" code. Both to provide an incentive for the sojourning husband to remain loyal and send money home and to sustain the kin and village networks without him, it was the Chinese custom for the wife to remain while her husband immigrated. See Stanford M. Lyman, "Marriage and Family Among Chinese Immigrants to America, 1880–1960," *Phylon*, 29, no. 4, pp. 321–30.
11. For the lurid details see Seward, pp. 261ff.; Kane, pp. 8ff.; and *The Social, Moral and Political Effect of Chinese Immigration,* A report of Public Hearings Conducted by the Committee of the Senate of California, printed by the Committee on Education and Labor, House of Representatives, 45th Congress, 1st Sess., 1877, Misc. Document 9.
12. In no year did the Persian imports exceed 10 percent of the Indian shipments; Owen, p. 287.
13. Figures on the India-China trade are from Owen, *British Opium Policy*, p. 281; on U. S. imports, from Hamilton Wright, *Report on the International Opium Commission for the Opium Problem as Seen within the United States and its Possessions,* published as *Message from the President of the United States of America,* 61st Congress, 2nd Sess., 1910, Senate Document 377, pp. 81–83.
14. In judging magnitudes like this, caution must be used, because side by side with the recorded entry of imported opium, there was a fairly brisk and unrecorded smuggling trade. The relative volumes of the two trades varied largely according to the attitude displayed toward the drug by U. S. Customs. According to Wright, between 1864 and 1870, when a 100 percent ad valorem tax was levied on imports, smuggling was particularly heavy. This then dropped between 1870 and 1883, when duties were reduced. Smuggling picked up in response to a provision in the 1880 treaty with China, according to which the importation of opium by Chinese subjects was prohibited (which left Americans free to import the drug and then sell it back to the Chinese). It got its biggest lift when duties rose again to $10 and $12 a pound.
15. See O. N. Reynolds, "The Chinese Tongs," *American Journal of Sociology*, 40, no. 5 (March 1935), 612–23; also, H. M. Lai, "A Historical Survey of Organizations of the Left Among the Chinese in America," *Bulletin of the Committee of Concerned Asian Scholars*, 4, no. 3 (Fall 1972), 10–20.
16. See Light, "From Vice District to Tourist Attraction," passim. For an account of contemporary *tong* roles and activities, see Virginia Heyer, "Patterns of Social Organization in New York City's Chinatown," Ph.D. diss., Columbia Univ. 1953.
17. Light, pp. 19–29.
18. Although there is little concrete evidence of this for this period, that the

involvement existed and continued for quite a while among the "legiti-mate" merchants is clear from the following news item which appeared in the *New York Times,* February 27, 1915, p. 7: "Tam Shi Yan, who was elected President of the Chinese Merchants Association of New York, an office to which the title of 'mayor of Chinatown' is accorded, was found guilty at his second trial in the Federal District Court yesterday of manu-facturing opium for smoking in Doyers Street. His defense was that mem-bers of a rival *tong* planted the opium and apparatus in his room during his absence."

19. Gunther P. Barth, *Bitter Strength,* pp. 196–97.
20. Wright, p. 41. Indirect support for this can be inferred from what we know of the social class in China from which the immigrants of this peri-od came and from the rough correlation that holds between this and the incidence of the opium habit. Earlier I made the point that the first wave of the Chinese immigration was a petite-bourgeoisie one, that only later did a laborer class predominate. In fact, even among the latter group, there were few who were from poor peasant or urban laborer strata in China, among which opium use was prevalent. James W. Loewen's findings for the Chinese immigrants entering the Mississippi delta be-tween 1870 and 1880 have general applicability: "the Delta Chinese prob-ably came from peasant and artisan families who because of their earlier emigrant connections were better off than the mass of rural Chinese but who were clearly not in the landlord class. Within their families the in-dividuals who left were probably those least well off. Most had little busi-ness background but were oriented toward independent business as a means of future advancement." Loewen, *The Mississippi Chinese: Be-tween Black and White,* Cambridge: Harvard Univ. Press, 1971, p. 28. Loewen recorded no use of opium in a century of Chinese life in the Mis-sissippi Delta.
21. Reynolds, "Chinese Tongs," p. 616.
22. Wright's arithmetic is off. The total population represented fractionally by his percentages is approximately 149,000, but not until 1950 did the Chinese population of the country actually reach this number. According to the census, population figures were as follows:

1860	34,933
1870	63,199
1880	105,465
1890	106,488
1900	118,746
1940	106,334
1950	150,005
1960	237,292
1970	435,062

It seems reasonable to conclude, therefore, that Wright overstated the incidence of opium-smoking among the Chinese. Since he further relied on these numbers to obtain estimates for the total amount of opium consumed by Chinese and non-Chinese for the period 1900–1909, it is highly probable that he underestimated the extent of opium use among the non-Chinese of the time.

23. Treadway reported in 1930 that nearly 21 percent of the narcotics violators reported to the U. S. Public Health Service during 1929 were Chinese. *Public Health Reports,* 45, No. 11 (1930), pp. 541–53. A California State Narcotic Committee report on arrests for narcotics violations during 1928 showed nearly 28 percent Chinese (*The Trend of Drug Addiction in California,* Sacramento: State Printing Office, 1930). A report by the same Committee for 1931–32 showed 26 percent Chinese statewide. In 1935 the Federal Bureau of Narcotics annual report, *Traffic in Opium and Other Dangerous Drugs,* indicated 9 percent "Oriental" among 946 addicts reported for the year. The following year, the California Senate Interim Narcotic Committee reported 16 percent Chinese among federal narcotic law violators for the year (*Report on Drug Addiction in California,* Sacramento: State Printing Office, 1936). In Chicago for 1937 Dai found 5.6 percent "yellow and red" addicts among the institutionalized population of Cook County over the six-year period, 1931–37 (Bingham Dai, *Opium Addiction in Chicago,* Shanghai: Commerical Press, 1937). In 1943 Pescor reported on addict patients admitted to Lexington Hospital from 1936 to 1937 and found 0.9 percent Chinese. Finally, in 1966 Ball and Lau, summarizing the ethnic data on all male addicts treated at Lexington from 1935 to 1964, found nearly 3 percent Chinese, as compared with 0.2 percent Chinese in all of the male population of the United States (John C. Ball and M. P. Lau, "The Chinese Narcotic Addict in the U. S.," *Social Forces,* 45, no. 1 [1966], pp. 68–72).

24. The California state legislature had preceded this action with a bill in 1872 to outlaw the administration of a narcotic drug to any person where there was intent to facilitate commission of a felony. Possession of the drug, smoking, or the operation of an opium den were made illegal in Arizona and Californaia in the early 1880s. Nevada prohibited the retail sale of opiates for nonmedical purposes in 1877. Data from Richard J. Bonnie and Charles H. Whitebread II, "The Forbidden Fruit and the Tree of Knowledge: An Inquiry into the Legal History of American Marijuana Prohibition," *Virginia Law Review,* 56, 6 (October 1970), 970–71.

25. Loewen, *Mississippi Chinese,* p. 23.

26. For a useful summary of historical material, see Edna Bonacich, "A Theory of Ethnic Antagonism: The Split Labor Market," *American Sociological Review,* 37, no. 5 (October 1972), 547–49. "To be split, a labor market must contain at least two groups of workers whose price of labor differs for the same work, or would differ if they did the same work. The concept 'price of labor' refers to labor's total cost to the employer, including not

only wages, but the cost of recruitment, transportation, room and board, education, health care, and the costs of labor unrest," p. 549.

27. *Social, Moral and Political Effect of Chinese Immigration,* p. 19.
28. Kane, *Opium-Smoking in America and China,* p. 3.
29. Seward, *Chinese Immigration,* pp. 217–22, 261–91.
30. Mayo-Smith, *Emigration and Immigration—A Study in Social Science,* New York: Scribner's, 1890, p. 244.
31. *Use of Opium and Traffic Therein,* p. 79.

CHAPTER 3. BLACKS AND COCAINE

1. The available history of drug use in those years and of narcotics policy appears almost completely divorced from the affairs of the rest of America. As a result, the forces which shaped that history are not easy to see. For general histories see Charles E. Terry and Mildred Pellens, *The Opium Problem,* New York: Bureau of Social Hygiene, 1928, reprint, Montclair, N. J.: Patterson Smith, 1970, chaps. 10–13; Rufus King, *The Drug Hang-Up, America's Fifty-Year Folly,* New York: Norton, 1972; David Musto, *The American Disease: Origins of Narcotic Control,* New Haven: Yale University Press, 1973. An article by Musto, "The American Anti-Narcotic Movement: Clinical Research and Public Policy," in *Clinical Research,* 29, 3 (1971), 601–605, is an unanalytical but useful account of the role of the medical profession in the early years of the Harrison Act; the thesis by James W. Hughes, *The American Medical Profession and the Narcotics Policy Controversy,* Ph.D. diss., Indiana Univ., 1967, covers similar ground over a longer time span and is equally uninformative on the deeper roots, though it is descriptively worthwhile. There is a comparable study of the legal history: Richard J. Bonnie and Charles H. Whitebread, II, "The Forbidden Fruit and the Tree of Knowledge: An Inquiry into the Legal History of American Marijuana Prohibition," *Virginia Law Review,* 56, 6 (October 1970), 971–1,220. There is no adequate, or even approximate, study of the narcotics enforcement bureaucracy; Laurence F. Schmeckebier, *The Bureau of Prohibition, Its History, Activities and Organization,* Washington, D. C.: Brookings Institution, 1929, is a simpleminded manual of the government's approaches; Arnold H. Taylor, *American Diplomacy and the Narcotics Traffic, 1900–1939,* Durham: Duke Univ. Press, 1969, has limited relevance for an understanding of the domestic situation.
2. See James Harvey Young, *The Toadstool Millionaires, A Social History of Patent Medicines in America Before Regulation,* Princeton: Princeton Univ. Press, 1961, pp. 228ff.
3. *Ibid.,* p. 161.
4. See Terry and Pellens, *The Opium Problem,* pp. 631ff, 745.

5. Quoted by Terry and Pellens, p. 750.
6. Wright, pp. 50–51.
7. *Ibid.*, p. 48.
8. For a full account see Musto, "American Anti-Narcotic Movement."
9. *Ibid.*, p. 604.
10. Quoted by Hughes, *American Medical Profession*, p. 20.
11. The case was *Ex parte Yung Jon* (1886); judgement quoted by Bonnie and Whitebread, "Forbidden Fruit," p. 997.
12. *Ibid.*, pp. 999ff.
13. Both quotations, *ibid.*, p. 1,003.
14. Terry and Pellens, pp. 757ff.
15. Brooks Adams (1913), quoted by Bonnie and Whitebread, "Forbidden Fruit," p. 1,009.
16. Terry and Pellens, p. 478. The same judge, Justice Collins, told a New York State joint legislative committee in 1916: "from my observation I would say it is the young men generally who are affected," *New York Times*, December 6, 1916, p. 6.
17. Bloedorn, "Studies of Drug Addicts," *United States Naval Medical Bulletin*, 11, no. 3 (1917), 315–16.
18. Kane, *Opium-Smoking in America and China*, p. 2.
19. In a 1924 survey of the published data on addiction, Kolb and DuMez raised an objection to extrapolating from New York City data to the situation throughout the country. They argued that this data overstated the youth of addicts because "young addicts are attracted to large cities, and conditions exist in them which cause a delinquent type of addiction, and it is also due in part to the fact that some of the older addicts were being taken care of (privately) by physicians and were not counted when the survey was made"; Lawrence Kolb and A. G. DuMez, "The Prevalence and Trend of Drug Addiction in the United States and Factors Influencing It," *Public Health Reports*, 39, no. 21 (May 23, 1924), p. 1,188. The claim that there was an unusual increase in adolescent drug use at this time must therefore be restricted to cross-time comparisons within the city of New York.
20. Bloedorn, "Studies of Drug Addicts," pp. 313–15.
21. Quoted by Lauretta Bender, "Drug Addiction in Adolescence," *Comprehensive Psychiatry*, 4, no. 3 (June 1963), 183.
22. Lichtenstein, "Narcotic Addiction," *New York Medical Journal* (November 14, 1914), p. 962.
23. *Ibid.*, p. 964. Lichtenstein was one of those who subscribed to the pusher theory of contagion, according to which drug pushers created a demand for the drug by giving it away free or in candy to school children. No evidence for this was or ever has been offered and substantiated. Cf. Terry and Pellens, *Opium Problem*, p. 481.
24. *New York Times*, December 5, 1916, p. 4.
25. Although no data of this type exist, I would guess that the high rates of

unemployment for teenagers that prevailed in 1914 and 1915 would have stimulated both drug use and the decision to enlist in the military. General unemployment rates for all persons 14 or over for 1914 and 1915 were 8 and 9.7 percent, respectively—almost double the average rate from 1910 to 1913; *Historical Statistics of the United States,* p. 73.

26. Review of article by S. R. Leaky, "Some Observations on Heroin Habitués," *United States Naval Medical Bulletin,* 10 (1916), pp. 129–30, published in *New York State Hospital Bulletin* (August 1915).

27. Kolb and DuMez, "Prevalence and Trend of Drug Addiction," p. 1,181.

28. *Ibid.,* p. 1,186.

29. *Ibid.,* p. 1,185.

30. King, "Use of Habit-Forming Drugs," p. 274.

31. Toward the end of the war, when the draft was first introduced, the prevalence of drug use came to light even more dramatically. In a report released by the New York City Parole Commission, approximately 8,000 men between 21 and 31 years of age were rejected from the call-up in New York because of alleged drug addiction, and a total of 80,000 men were rejected out of the draft of 1918 nationwide. *New York Times,* April 15, 1919, p. 24.

32. "I believe I am correct in saying that I can now name four interior ports and several points along the Mexican border in which distinctive 'epidemics' of drug using have occurred since 1912"; King, "Use of Habit-Forming Drugs," pp. 383–84. Since it was well known that heroin had been developed by German chemists, the patriotic fervor of the war years made current the notion that drug addiction was being spread in the United States by enemy agents; see *The Drug Hang-Up,* p. 25.

33. Bloedorn, "Studies of Drug Addicts," p. 309.

34. Lichtenstein, "Narcotic Addiction," p. 964.

35. *Ibid.,* p. 964.

36. *New York Times,* July 15, 1914, p. 18.

37. *Ibid.,* June 24, 1914, p. 6. This article is especially interesting, for it summarizes the confession of Annie Goldstein, a dealer who turned state's evidence against her lover and his associates. His name was James Blutier and his occupation was that of a truck driver. He had begun his career as a cocaine dealer in an operation run by Jack Sirocco in the Bowery. But Blutier broke away to set up for himself, and, according to Goldstein, the two did well. It was not uncommon for them to make $35 a day. After all expenses were paid, they were saving $600 a year of the proceeds.

38. See, for example, Troy Duster, *The Legislation of Morality, Law, Drugs and Moral Judgment,* New York: Free Press, 1970; Bonnie and Whitebread, pp. 981ff: Patricia M. Wald et al., *Dealing with Drug Abuse: A Report to the Ford Foundation,* New York: Praeger, 1972.

39. J. M. Hull, in *Biennial Report of the State Board of Health of Iowa* (1885), summarized in Terry and Pellens, pp. 16–18, 99.

40. O. Marshall, "The Opium Habit in Michigan," in *Annual Report, Michigan State Board of Health* (1878), *ibid.*, pp. 9–16, 96–97.
41. E. G. Eberle, "Report of Committee on Acquirement of Drug Habits," *American Journal of Pharmacology* (October 1903), *ibid.*, p. 23.
42. Wright, p. 49.
43. Lichtenstein, "Narcotic Addiction," p. 962.
44. Dr. Jackson R. Campbell, in *New York Times*, December 6, 1916, p. 6.
45. Wright, p. 50.
46. Lawrence Kolb, "Drug Addiction in Its Relation to Crime," *Journal of Mental Hygiene*, 9, no. 1 (January 1925), 88.
47. Major Sylvester, in a letter quoted by the *Reports of the President's Homes Commission*, 61st Congress, 1st Sess., 1909; Senate Document #644, p. 255.
48. Statement by Dr. Lyman F. Kebler, chief of the Division of Drugs, Bureau of Chemistry, U. S. Department of Agriculture, as quoted in the Homes Commission Report, p. 254; also quoted (though without acknowledgement) by Wright, p. 48.
49. *New York Times*, August 1, 1914, p. 16.
50. William M. Tuttle, Jr., *Race Riot, Chicago in the Red Summer of 1919*, New York: Atheneum, 1970, pp. 22–31.
51. Green, "Psychoses Among Negroes—A Comparative Study," *Journal of Nervous and Mental Disease*, 41 (1914), 697–708. It may be of interest that the psychoses attributed to a larger population of blacks than whites were schizophrenia and manic-depressive syndrome.
52. *Ibid.*, pp. 701–702.
53. *Reports of the President's Homes Commission*, pp. 252, 254.
54. *Ibid.*, p. 255. The date this was written was December 1908.
55. Wright, p. 50.
56. *Reports of the President's Homes Commission*, p. 210.
57. W. E. B. DuBois, ed., *The Negro American Family*, (originally published in 1909), Cambridge: MIT Press, 1970, pp. 111–122.
58. John C. Kennedy et al., *A Study of Chicago's Stockyards Community III: Wages and Family Budgets in the Chicago Stockyards*, Chicago: Univ. of Chicago Press, 1914, p. 74.
59. Testimony of John C. Kennedy, in *Life and Labor Conditions of Chicago Stockyards Employees*, Final Report and Testimony, Commission on Industrial Relations, vol. 4, Washington, D. C.: U. S. Government Printing Office, 1916, pp. 3,468ff.
60. G. H. Weber, "Sociological Study of 1,251 Families," *Reports of the President's Homes Commission*, p. 288.
61. Lyman F. Kebler, "Soft Drinks Containing Caffeine and Extracts of Coca Leaf and Kola Nut," appendix, *Reports of the President's Homes Commission*, pp. 372–73, notes that some of the manufacturers of the drinks cited as containing extract of coca leaf claimed to use only the de-

cocainized leaf, a by-product of the manufacture of cocaine but without the drug's potent properties.

62. *Ibid.*, p. 372.
63. For example, Magistrate Simms of the Yorkville District Court, New York, in *New York Times,* December 15, 1916, p. 19.
64. Wright, p. 49.
65. Wright, p. 33. These statistics may not be correct; Kolb and DuMez report that between 1908 and 1915, 962, 281 pounds were imported legally (smuggling began after the 1909 act), whereas for two years alone, 1908 and 1909, Wright gives the total imports as 1,733,770 pounds.
66. *New York Times,* May 6, 1915, p. 22.
67. *Ibid.,* May 27, 1919, p. 17.
68. For the role of the newspapers in the Washington riot in July 1919 see Arthur I. Waskow, *From Race Riot to Sit-In, 1919 and the 1960s,* Garden City: Doubleday, 1967, pp. 22–33.
69. Tuttle, *Race Riot,* pp. 22–23.
70. *New York Times,* October 19, 1919, p. 6. The reference here was to W. E. B. DuBois, editor of a radical black journal, *The Crisis,* and a Ph. D. graduate of Harvard.
71. Wright, p. 51.
72. See James Arthur Estey, *Business Cycles, Their Nature, Cause and Control,* Englewood Cliffs: Prentice-Hall, 1956, p. 20.
73. For the details, see Tuttle, *Race Riot,* Graham Adams, *The Age of Industrial Violence,* New York: Athenum, 1965; Jeremy Brecher, *Strike!,* San Francisco: Straight Arrow Books, 1972.

CHAPTER 4. MEXICANS AND MARIJUANA

1. Throughout this chapter the term *marijuana* refers to each and every preparation of *cannabis sativa,* or the hemp plant. Although a few early writers on the drug were acquainted with the Indian preparations known as *ganja, bhang* and *chores,* there was almost no awareness of the difference between them or between marijuana and hashish in pharmacological or psychological terms.
2. Dr. George F. Roeling, city coroner, had sent inquiries to the United States Dispensary and to the botanical division of the Department of Agriculture, which were fruitless. See A. E. Fossier, "The Marihuana Menace," *New Orleans Medical and Surgical Journal,* 84, no. 4 (October 1931), 250.
3. Washington, California, and Texas had felony laws; Mississippi, Louisiana, and Kansas had misdemeanor laws. For a full account see Bonnie and Whitebread, "Forbidden Fruit," pp. 1,010–20.
4. Paul Livingstone Warnshuis, "Crime and Criminal Justice Among the

Mexicans of Illinois," part 3, section 3 of *Report on Crime and the For-eign Born*, report no. 10, *National Commission on Law Observance and Enforcement*, Washington, D. C.: U. S. Government Printing Office, 1931, p. 281. Hereafter cited as *Crime and the Foreign Born*.

5. Quoted by David Musto, "The Marihuana Tax of 1937," *Archives of General Psychiatry*, 26 (February 1972), 104. Anslinger had insisted ear-lier, in 1932, on the reintroduction of marijuana as a "narcotic drug" to the draft provisions of the Uniform Narcotic Drug Act which was passed by Congress in the same year. See Bonnie and Whitebread, "Forbidden Fruit," pp. 1,030–34.

6. King, *Drug Hang-Up*, p. 75.

7. Musto, "Marihuana Tax," p. 105. Let it be noted that 1936 was a presi-dential election year.

8. *Ibid.*, p. 105; Bonnie and Whitebread, "Forbidden Fruit," p. 1,037. Mus-to, who wrote two years after Bonnie and Whitebread, appears to have been unaware of their article, as was I when the first draft of this chapter was composed.

9. Sources for these figures are the *Fifteenth Census of the United States: 1930*, vol. 1, pp. 149, 153; vol. 3, part 1, Table 17; and the *Sixteenth Cen-sus of the United States: 1940*, vol. 2, part 1, pp. 711, 718, 743.

10. Cf. Paul S. Taylor, *Mexican Labor in the United States: II. Valley of the South Platte*, Univ. of California Publications in Economics, 6, no. 2, (1929). Also, in the first volume of this work, Taylor provides estimates for harvest labor requirements for various crops and by each month of the year. See *Mexican Labor in the United States Imperial Valley*, Univ. of California Publications in Economics, 6, no. 1, (1928), p. 36.

11. For the details of nativity and country of birth of the foreign-born resi-dents of the county, see *Fifteenth Census*, vol. 3, part 1, Table 17.

12. See the *Annual Report of the Secretary of the Treasury* for fiscal years 1938, 1939, 1940: Report of the Bureau of Narcotics.

13. H. J. Anslinger and William F. Tompkins, *The Traffic in Narcotics*, New York: Funk and Wagnalls, 1953, pp. 18–26.

14. *Sixteenth Census*, vol. 2, part 1, p. 743.

15. The crusade of the Rowells may be mentioned in this context as forming popular ideas about the drug without any predisposing experience of the "Mexican problem." See Earl A. and Robert Rowell, *On the Trail of Ma-rijuana, the Weed of Madness*, Mountain View, Cal.: Pacific Press, 1939.

16. Although marijuana is not regarded as a narcotic drug today, it was con-sidered so during the Depression. When the Marijuana Tax Act was intro-duced in Congress, the following exchange occurred:

Mr. Snell. *What is the bill?*

Mr. Rayburn. *It has something to do with something that is called marihuana. I believe it is a narcotic of some kind.*

Quoted by Bonnie and Whitebread, "Forbidden Fruit," p. 971. For the text of the Marihuana Tax Act see the *Annual Report of the Secretary of the Treasury for the Fiscal Year Ended June 30, 1938,* Washington, D. C., 1938, Exhibit 43, pp. 275–79.

17. Immigration statistics are a poor measure of the actual numbers of Mexicans moving into the United States in any particular period. This is because an uncounted number did not register at a border station or paid no head tax, worked only temporarily in the United States, and then moved back home. These statistics are, however, a useful guide to the *relative magnitude* of population movements from period to period. For an early analysis of these statistics and their problems, see Paul S. Taylor, *Mexican Labor in the United States Migration Statistics,* vols. 1–3. Volume 1 was published as *University of California Publications in Economics,* 6, no. 3, (1929); Volumes 2 and 3 appeared in the same series, 12, nos. 1 and 2 (1933).

18. Between 1916 and 1917 agricultural wages in California rose by 40 percent, and losses of crops were reported in the state for lack of labor to harvest them. Before recruiting Mexicans, the state's agriculturalists tried raising a work force from among women, children on school vacation, and convicts. Drinking saloons were closed and antivagrancy laws were stiffly enforced. See Vanden Fuller, *The Supply of Agricultural Labor as a Factor in the Evolution of Farm Organization in California,* printed in Hearings before a Subcommittee of the Committee on Education and Labor, United States Senate, 66th Congress, 3rd Session, 1940, *Violations of Free Speech and Rights of Labor,* Part 54, Exhibit 8762-A, pp. 19,847ff.

19. Carey McWilliams, *North from Mexico, the Spanish-Speaking People of the United States,* New York: Monthly Review Press, 1948 and 1961, p. 181.

20 Fuller, *Supply of Agricultural Labor,* pp. 19,854, 19,865. See also Musto, "Marihuana Tax of 1937," pp. 103–104.

21. *Ibid.*

22. *Sixteenth Census,* vol. 2, p. 41ff. See also, Fuller, *Supply of Agricultural Labor,* p. 19,852.

23. Max Sylvius Handman, *Preliminary Report on Nationality and Delinquency: The Mexican in Texas,* in *Crime and the Foreign Born,* part 3, section 2, p. 250.

24. *Ibid.,* p. 254.

25. *Ibid.,* pp. 256–57.

26. Paul S. Taylor, *Crime and the Foreign Born: The Problem of the Mexican,* in *Crime and the Foreign Born,* part 3, section 1, pp. 218–19.

27. In 1930 Colorado had just over 4 percent of the Mexicans in the United States; in terms of state population they amounted to 5.6 percent of the total.

28. Taylor, *Crime and the Foreign Born,* pp. 216–17.

29. Table appears in Fuller, *Supply of Agricultural Labor*, p. 19,860. Source of data: United States Department of Agriculture, *Crops and Markets*, monthly supplement.
30. *Mexicans in California, Report of Governor C. C. Young's Mexican Fact-Finding Committee*, orig. San Francisco: State Printing Office, 1930, reprint, San Francisco: R&E Research Associates, 1970, p. 168. This section of the report summarizes questionnaire responses to a query about the effect putting the Mexicans on a quota basis would have.
31. Taylor, *Imperial Valley*, p. 31.
32. Fuller, *Supply of Agricultural Labor*, p. 19,861.
33. For a valuable analysis of Japanese farming methods and economic organization, see Ivan H. Light, *Ethnic Enterprise in America: Business and Welfare Among Chinese, Japanese and Blacks*, Berkeley: Univ. of California Press, 1972, pp. 72–78.
34. Taylor, *Mexican Labor in the Imperial Valley*, pp. 70–71.
35. Quoted by Fuller, *Supply of Agricultural Labor*, p. 19,864.
36. Taylor, *Crime and the Foreign Born*, p. 212.
37. The sheer physical and social isolation enforced on Mexicans when they lived in California made a custom such as smoking marijuana more or less invisible to the Anglo population until other factors led to the belief that the drug, in fact, encouraged its users to cross racial boundaries and attack whites.
38. See H. M. Lai, "A Historical Survey of Organizations of the Left Among the Chinese in America," *Bulletin of the Committee of Concerned Asian Scholars*, 4, no. 3 (Fall 1972), p. 11.
39. See Light, *Ethnic Enterprise in America*, pp. 72–78.
40. For an account of the ruthless profiteering involved in the labor contract system for Mexicans, see McWilliams, *North from Mexico*, "Coyotes and Man-Snatchers," pp. 178–79. Among the native American unions in the 1920s, only the socialist International Workers of the World did not bar Mexicans from membership.
41. Taylor, *Mexican Labor in the Imperial Valley*, pp. 61–64.
42. The first labor unions established among Mexicans were chapters of the Confederacion de Uniones Obreras Mexicanas which began in November 1927 in Los Angeles, also at the initiative of the mutual aid associations. At the first convention of this group in May 1928, 24 unions were represented from all over the United States.
43. For comparable, if biased, accounts see Taylor, *Mexican Labor in the Imperial Valley*, pp. 45–54; *Mexicans in California*, pp. 135–150.
44. Taylor, *Mexican Labor in the Imperial Valley*, p. 41.
45. Fuller, *Supply of Agricultural Labor*, p. 19,874.
46. *Ibid.*, p. 19,866; and Max Sylvius Handman, "Economic Reasons for the Coming of the Mexican Immigrant," *American Journal of Sociology*, 35, no. 4 (January 1930), 601–11.

47. *Brawley News,* April 15, 1930, quoted by Paul S. Taylor and Clark Kerr, "Documentary History of the Strike of the Cotton Pickers in California 1933," in *Violation of Free Speech and Rights of Labor,* p. 19,953. This is an excellent source for the details of labor strife in the early Depression years in California.

48. Quoted by M. H. Hayes and L. E. Bowery, "Marihuana," *Journal of Criminal Law and Criminology,* 23, no. 6 (March-April 1933), 1,071, 1,088.

49. Vernon Monroe McCombs, *From Over the Border, A Study of the Mexicans in the United States,* New York: Council of Women for Home Missions and Missionary Education Movement, 1925, reprint (San Francisco: R&E Research Associates, 1970), p. 36.

50. Taylor, *Crime and the Foreign Born: The Problem of the Mexican,* p. 205.

51. *Ibid.*

52. Robert M. Fogelson, *The Fragmented Metropolis, Los Angeles, 1850–1930,* Cambridge: Harvard Univ. Press, 1967, pp. 76–79.

53. *Mexicans in California,* pp. 97–121.

54. Jacqueline Rorabeck Kasun, *Some Social Aspects of Business Cycles in the Los Angeles Area, 1920–1950,* Los Angeles: Haynes Foundation, 1954, pp. 96–97.

55. *Mexicans in California,* p. 186.

56. McCombs, *From Over the Border,* p. 36.

57. *Ibid.,* p. 37.

58. Computed by Kasun, *Social Aspects of Business Cycles,* p. 122.

59. *Ibid.,* pp. 120–21.

60. *Ibid.,* p. 135.

61. Paul S. Taylor, *Crime and the Foreign Born: Stockton, California,* in *Crime and the Foreign Born,* part 4, section 3, p. 380. "In commenting upon the use of marijuana, our informant said that its use was not extensive and was usually limited to unmarried men working under unendurable conditions who used it to relieve the dreariness of their existence," p. 381. Only 3.3 percent of all offenses involving Mexicans in Stockton were for violations of the State Poison Act (marijuana).

62. *Mexicans in California,* pp. 123ff.

63. Taylor, *Crime and the Foreign Born: Stockton, California,* pp. 379–81.

64. Taylor, *Crime and the Foreign Born: The Problem of the Mexican,* p. 243.

65. See Kasun, *Social Aspects of Business Cycles,* p. 32.

66. Quoted by McWilliams, *North from Mexico,* p. 193.

67. Leo Grebler et al., *The Mexican-American People: The Nation's Second Largest Minority,* New York: The Free Press, 1970, p. 538.

68. McWilliams, *North from Mexico,* p. 193.

69. Emory S. Bogardus, "Repatriation and Adjustment," in Manuel P. Servin, *The Mexican-Americans: An Awakening Minority,* Beverly Hills: Glencoe Press, 1972, p. 90.

70. McWilliams, *North from Mexico*, p. 193.
71. The text of a resolution adopted at the convention of the Confederacion de Uniones Obreras Mexicanas, Los Angeles, May 1928. See *Mexicans in California*, pp. 125, 127.
72. The California State Narcotic Committee did acknowledge the qualitative difference between marijuana and the drugs we are accustomed today to calling narcotics, even if few police officers or ordinary citizens realized this. "Fortunately," the committee reported in 1931, marijuana "will never be as serious a problem as the narcotic drugs, because it is not cumulative in its effect and the sudden discontinuance of its use produces no withdrawal symptoms"; quoted by Taylor, *Crime and the Foreign Born: The Problem of the Mexican*, p. 205.
73. E. Stanley, in *American Journal of Police Science*, 2 (1931), 252.
74. Bonnie and Whitebread, "Forbidden Fruit," pp. 1,026, 1,044.
75. A. E. Fossier (with comments by others), "The Marihuana Menace," *New Orleans Medical and Surgical Journal*, 84, no. 4 (October 1931), 247–52.
76. *Ibid.*, p. 250.
77. *Ibid.*, p. 249.
78. *Ibid.*, p. 250. For a more elaborate and quasi-empirical version of this, see Hayes and Bowery, "Marihuana," p. 1,092.
79. F. F. Young, "The Marihuana Menace," p. 251.
80. *Ibid.*, p. 251.
81. Anslinger and Tompkins, *Traffic in Narcotics*, p. 283.
82. Jesse F. Steiner, *Crime and the Foreign Born: New Orleans*, in *Crime and the Foreign Born*, part 4, section 1, p. 337.
83. Kasun, *Social Aspects of Business Cycles*, pp. 127–34.
84. Steiner, *Crime and the Foreign Born: New Orleans*, p. 336.
85. Musto, "Marihuana Tax of 1937," p. 102.
86. Steiner, *Crime and the Foreign Born: New Orleans*, pp. 341–42.
87. *Ibid.*, p. 344.
88. Walter Bromberg, "Marihuana Intoxication: A Clinical Study of Cannabis Sativa Intoxication," *American Journal of Psychiatry*, 91, no. 2 (September 1934), 303–30. Bromberg identified marijuana use as being most common among Puerto Ricans, Mexicans, and blacks (p. 307). He was one of the early proponents of the view that the use of marijuana may lead to heavier drugs such as heroin. Commissioner Anslinger frequently resorted to this view when challenged to demonstrate the harmfulness of marijuana per se. See Anslinger and Tompkins, *Traffic in Narcotics*, p. 168.
89. *Sixteenth Census*, vol. 2, pp. 67ff.: *Historical Statistics of the United States*, p. 47.
90. Perry H. Howard, *Political Tendencies in Louisiana*, rev. ed., Baton Rouge: Louisiana State Univ. Press, 1971, pp. 243–50. For general back-

ground see George M. Reynolds, *Machine Politics in New Orleans, 1897–1926,* New York: Columbia Univ. Press, 1936.

91. *Montana Standard,* January 27, 1929; quoted by Bonnie and Whitebread, "Forbidden Fruit," p. 1,014.
92. Quoted from the Tax Act Hearings by Bonnie and Whitebread, *ibid.,* p. 1,055.

CHAPTER 5. RACE OR CLASS, 1949–1953

1. Patricia M. Wald et al., *Dealing with Drug Abuse: A Report to the Ford Foundation,* New York: Praeger, p. 4. In terms of arrests, only between 1950 and 1960 did blacks outnumber whites.
2. According to the 1970 Census there are still more blacks in the South (nearly 12 million) than the total from all other regions combined, and it is likely to stay that way. For a discussion of the Southern pattern of addiction predominant among whites, see John C. Ball, "Two Patterns of Narcotic Drug Addiction in the United States," *Journal of Criminal Law, Criminology and Police Science,* 56, no. 2 (June 1965), 203–11; William M. Bates, "Narcotics, Negroes and the South," *Social Forces,* 45, no. 1 (September 1966), 61–67.
3. J. D. Roberts, "Opium Habit in the Negro," *North Carolina Medical Journal,* 16 (1885), 207.
4. *Ibid.*
5. Green, "Psychoses Among Negroes—A Comparative Study," *Journal of Nervous and Mental Disease,* 41 (1914), p. 110.
6. Charles E. Terry and Mildred Pellens, *The Opium Problem,* New York: Bureau of Social Hygiene, 1928, p. 25.
7. Lucius P. Brown, "Enforcement of the Tennessee Anti-Narcotic Laws," reprinted in John A. O'Donnell and John C. Ball, eds., *Narcotic Addiction,* New York: Harper & Row, 1966.
8. According to the survey of physicians reported in *Traffic in Narcotic Drugs,* Report of the Special Committee of Investigation, U. S. Department of the Treasury: Washington, D. C., 1919. It is also confirmed by reports on the major narcotics clinics in operation in the early 1920s; for example, see the report on the Shreveport (La.) Clinic by Willis P. Butler, *American Medicine,* 17 (1922), pp. 154–162. In 1923 the Bureau of the Census carried out an extensive survey of all prisoners and commitments to penal institutions throughout the country. By this time, *and for this category of drug offender* (including marijuana offenders), the Middle Atlantic, Mountain, and Pacific states had supplanted the Southern states in their totals. Expressed as rates per 100,000 population, the Pacific states (primarily California) led the country with 11.1 commitments for drug offenses; the Middle Atlantic states (primarily New York) fol-

lowed with 5.2; in contrast, the Southwest region had a rate of 1.3. See Bureau of the Census, *Prisoners, 1923: Crime Conditions in the United States as Reflected in Census Statistics of Imprisoned Offenders*, Washington, D.C., 1926, p. 41.

9. Kolb and DuMez, "The Prevalence and Trend of Drug Addiction in the United States and Factors Influencing It," *Public Health Reports*, 39, no. 21 (May 23, 1924), p. 1,184.

10. Green, "Psychoses Among Negroes," p. 702.

11. *Sources*:

> 1913—C. E. Terry, *Annual Report of the Board of Health, Jacksonville, Florida*, 1913, quoted by Terry and Pellens, *The Opium Problem*, p. 25.

> 1915—L. P. Brown, "Enforcement of the Tennessee Anti-Narcotic Law," *American Journal of Public Health*, 5, no. 4 (1915), quoted by Terry and Pellens, *The Opium Problem*, pp. 27–29.

> 1919–20—S. Dana Hubbard, "The New York City Narcotic Clinic and Differing Points of View on Narcotic Addiction," *Monthly Bulletin of the Department of Health, City of New York* (February 1920), reprinted in *Illicit Narcotics Traffic*, Hearings Before the Subcommittee on Improvements in the Federal Criminal Code, Committee on the Judiciary, U.S. Senate, 84th Congress, 1st Sess. (September 1955), part 5, p. 1,719 (hereafter cited as *Daniel Hearings*).

> 1926—Percent distribution of male prisoners received in federal and state prisons and reformatories during 1926 by race and nativity and by offense: Alida C. Bowler, "Recent Statistics on Crime and the Foreign Born," in *Crime and the Foreign Born*, part 2, p. 153.

> 1928—Arrests, drug offenses, California Narcotic Division: Paul S. Taylor, "Crime and the Foreign Born: The Problem of the Mexican," in *Crime and the Foreign Born*, part 3, p. 206.

> 1929—Walter L. Treadway, "Further Observations on the Epidemiology of Narcotic Drug Addiction," *Public Health Reports*, 44, no. 45 (1929), 2,702–2,704.

> 1930—Walter L. Treadway, "Further Observations on the Epidemiology of Narcotic Drug Addiction," *Public Health Reports*, 45, no. 11 (1930), 541–53.

> 1935(1)—Arrests, Federal Bureau of Narcotics: *Traffic in Opium and Other Dangerous Drugs*, U. S. Treasury Department (1936), quoted by Alan S. Meyers, ed., *Social and Psychological Factors in Opiate Addiction*, New York: Bureau of Applied Social Research, Columbia Univ. (1959), p. 33.

> 1935(2)—Arrests, drug offenses, California Senate Interim Narcotic Committee, *A Report on Drug Addiction in California* (1936), quoted by Meyers, p. 34.

1930—36—Sample derived from a variety of institutional and police sources: Bingham Dai, *Opiate Addiction in Chicago*, Shanghai: Commercial Press, 1937.

1931–36—Records of 300 male addicts in Detroit House of Corrections: Edward C. Jandy and Maurice Bloch, *Narcotic Addiction as a Factor in Petty Larceny in Detroit*, Detroit: Bureau of Governmental Research, 1937, Report #145. Quoted in Meyers, *Social and Psychological Factors*, p. 35.

12. Royal S. Copeland, "The Narcotic Drug Evil and the New York City Health Department," *American Medicine*, 15 (January 1920); reprinted in *Daniel Hearings*, p. 1,707.

13. Hubbard said: "Cocaine was distributed on the first day the clinic operated, but on ascertaining the fact regarding its effect on the individual [depressive], it was immediately discontinued and not again prescribed or dispensed," *Daniel Hearings*, p. 1,715.

14. A third usable source of time series statistics is the Census of Prisoners compiled for 1923 and then from 1926 through 1946 by the Bureau of the Census. The annual publication was titled *Prisoners in State and Federal Prisons and Reformatories*.

15. Computed from figures supplied as Exhibit 8, *Daniel Hearings*, pp. 272–75.

16. *Daniel Hearnings*, p. 30.

17. Alfred R. Lindesmith, *The Addict and the Law*, Bloomington: Indiana Univ. Press (1965), pp. 122–24.

18. *Ibid.*, p. 121.

19. Ortiz M. Walton, *Music: Black, White and Blue*, New York: William Morrow, 1972, p. 98.

20. *Race Riot*, p. 104.

21. David Katzman, personal communication, November 13, 1972.

22. Testimony of Harry J. Anslinger, *Daniel Hearings*, p. 10.

23. In 1954, 85 percent of narcotics violators arrested by the Chicago police were repeat offenders. See the testimony of Lt. Joseph J. Healy (Narcotics Bureau, C. P. D.) in *Daniel Hearings*, p. 4,252.

24. *The Kefauver Committee Report on Organized Crime* [Report of The Special Senate Committee to Investigate Organized Crime in Interstate Commerce], New York: Didier, 1951, p. 146.

25. FBN figures for 1954 indicated that among reported addicts, 35 percent were from New York State, 27 percent from Illinois, and 9 percent from California, for a total share of 71 percent. Arrests were somewhat differently distributed, but these states alone shared 66 percent of the national total; *Daniel Hearings*, p. 110.

26. *Ibid.*, p. 1,643.

27. *Ibid.*

28. Joseph L. Coyle, "The Illicit Narcotics Problem," *New York Medicine*, 14 (1958), 528.

29. *Daniel Hearings,* p. 10.
30. Terranova, p. 81.
31. Isidor Chein et al., *The Road to H: Narcotics, Delinquency and Social Policy,* New York: Basic Books, 1964, p. 32. According to Dr. Harold Jacobziner, assistant commissioner of health in New York City, no cases of narcotics use were known to the school health service until the summer of 1950. "The epidemic reached its peak in May 1951 and then gradually abated toward the end of the school year." Thirty percent of the cases surveyed by Jacobziner were aged 16; 60 percent were 16 or older. Among 754 schools surveyed, drug use was concentrated in the vocational high schools; three schools alone were responsible for 54 percent of all cases, and over 25 percent came from just one school. See Harold Jacobziner, "Epidemic of Narcotic Use Among Schoolchildren in New York City," *Journal of Pediatrics,* 42 no. 1 (January 1953), 65–74.
32. Chein et al., *Road to H,* p. 39.
33. *Ibid.,* pp. 57–65.
34. *Ibid.,* p. 73.
35. Testimony of Lt. Joseph J. Healy, Narcotics Bureau, Chicago Police Department, *Daniel Hearings,* p. 4,256.
36. Solomon Kobrin and Harold Finestone, *Drug Addiction Among Young Persons in Chicago, A Report of a Study of the Prevalence, Incidence, Distribution and Character of Drug Use and Addiction in Chicago During the Years, 1947–53,* in James F. Short, ed., *Gang Delinquency and Delinquent Subcultures,* New York: Harper & Row, 1968, p. 113.
37. Dr. Edward Kelleher, testimony given before a meeting of the Legislative Committee of the Chicago Crime Prevention Bureau, printed in *Control of Narcotics, Marihuana and Barbiturates,* Hearings before a Subcommittee of the Committee on Ways and Means, U.S. House of Representatives, 82nd Congress, 1st Session, April 1951, p. 100. This will be cited hereafter as *Boggs Hearings.*
38. *Daniel Hearings,* p. 4,238.
39. *Daniel Hearings,* pp. 4,295–96.
40. Testimony of Peter Grosso, assistant state's attorney for Cook County, *Daniel Hearings,* p. 4,297.
41. *Daniel Hearings,* p. 4,252.
42. *Ibid.,* pp. 4,247–48.
43. Kobrin and Finestone, p. 114.
44. Chein *et al.,* p. 123.
45. Kobrin and Finestone, p. 115.
46. *Daniel Hearings,* p. 4,227.
47. Kobrin and Finestone, *Drug Addiction,* p. 115.
48. *Report on Organized Crime,* p. 146.
49. *Ibid.,* p. 131.

50. *Ibid.*, pp. 19, 63, 130, 148–49.
51. *Ibid.*, p. 149.
52. *Ibid.*, p. 147.
53. *Boggs Hearings,* p. 48.
54. Of all cases brought to court, the national conviction rate was 89 percent, imprisonment in 69 percent of all cases, and an average sentence of 21.9 months. In Louisiana (eastern division) the corresponding figures were 94 percent, 85 percent, and 24.7 months. From *1950 Narcotic Violations,* data supplied by the Administrative Office of the United States Courts, *Boggs Hearings,* p. 109.
55. See testimony of Sheriff Frank J. Clancy, Hearings Before the Special Committee to Investigate Organized Crime in Interstate Commerce, U.S. Senate, 82nd Congress, 1st Session, Part 8 (Louisiana), January–February 1951, p. 413. Hereafter cited as *Kefauver Hearings (Louisiana).*
56. *Ibid.*, p. 427.
57. *Political Tendencies in Louisiana,* pp. 280–87.
58. *Report on Organized Crime,* p. 128.
59. In the end he lost, but more successful was Senator Price Daniel, chairman of the Senate narcotics hearings in 1955. He ran for governor of Texas the year after the hearings and won.
60. Testimony of Mrs. Lois Higgins of the Crime Prevention Bureau, Chicago, *Boggs Hearings,* p. 104.
61. Testimony of Congressman Sidney R. Yates, *ibid.*, p. 44; see also pp. 1, 46.
62. *Ibid.*, p. 111.
63. *Ibid.*, p. 206.
64. *Ibid.*, p. 53.
65. *Ibid.*, p. 59.
66. *Ibid.*, p. 208.
67. The one exception occurs in the testimony of Dr. Harris Isbell, director of research at the Public Health Service hospital at Lexington: "in recent years the increase has been particularly bad among the colored population in the large cities in the East and Middle West," *Boggs Hearings,* p. 202.
68. *Ibid.*, p. 203.
69. *Daniel Hearings,* pp. 657, 4,184; *Treatment and Rehabilitation of Juvenile Drug Addicts,* p. 81.
70. Cf. testimony of FBN agent, James C. Ryan, in *Daniel Hearings,* p. 796.
71. *Boggs Hearings,* p. 56.
72. *Report on Organized Crime,* p. 149.
73. *Ibid.*
74. *Ibid.*, p. 203.
75. *Ibid.*, p. 84.

76. Text of Anslinger's remarks before Tenth Session of the UN Commission on Narcotic Drugs, April–May, 1955; reprinted in *Traffic in and Control of Narcotics, Barbiturates and Amphetamines*, Hearings before a subcommittee of the Committee on Ways and Means, U.S. House of Representatives, 84th Congress, October–December 1955, January 1956, pp. 200–203.

77. *Daniel Hearings*, pp. 205, 701, 771, 1,305.

78. *Ibid.*, p. 205.

79. Testimony of Robert A. Neeb, Jr., in *Treatment and Rehabilitation of Juvenile Drug Addicts*, p. 8.

80. See Alfred W. McCoy et al., *The Politics of Heroin in Southeast Asia*, New York: Harper & Row, 1972.

81. *Ibid.*, pp. 30–47.

82. See, for example, the case and testimony of Edward Y.T. Lin, *Daniel Hearings*, pp. 710–44. Lin was alleged to have been a Communist who organized a *tong* to cover heroin smuggling from Hong Kong.

83. Cited above as *Traffic in and Control of Narcotics, Barbiturates and Amphetamines* and *Treatment and Rehabilitation of Juvenile Drug Addicts*, respectively.

84. Copeland, "Narcotic Drug Evil," p. 1,707.

85. Even among the foreign-born white patients, the number of Jews was over 45 percent—assuming that those listing their nationality as Russian or Rumanian were in all likelihood Jewish. See Hubbard, p. 1,720, and Lichtenstein (1914), p. 964.

86. Hubbard, "New York City Narcotic Clinic," p. 1,720.

87. *Historical Statistics of the U.S., From Colonial Times to the Present*, p. 66. Statistics cover the United States as a whole.

88. Paul S. Taylor, "Mexican Labor in the United States, Chicago and the Calumet Region," *University of California Publications in Economics*, 7, no. 2 (1932), 40.

89. *Ibid.*, pp. 42–43.

90. Cf. Gerald Rosenblum, *Immigrant Workers, Their Impact on American Labor Radicalism*, New York: Basic Books, 1972.

91. Cf. Tuttle on the latent functions of the YMCA and the Urban League from 1917, pp. 98–102.

92. Thomas Vietorisz and Bennett Harrison, "A Theory of Sub-employment and the Labor Market," paper presented to annual meeting of the American Economic Association, Toronto, December 1972, p. 5. Cf. Edna Bonacich, "A Theory of Ethnic Antagonism: The Split Labor Market," *American Sociological Review*, 37, no. 5 (October 1972), 549.

93. Vietorisz and Harrison, "Theory of Sub-employment," passim.

94. Frank G. Davis, "Problems of Economic Growth in the Black Community: Some Alternative Hypotheses," *Review of Black Political Economy*, 4, no. 1 (1972), 75–107.

95. *Ibid.*, pp. 94–97.

96. Note that this was not true in 1940. That year unemployment was very high, at 14.6 percent, and the labor force participation rate of teenagers (male) was at the wartime low of 35.4 percent. At the same time, drug arrests (FBI series) shot up nearly 130 percent.

97. Quoted by Bonnie and Whitebread, "Forbidden Fruit," pp. 1,009–10.

98. For a discussion of theories as to why this is so, see Edward Kalachek, "Determinants of Teenage Employment," *Journal of Human Resources*, 4, no. 1 (1969), 3–4.

99. Robert I. Lerman, "Some Determinants of Youth School Activity," *Journal of Human Resources*, 7, no. 3 (1972). Also by the same author, "An Analysis of Youth Labor Force Participation, School Activity and Employment Rates, " Ph.D. thesis, MIT, 1970.

100. *Youth Unemployment and Minimum Wages*, U.S. Department of Labor, Bureau of Labor Statistics Bulletin No. 1657, Washington, D.C., 1970, pp. 4–29.

101. *Historical Statistics*, p. 71.

102. This describes the national situation. In New York and Chicago labor statistics for the period are not exactly comparable in age group. However, the evidence (for 16–26 year olds) clearly shows the same pattern—a rise in white participation and a decline in black.

103. A teenager cannot qualify for unemployment compensation unless he or she can show earnings of no less than $900 in the preceding 12 months. The only other option is welfare—either aid for dependent children or general relief—which is applied for and received by the individual's family. It is contingent not only on family cohesion and living together at this stage but on the individual's willingness to satisfy a complex system of registration and job search rules.

104. Another source of statistics on this, *Youth Unemployment and Minimum Wages*, p. 20, shows a steady increase in the gap between the black and white jobless rates between 1948 and 1951.

105. *Ibid.*, p. 19.

106. In 1949 there were more black families than white in New York earning up to $2,499, up by a factor of two. The difference was only a little less in Chicago.

107. *Youth Unemployment and Minimum Wages*, pp. 104–105. The data is for 1967.

108. From Chein (see Table 5–3) we can see that adding a specific race variable to his multiple correlation of economic (class) factors with drug use adds a very small amount to the variance explained—about 7 percent for Manhattan and none at all in the Bronx and Brooklyn. Eisner, who analyzed juvenile delinquency in general in San Francisco during the 1960s, found that most changes in time between racial or ethnic groups and their delinquency rates were due to demographic changes. See Victor Eisner, *The Delinquency Label: The Epidemiology of Juvenile Delinquency*, New York: Random House, 1970.

CHAPTER 6. VIETNAM

1. *Traffic in and Control of Narcotics, Barbiturates and Amphetamines* (October 1955–January 1956), p. 88.
2. Provisions of this kind were held unconstitutional by the U.S. Supreme Court in *Robinson* v. *California,* 1963.
3. *Traffic in and Control of Narcotics, Barbiturates and Amphetamines,* p. 1,230.
4. *Ibid.,* pp. 89–100.
5. *Ibid.,* p. 1,229.
6. *Ibid.,* p. 1,230.
7. *Ibid.,* p. 158.
8. The text of the original bill and related resolutions is printed at the beginning of the hearings document, *ibid.,* pp. 3–21.

An important but often overlooked provision in the legislation when it was first introduced was that it ordered a complete overhaul of the Bureau of Narcotics and substantially expanded its operating powers. The overhaul was planned under congressional authorization to transfer the organization from the Treasury Department, where it had been since the Harrison Act of 1914, to the Department of Justice. Undoubtedly this was looked for by Commissioner Anslinger in order to raise the status and appropriations of his unit on a par with the FBI. This was not just a matter of status and prestige but of manpower, money, and a degree of bureaucratic independence which the Bureau of Narcotics did not have in the Treasury where historically it had been overshadowed (and outreached at budget time), first by the Bureau of Prohibition and then by the Internal Revenue Service and Customs units.

Additional powers proposed for the federal narcotic agents by the legislation included the power to subpoena witnesses and records and to issue and execute search warrants, together with the right to carry firearms and make arrests without warrants so long as the agents had "reasonable grounds" for suspecting an offense had been committed. This last represented a big step in allowing the FBN to operate exactly as it wished, and in the reports on the legislation submitted to Congress by various departmental officials, no objections to this were raised on legal or any other grounds.

However, Justice, Treasury, and other agency representatives were united in opposing the transfer of the bureau. As Chapman Ross, the acting Treasury secretary, wrote in his report, "the federal narcotic laws are primarily revenue rather than police measures and the agency which administers them should be in the same department as the revenue agency" (*ibid.,* p. 16). This pointed up the fragile constitutional nature of the entire federal system of narcotics policy, which was indeed based on revenue or tax measures in the case of both the standard narcotics and marijuana. These, of course, had been written that way in order to provide the government with real police powers while sidestepping the big constitutional issue of whether self-administered, voluntary use of such drugs amounted to a crime.

To his superiors Commissioner Anslinger's ambitions looked likely to blow the cover on a legal subterfuge which had secured the government's drug legislation from the beginning.

This was just one of the chronic dilemmas confronting the policy makers on the drug issue. The legal rationale for a powerful police apparatus virtually denied that that was what it was, and the rationale for progressively increasing its powers, as had occurred at the end of each of the episodes we have looked at, was that the drug problem was getting out of hand. But since increased statutory power, as well as manpower, can result in increased arrest totals, and since the size of the addict population is figured from these, the problem may only *seem* to get worse, and a vicious cycle results. An improvement, as reportedly occurred in the late 1930s and early 1940s, can do the police organization no good either, for it is threatened with cutbacks appropriate to the diminished need for enforcement. Precisely this threat had faced the Bureau of Narcotics at the end of the war until Anslinger, with the help of Senator Kefauver and Congressman Boggs, was able to mobilize new public concern.

In any event, the plan to move the Bureau of Narcotics was dropped before the bill went to a vote. The loss was not complete, however, for the expanded powers passed intact.

Twelve years later, in 1968, the reorganization plan was finally implemented, the old Bureau of Narcotics becoming the Bureau of Narcotics and Dangerous Drugs (BNDD) within the Justice Department. The Treasury retained a portion of its old sovereignty by keeping Customs on the track of drug smuggling (i.e., almost the whole of the drug traffic), and a situation of intense interorganizational rivalry arose between the two units and departments in this area. For a description of this see John Rothchild and Tom Ricketts, "The American Connection," *Washington Monthly*, 4, no. 4 (June 1972), 33–44.

The Nixon Administrion's contribution to this bureaucratic evolution was, first of all, to bypass the existing authorities and create the brand new executive agency, the Special Action Office for Drug Abuse Prevention (SAODAP), which had great policy powers by virtue of the enormous appropriations at its disposal but no enforcement authority as such. Subsequently the President proposed to eliminate interagency competition and facilitate more centralized control of the burgeoning police apparatus by amalgamating all units into a single agency to be known as the Drug Enforcement Administration. In departmental terms, victory went to Justice, under which the new unit will operate.

9. *Narcotics Research, Rehabilitation and Treatment,* Hearings before the Select Committee on Crime, House of Representatives, 92nd Congress, 1st Sess. (April 1971), p. 1 (hereafter cited as *Pepper Hearings*). For a

survey of Congressional testimony on the amphetamine, barbiturate, LSD, and heroin epidemics during the 1960s, see Rufus King, *The Drug Hang-Up, America's Fifty-Year Folly,* New York, Norton, 1972, pp. 247–322.

10. *Youth Unemployment and Minimum Wages,* pp. 19–20.

11. *The Employment Situation: January 1973,* release from Bureau of Labor Statistics, U.S. Department of Labor, Washington, D.C., February 2, 1973, Table A–6.

12. Bureau of the Census, *Employment Profiles of Selected Low-Income Areas—New York, N.Y.—All Survey Areas,* PHC[3]-2, Washington, D.C., 1972, pp. 3, 5.

13. *Employment Profiles of Selected Low-Income Areas—United States Summary,* PHC[3]-1, pp. 145–47.

14. Frank G. Davis, "Problems of Economic Growth in the Black Community, Some Alternative Hypotheses," *Review of Black Political Economy,* 4, no. 1 (1972), pp. 85ff.

15. R. Levengood, P. Lowinger, and K. Schooff, "Heroin Epidemics in the Suburbs: An Epidemiological Study," paper presented at 99th Annual Meeting, American Public Health Association, Minneapolis, 1971. Also P. Kroll, P. Diamond, and K. Schooff, "Psychodynamics of a Group of Middle Class Heroin Addicts from a Suburban Community," addendum 3, vol. 2, Committee on Problems of Drug Dependence, Washington, D.C., National Academy of Sciences, 1971.

16. Statement of Howard A. Jones, chairman of the New York State Narcotic Addiction Control Commission, *Pepper Hearings,* p. 581; Patricia M. Wald et al., *Dealing with Drug Abuse: A Report to the Ford Foundation,* New York: Praeger, 1972, p. 4.

17. Narcotic Addiction Control Commission (NACC), State of New York, *First Annual Statistical Report—For the Fiscal Yar Ended March 31, 1968,* Albany: NACC, 1968, pp. 81, 86.

18. NACC. *Fourth Annual Statistical Report,* Albany: NACC, May 1971, p. 132.

19. Carl D. Chambers, *An Assessment of Drug Use in the General Population,* Special Report No. 1, *Drug Use in New York State,* Albany: NACC, May 1971, p. 132.

20. S. Dana Hubbard, "The New York City Narcotic Clinic and Differing Points of View on Narcotic Addiction," reprinted in *Daniel Hearings,* p. 1,720.

21. David H. Nurco et al., "Drug Abuse Known to the Maryland Psychiatric Case Register," in vol. 1, Committee on Problems of Drug Dependence, Washington, D.C.: National Academy of Sciences, 1971, pp. 901–48.

22. *NACC Report, 1968,* p. 44.

23. Chambers, *Assessment of Drug Use,* p. 132.

24. Ursula M. von Eckhardt, "Cultural Factors in Heroin Addiction in Puerto Rico," paper presented at 17th Winter Meeting, American Academy of Psychoanalysis, New York, December 1972, p. 5.

25. *NACC Report, 1968,* p. ix. The general distribution of the two Puerto Rican racial categories in the sections of New York surveyed by the Census in its low-income area analyses in 1970 was 80.4 percent white and 19.6 percent black.

26. For detailed data see two reports from the Bureau of Labor Statistics, U.S. Department of Labor: *Labor Force Experience of the Puerto Rican Worker,* Regional Reports No. 9 (June 1968); *The New York Puerto Rican: Patterns of Work Experience,* Regional Reports No. 19 (May 1971); both were published by the Middle Atlantic Regional Office, New York.

27. *Employment Profiles of Selected Low-Income Areas—New York,* p. 5.

28. Similar findings have been reported from both Washington, D.C. and Boston.

29. Addiction Services Agency, City of New York, *A Plan to Rehabilitate Addicted and Drug-Abusing Veterans in New York City* (November 1971), p. 40.

30. Addiction Services Agency, Ambulatory Detoxification Program, *Program Report* (preliminary) (April 25, 1972); supplied by Alan J. Gibbs, Department of Health, New York.

31. *Plan to Rehabilitate,* p. 40.

32. Nicholas J. Kozel, *et al.,* "Narcotics and Crime: A Study of Narcotic Involvement in an Offender Population," *International Journal of the Addictions,* 7, 3 (1972), p. 445.

33. John Helmer, *Bringing the War Home: The American Soldier in Vietnam and After,* New York: Free Press, 1974, p. 82.

34. *Ibid.,* p. 87.

35. Vernon D. Patch et al., "Vietnam Heroin Addicts in Boston," *Proceedings, Fourth National Conference on Methadone Treatment,* Washington, D.C.: National Institute of Mental Health, 1971.

36. *Profile of Drug Abusers in Vietnam,* release of Department of Defense, Office for Health and Environment (December 1971). The benchmarks against which these percentages should be compared are themselves difficult to establish. One source of figures has estimated there to have been 11.7 percent blacks among army men assigned to Southeast Asia in the first six months of 1968; 10.5 percent in the armed forces altogether (Charles C. Moskos, Jr., *The American Enlisted Man,* New York: Russell Sage, 1970, p. 218). This includes all ranks, unfortunately, and the available racial breakdown by rank or pay grade does not count Vietnam or Southeast Asian assignees separately. In 1967 blacks made up 12.1 percent of all army enlisted men (from grades E–1 through E–9) (Moskos, *American Enlisted Man,* p. 215). On the other hand, blacks were much more numerous in the combat arms. In 1967, 28.6 percent of en-

listed personnel in these arms were black (Moskos, *ibid.*, p. 216). According to Veterans' Administration data, whites make up 84 percent of all Vietnam era veterans (all personnel serving after August 5, 1964); blacks, 11 percent (Louis Harris et al., *A Study of Problems Facing Vietnam Era Veterans: Their Readjustment to Civilian Life*, Washington, D.C., 1971, p. 265).

37. *Fact Sheet to Commanding General, U.S. Army Support Command, Saigon, 27 September 1971, concerning command-wide attitude survey of 530 lower-ranking EM;* unpublished document made available by Capt. J.E. Engstrom, retired, former SSC Command Drug Control Officer.

38. Letter from J.A. McIntyre, Director, Reports and Statistics Service, Veterans' Administration, March 20, 1972.

39. Lee N. Robins et al., *A Follow-up of Vietnam Drug Users*, Interim Final Report, Washington, D.C.: Special Action Office for Drug Abuse Prevention, Monograph Sec. A, no. 1 (April 1973), p. 8; also, Lee N. Robins et al., *The Vietnam Drug User Returns*, Final Report (same place, same issuing authority, May 1974).

40. From statistics supplied by the Veterans' Administration (Reports and Statistics Service).

41. Both the prewar Japanese and Communist Chinese regimes have had unusual success in eliminating the use of opiates in their societies. Field reports also indicate that the North Vietnamese and N.L.F. forces rarely used opiates or marijuana during the Vietnam War.

42. Thomas Flemming, *The Forgotten Victory—The Battle for New Jersey*, n.p., n.d., quoted in *New York Times*, August 30, 1973, p. 37.

43. Charles E. Terry and Mildred Pellens, *The Opium Problem*, New York: Bureau of Social Hygiene, 1928, p. 69.

44. Figures provided by Hamilton Wright in *Report on the Opium Commission . . .* (1910), pp. 81–83.

45. E.G. Eberle, "Report of Committee on Acquirement of Drug Habits," *American Journal of Pharmacology* (October 1903); quoted by Terry and Pellens, *Opium Problem*, pp. 23–24.

46. R.M. Blanchard, "Heroin and Soldiers," *Military Surgeon*, 33, no. 2 (August 1913), 142.

47. Cf. King, "The Use of Habit-Forming Drugs (Cocaine, Opium and Its Derivatives) by Enlisted Men: A Report Based on the Work Done at the United States Disciplinary Barracks," *Military Surgeon*, 39 (1916), 277.

48. W.B. Meister, "Cocainism in the Army," *Military Surgeon*, 34, no. 4 (April 1914), 348.

49. King, "Use of Habit-Forming Drugs," pp. 273–74.

50. Pearce Bailey, "Nervous and Mental Disease in United States Troops," *Medical Progress*, 36, no. 416 (September 1920), pp. 193–97.

51. J.F. Siler, "Marijuana Smoking in Panama," *Military Surgeon*, 73, no. 5 (November 1933), 269–70.

52. *Ibid.*, p. 274.

53. *Ibid.*, p. 275.
54. *Ibid.*, p. 280.
55. The typical use of these quasi-psychiatric labels to refer to working-class drug-users (delinquents, criminals, etc.) has been noted. One study of "mental deficiency" among World War I servicemen found a close correlation between psychopathology, the prevalence of "morons," and such typical class indices as educational attainment, occupation, immigration status, and race (large black representation). See Pearce Bailey and Roy Haber, "Mental Deficiency," *Mental Hygiene,* 4, no. 3 (July 1920), 589ff.
56. Siler, "Marijuana Smoking in Panama," pp. 277–78.
57. *Ibid.*, p. 279.
58. "The Marihuana Bugaboo," editorial, *Military Surgeon,* 93, no. 1 (July 1943), 94–95.
59. H.L. Freedman and M.J. Rockmore, "Marihuana: A Factor in Personality Evaluation and Army Maladjustment," *Journal of Clinical Psychopathology,* 7, no. 2 (1946), 765–82; and 8, no. 1 (1947), 221–36.
60. Eli Marcovitz and Henry J. Meyers, "The Marihuana Addict in the Army," *War Medicine,* 6, no. 6 (December 1944), 387.
61. D. B. Davis et al., "Absence Without Leave," *War Medicine,* 7, no. 2, (1945), 145–51.
62. A.C. Cornsweet and B. Locke, "Alcohol as a Factor in Naval Delinquency," *U.S. Navy Medical Bulletin,* 46 (1946), 1,690–95.
63. See note 59.
64. *Daniel Hearings,* pp. 224–27.
65. Data for 1953–54 only. Other reports put the percentage of blacks at 78. See *Daniel Hearings,* pp. 176, 224–27.
66. *Ibid.*, pp. 176–77.
67. Testimony of Major General William H. Maglin, Army Provost General, and Lt. Colonel George C. Williams, in *Traffic in and Control of Narcotics, Barbiturates and Amphetamines,* p. 1,092.
68. *Ibid.*, pp. 1,090, 1,092.
69. *Ibid.*, p. 1,093.
70. Alfred W. McCoy et al., *The Politics of Heroin in Southeast Asia,* New York: Harper & Row, 1972, pp. 72–75. This is the best book to date on the drug trade.
71. Raw opium is obtained from a variety of poppy plant by extracting and drying its juice. By boiling this to 143°F, a derivative alkaloid, morphine, can be collected as the condensation. This much is easy. The morphine is then treated with acetic acid to obtain heroin, which is about three times more potent than morphine. The use of other chemical reagents has been developed for refining to grades of extremely high purity and potency. The last stage is the dangerous one and requires skill in handling.
72. McCoy, *Politics of Heroin,* pp. 75, 183.

73. *Report concerning command-wide attitude survey of 570 lower-ranking Ems,* (results, p. 3).
74. *New York Times,* May 16, 1971, p. 1.
75. Allen H. Fisher, Jr., *Preliminary Findings from the 1971 Department of Defense Survey of Drug Use,* Human Resources Research Organization (HumRRO) Technical Report #72-8 (March 1972).
76. *New York Times,* April 24, 1973, p. 1, reporting on the release of Robins et al., *A Follow-Up of Vietnam Drug Users* (see note 39 above).
77. As reported in *Staff Report on Drug Abuse in the Military,* Report of the Subcommittee on Drug Abuse of the Senate Committee on Armed Services, 92nd Congress, 1st Sess. (1971), p. 8. Also, Alfred V. McCoy et al., *The Politics of Heroin in Southeast Asia,* New York: Harper & Row, 1972, p. 181.
78. The Army Provost Marshal reported from Saigon in 1971 that North Vietnamese opium cultivation was strictly for the production of morphine for medical purposes: "the Drug Abuse Problem in Vietnam," U.S. Military Assistance Command Vietnam, quoted by McCoy, *Politics of Heroin,* p. 182.
79. *Ibid.,* pp. 185ff.
80. *Ibid.,* p. 184.
81. See C. R. Sanders, "Doper's Wonderland: Functional Drug Use by Military Personnel in Vietnam," *Journal of Drug Issues,* 3, *1* (Winter 1973), pp. 65–78; John Helmer, *Bringing the War Home: The American Soldier in Vietnam and After* (New York: The Free Press, 1974), pp. 76–77.
82. Robins, *The Vietnam Drug User Returns,* p. 25.
83. *Ibid.* p. 38; Larry H. Ingraham, " 'The Nam' and 'The World', Heroin Use by U.S. Army Enlisted Men Serving in Vietnam," *Psychiatry,* 37, 1 (May 1974), 121–22; M.A. Farber, "Veterans Still Fight Vietnam Drug Habits," *New York Times,* June 2, 1974, p. 1.
84. Robins, *Vietnam Drug User Returns,* p. 33.
85. "Here I must emphasize that the Vietnam War was planned by college-educated and relatively affluent Americans in Washington and fought in the field by the less educated, the economically disadvantaged, and the poor. For no other war in our history can it be said that the American Army was a poor man's army and that this was so by design"; Helmer, *Bringing the War Home,* pp. 9–10.
86. Harvey Feldman, "The Sheet System, Drugs and Military Service," in Andrew Swenson, ed., *Confronting Drug Abuse,* Philadelphia: Pilgrim Press, 1972; Vernon Patch, personal communication, January 24, 1972.
87. The same finding has been noted by Norman Zinberg, "Rehabilitation of Heroin Users in Vietnam," unpub. ms., 1971, p. 6.
88. Helmer, *Bringing the War Home,* pp. 328–30.
89. Engstrom, *Fact Sheet,* p. 5.
90. A revised text is in *Journal of Drug Issues,* 4, 1 (Winter 1974), 11–31. See also the text for Wilbur's Press Conference, releasing the Interim Final

Report by Robins, April 23, 1973, p. 11, and the departmental news release of the same date.

91. *New York Times,* June 2, 1974, p. 1.
92. See Helmer, *Bringing the War Home,* p. 184.
93. Robins, *Vietnam Drug User Returns,* p. 42.
94. *Ibid.,* p. 38.
95. *Ibid.,* p. 40.
96. For a complementary account of the heads and juicers, see Ingraham, Walter Reed Army Institute of Research, pp. 124–28.
97. Zinberg, p. 6; Ingraham, p. 119.
98. *New York Times,* June 2, 1974, p. 1.
99. Richard G. Wilbur, *Text for Press Conference, April 23, 1973,* pp. 11–12.
100. Helmer, *Bringing the War Home,* p. 84.
101. *Ibid.*
102. Robins, *Vietnam Drug User Returns,* p. 80.
103. *Ibid.,* p. 80.
104. *Hearings of the Subcommittee on Drug Abuse, Committee on Armed Services,* U.S. Senate, 92nd Congress, 2nd Sess: (June 1972), pp. 5ff.
105. Robins, *Vietnam Drug User Returns,* pp. 35, 36, 61.
106. *Ibid.,* p. 67.
107. Senator Alan Cranston, "Legislative Approaches to Addiction Among Veterans: The Nation's Unmet Moral Responsibility," *Journal of Drug Issues,* 4, 1 (Winter 1974), 1–10.
108. *New York Times,* June 2, 1974, p. 1. For corroboration see Paul Starr et al., *Epilog to Vietnam,* New York: Charterhouse, 1974.
109. Robins, *Vietnam Drug User Returns,* pp. 93–94.
110. *Ibid.,* pp. 57, 79.
111. *Separations from the Armed Forces of Veterans Who Served in the Vietnam Theater of Operations,* Office of Controller, Veterans' Administration, April 11, 1972. The total for 1971 was 560,000.
112. The Assistant Secretary of Defense for Health and Environment was an M.D. and occupied his Pentagon office while on leave from his permanent job as deputy executive vice-president of the AMA.

CHAPTER 7. DRUGS AND CLASS CONFLICT

1. News item from the *Badger State Banner* (Wisconsin), April 2, 1885; quoted by Michael Lesy, *Wisconsin Death Trip,* New York: Pantheon Books, 1973, n.p.
2. *New York Times,* August 1, 1914, p. 16.
3. *Denver Post* (Colorado), April 17, 1929, p. 2, quoted by Richard J. Bonnie and Charles H. Whitebread II, "The Forbidden Fruit and the Tree of Knowledge: An Inquiry into the Legal History of American Marijuana Prohibition," *Virginia Law Review,* 56, 6 (October 1970), p. 1,015.

4. From Nelson Algren, *The Man with the Golden Arm*, New York: Pocket Books, 1951, p. 79.
5. Helmer, *Bringing the War Home: The American Soldier in Vietnam and After*, New York: Free Press, 1974, pp. 205–6.
6. See Robert P. Bomboy, *Major Newspaper Coverage of Drug Issues*, Washington, D.C.: Drug Abuse Council, 1974, p. 2.
7. Thus, from the judicial opinion in an 1890 case:

   > Smoking or inhaling opium injures the health of the individual, and in this way weakens the state . . . it tends to the increase of pauperism . . . it destroys the moral sentiment and leads to the commission of crime. In other words . . . it has an injurious effect upon the individual, and, consequently, results indirectly in an injury to the community.

   (Quoted by Bonnie and Whitebread, "Forbidden Fruit," p. 1,004.) From the Chairman of the National Advisory Commission on Drug Abuse Prevention, 1972:

   > A society is therefore unworthy if it permits, or is indifferent to, any activity that renders its members inhuman or deprives them of their essential (or "natural") capacities to judge, choose, and act. If heroin use is such an activity, then its use should be proscribed.

   James Q. Wilson et al., "The Problem of Heroin," *The Public Interest*, no. 29 (Fall 1972), 7.
8. For a broad review of and full bibliographical references to the literature, see John H. McGrath III, "A Comparative Study of Adolescent Drug Users, Assaulters, and Auto Thieves, New Brunswick: Department of Sociology, Rutgers Univ., Ph.D. diss., 1967, pp. 1–44. Also, Richard H. Blum, ed., "Origins of Drug Use and Drug Problems: Fact, Theory and Implications for Public Action, Washington, D.C.: Special Action Office for Drug Abuse Prevention, unpub. doc., 1972, part 4.
9. *Ibid.*, p. 14.
10. McGrath, "Comparative Study," p. 8.
11. Isidor Chein et al., *The Road to H: Narcotics, Delinquency and Social Policy*, New York: Basic Books, 1964, p. 255.
12. See, inter alia, Percy Mason, "The Mother of the Addict," *Psychiatric Quarterly Supplement*, 32 (1958), 189–99; C. M. Rosenberg, "Determinants of Psychiatric Illness in Young People," *British Journal of Psychiatry*, 115 (1969), 907–15; McGrath, "Comparative Study," p. 7. For a general review of the literature, see David Paul Leeds, "Personality Patterns and Modes of Behavior of Male Adolescent Narcotic Addicts and Their Mothers, Yeshiva University, Ph.D. diss., 1965, pp. 20–53; Robert S. Lee, "The Family of the Addict: A Comparison of the Family Experiences of Male Juvenile Heroin Addicts and Controls," New York University, Ph.D. diss., 1960.

13. See, for example, Chein et al., *Road to H,* pp. 256–65.
14. Conalee Levine, "A Comparison of the Conscious and Unconscious Identification with Both Parental Figures among Addicted and Non-Addicted Male Adolescent Character Disorders," New York University, Ph.D. diss., 1959.
15. Leeds, "Personality Patterns," p. 242.
16. George D. Jackson, "Personality Characteristics of Narcotics Users," New York University, Ph.D. diss., 1970.
17. McGrath, "Comparative Study," 98, 190, 192, 222.
18. *Ibid.,* p. 208.
19. *Ibid.,* p. 209.
20. From the report in the *New York Times,* January 21, 1914, p. 3.
21. See Rufus King, *The Drug Hang-Up, America's Fifty-Year Folly,* New York: Norton, 1972, p. 52.
22. This is the key to the comparison at the most general level between those who use narcotics and those who do not, which is roughly all the difference public policy and the law have essentially been concerned with. That users differ among themselves is not to be denied; indeed, the analysis of this will take up a full and subsequent book. But see, for example, Zinberg and Jacobson, *The Social Basis of Drug Abuse Prevention* Washington, D.C.: The Drug Abuse Council, 1974; Patrick H. Hughes et al., "The Social Structure of a Heroin Copping Community," *American Journal of Psychiatry,* 128, 5 (November 1971), 551–58; Peter Albin, John Helmer, Thomas Vietorisz, et al., *Labor Markets and Drug Involvement,* research proposal submitted to the National Institute of Mental Health, Center for Studies on Narcotic Addiction and Drug Abuse (May 1974).
23. "On the General Features and the Medical Aspects of the Opium Habit in India," Memorandum I, *Royal Commission on Opium,* part 1, vol. 6, London: HMSO, 1895.
24. The initial announcement and supporting papers were released on May 10, 1972. See *New York Times,* May 11, 1972.
25. Cf. Edward Jay Epstein, "Methadone: the forlorn hope," *The Public Interest,* no. 36 (Summer 1974), 3–24.

Index